Capitalist Diversity an

Capitalist Diversity and Change

Recombinant Governance and Institutional Entrepreneurs

COLIN CROUCH

OXFORD
UNIVERSITY PRESS

OXFORD
UNIVERSITY PRESS

Great Clarendon Street, Oxford OX2 6DP

Oxford University Press is a department of the University of Oxford.
It furthers the University's objective of excellence in research, scholarship,
and education by publishing worldwide in

Oxford New York

Auckland Cape Town Dar es Salaam Hong Kong Karachi
Kuala Lumpur Madrid Melbourne Mexico City Nairobi
New Delhi Shanghai Taipei Toronto

With offices in

Argentina Austria Brazil Chile Czech Republic France Greece
Guatemala Hungary Italy Japan Poland Portugal Singapore
South Korea Switzerland Thailand Turkey Ukraine Vietnam

Oxford is a registered trade mark of Oxford University Press
in the UK and in certain other countries

Published in the United States
by Oxford University Press Inc., New York

British Library Cataloguing in Publication Data

Data available

Library of Congress Cataloguing in Publication Data

Data available

Typeset by SPI Publisher Services, Pondicherry, India
Printed in Great Britain
on acid-free paper by
Biddles Ltd., King's Lynn, Norfolk

ISBN 0–19–928647–7   978–0–19–928647–8
ISBN 0–19–928665–5 (Pbk.)   978–0–19–928665–2 (Pbk.)

1 3 5 7 9 10 8 6 4 2

For Joan

CONTENTS

ACKNOWLEDGEMENTS

In the preparation of this book I owe special debts to Henry Farrell and Maarten Keune, who were both doctoral students at the European University Institute (EUI), Florence, when I was teaching there. Henry helped me in particular with formalizing my ideas about path dependence, and Chapter 4 is based on an article written jointly with him (Crouch and Farrell 2004). Maarten worked for a time as my research assistant, helping especially with the ideas developed in Chapter 3. We also wrote an article together (Crouch and Keune 2005) that is used in Chapter 6.

More generally my thinking was helped considerably by seminars, workshops, and informal discussions with colleagues and students at the EUI, at the Max-Planck Institute for the Study of Societies, Cologne; CEPREMAP, Paris; and the Business School of the University of Warwick. Particularly helpful were meetings of the informal 'Complementarities' group organized in Cologne and Paris. Among many individuals from whom I have learned I would single out Bruno Amable, Robert Boyer, Luigi Burroni, Fabrizio Cafaggi, Ulrich Glassmann, Peter Hall, J. Rogers Hollingsworth, Martin Höpner, Renate Mayntz, Glenn Morgan, Fritz Scharpf, Philippe Schmitter, Wolfgang Streeck, Carlo Trigilia, and Helmut Voelzkow. The usual disclaimers about responsibility apply, as none of them has seen this final text.

1

Neo-institutional Analysis and Comparative Capitalism

The idea around which much of this book is centred first came to me looking at a temporary exhibition at Florence Airport in May 1999. It was an exhibition of photographs taken along what had been the mediæval pilgrimage and transport route, the Via Francigena, that led from the Lombard kingdom of the Po Valley to Rome. The text accompanying the photographs explained that the route was not a road in the sense we understand today, but a series of alternatives. At one point a river might be in flood on the way the pilgrims were using, and local people would tell them that when that happened they had to take a different path through the hills. Or there might be wolves in the hills; in which case another way through was advised. I had been reading one of the many studies that started appearing in the mid-1990s, that talked about the path dependence of public policy and national economic institutions. It occurred to me that perhaps the 'paths' used by social actors might often be far more like the pilgrims' route than the modern concept of a fixed, sign-posted road with clear boundaries and a certainty of moving along it from A to B. This might have implications for the gloomy determinism and inflexibility that filled the predictions of authors talking of path dependence.

Not long after that early papers from the Varieties of Capitalism project, led by Hall and Soskice (2001*b*) began to circulate. The main emphasis of the authors themselves was that there was no single form of capitalism. They were here building in a thorough and rigorous way on similar but looser claims by a variety of authors (Lazonick 1991; Albert 1991; Boyer 1996; Crouch and Streeck 1997). But I was increasingly struck by the paradoxical determinism behind this ostensibly liberating message: There were two but only two viable forms of capitalism. Nation-states possessed one or the other of these, the institutions appropriate to which extended in a coherent way across a wide range of economic, political, and social areas, determining their economic capacities over most products and types of production. And once a country had a particular set of such institutions, there was very little it could to change it. These paths were fixed, sign-posted roads with clear boundaries and a certainty of direction. Hall and Soskice were bringing to a brilliant fulfilment a project around which many of us had been skirting for the past quarter century. But now that I saw its perfectly logical culmination I was unsettled by it. And somehow the Via Francigena seemed to have something to do with my unease. I set about working out the link, setting off on many alternative paths of my own on the way. The following discussions present the result. Much is said in the following pages which is deeply critical of Hall and Soskice, and others have written even more pages of such criticism (e.g. Bertoldi 2003; Blyth 2003; Goodin 2003; Regini 2003; Watson 2003). However, this only emphasizes the extent of their achievement in defining the terms of an entire school of study. Certainly, without their work I could not have started the present task at all.

Problems of Neo-institutional Analysis

The school concerned is the application of neo-institutionalist analysis to the comparative study of capitalism, a task that has been particularly important in the context of globalization, which throws into question the viability of diverse forms of capitalism. Also relevant has been the collapse of the Soviet form of economic organization, the only alternative to capitalism, which collapse put into relief differences among capitalist economies. The other great achievement of neo-institutionalism in general is to have re-established the role of political science and sociology in the study of economic phenomena, something that they had lost after the Second World War. It does this by demonstrating how economic behaviour, and the market itself, exist within a framework of patterns, routines and rules which constrain the actions and choices of rational maximizing actors. This is an extremely valuable corrective to assumptions made in economic theory of the freedom that such actors have. It is, however, in the process of achieving this that neo-institutionalism has become rather deterministic. It draws much of the power of its analysis from its ability to depict a very limited number of institutional forms to which actors have access, and to show how particular forms are very homogeneous and monotonic. Very often mechanisms with similar characteristics are seen in the operation of institutions across a wide range of contexts within any individual society. It is in this way that whole societies can be characterized, the constraints on the scope available to actors within them delimited, and typologies drawn up of the different kinds of economy and society.

Actors seem to exist in an iron cage of institutions, which they cannot change. Yet we know that institutional innovation does take place. The problem therefore is to devise theories of action that retain all the insights of neo-institutionalism concerning the constrained nature of human action, while also being able to account for innovation. As Sewell (1992: 2) has pointed out, use of the metaphor of 'structure' in social analysis tends to reduce human actors to automata and implies too much stability; but it does make an important point about the patterned nature of human action, patterns that exist even when we neither want nor are aware of them (ibid.: 3). How can we sustain theoretical rigour in accounts that try to bridge that gap, rather than lapse into narrative description? And can we develop models of the kinds of operations that social actors perform when they innovate?

More specifically: Is it possible for social science to model the ways in which actors might change the terms of operation of an economy and society endowed with a particular type of capitalist institution, in order to enable it to perform in ways similar to societies that feature other types? From the point of view of institutional determinists the answer must clearly be no: A particular economy—usually defined as being a national one—is fated to continue along its path, unless perhaps it undergoes a profound crisis. But from the point of view of political and economic actors determined to seek change this negative answer merely invites attempts to refute it. In this book I call such people institutional entrepreneurs, because their approach to institutions is the same as that of an economic entrepreneur towards a business opportunity: They constantly seek ways to do things which until now have been impossible. They cast around for elements of institutions that they could *recombine* in unusual ways at opportune moments in order to produce change. 'Recombining' has become a much noted process ever since geneticists began to work on recombinant DNA (or rDNA). In this process, DNA from two or more sources, using matching genetic components from each, is incorporated into a single artificial, recombinant molecule, which has different qualities from those of the sources. I want in this book to provide a theoretical base for analysing how innovative social actors do something similar to institutions. It should be noted that my focus is not on innovation as such (in the sense that firms or scientists make innovations), but on what I might call meta-innovation: changing and creating the institutional contexts within which innovators in the normal sense operate.

To provide theoretical space in which institutional entrepreneurs can operate requires attacking part of the edifice of neo-institutionalism. This is in the first instance a negative task, knocking down major achievements in the recent work of macro analysis in social science. I therefore hope to do this in a way that involves challenging and building upon, rather than destroying those achievements. The challenge has to be made, or neo-institutionalism will become the new dismal science, endlessly demonstrating that actors within particular structures are doomed to keep re-enacting their past legacies. But the challenge has to be a constructive one, or the wisdom that has been accumulated concerning the way in which economic institutions work will be jettisoned. In particular, perhaps the most important achievement has been to demonstrate that capitalism exists in a number of different institutional forms, not as just the single model implied by neoclassical economic theory. But it has been important to theorists of this diversity to show that the number of such forms is very limited, and that once one has identified a form one can show how extensively it affects actors' behaviour. It was only with such limitations that neo-institutionalists could lay claim to having theoretical parsimony, an essential quality if the respect of economists was to be won. But it is the search for the same quality that leads to the determinism and functionalism that is making neo-institutionalism rigid and static. This defect has to be addressed without compromising the achievement. This is the spirit in which the following analysis is presented.

The Achievements of Neo-institutionalism

Human institutions oscillate between periods of specialization and differentiation, and those of recombination and the breach of barriers. Innovation derives from the clash and conflict produced by this oscillation. Academic study itself proceeds in the same way, as it is a human institution. For example, in the natural sciences, while until the late nineteenth century most scientists took pride in the breadth and range of their knowledge, for most of the twentieth century their increasingly professional successors moved into specialisms, perfecting subdisciplines and sub-subdisciplines, gaining thereby an intensity and depth of knowledge not possible for the grand generalist. Then, however, towards the end of that century developments in molecular biology and then new work on genetic structures began to bring together again, not just different branches of biology, but of chemistry too; and not just organic chemists, but physical chemists and then even physicists. The achievements of the past century or so of specialism were not thereby rendered redundant; nor did work advancing knowledge within the specialisms cease. But radical innovation increasingly took place on the boundaries and among those who communicated across them (Hollingsworth and Hollingsworth 2000).

The social sciences cannot yet claim to have made any breakthroughs as important and dramatic as the genome project, but the same oscillation between specialization and recombination can be seen. Until the 1960s practitioners of the different social sciences—anthropology, economics, politics, psychology, sociology, some approaches to geography, history, and law—would expect to understand and benefit from each other's work and from exchanges across subject boundaries. Degree courses would start from a common base in a number of constituent disciplines. Then, starting with economics departments in the USA but gradually becoming universal, the disciplines began to pull away from each other, to define jealously their field of study, and to deepen and intensify their specialist knowledge. Economics and psychology in particular began to develop in ways that took them closer to certain natural sciences. Economics became increasingly mathematical and defined its problems in terms of mathematical development rather than social questions. Psychology moved closer to biochemistry.

Political science and sociology became complicit in the process, the latter increasingly defining its concerns in terms of the gaps that other disciplines left behind—in particular departing the field of studying the economy. In his masterly study of the strong nineteenth- and early twentieth-century development of economic sociology and its curious disappearance during the 1950s and 1960s, Trigilia (1998: ch. VIII) sees part of the explanation of this retreat of sociology from the study of economic phenomena in the fact that, during the Keynesian period, the social problems of the economy seemed to have been resolved in the wealthy parts of the world. Economic sociology, he notes, continued to thrive in studies of third-world development, where the establishment of a market economy was still problematic. But he goes on to show how matters changed, and a recombination began to appear. The inflationary crises of the 1970s, and then the succeeding periods of returned economic insecurity, produced the change. First, political scientists, under the label of 'political economy', began to redefine certain economic issues as within their province. Later some economists and economic historians began to resist the lack of attention being paid to institutional context by neoclassical economics, culminating in the work of North (1990a). These varied groups started to come together under the banner of neo-institutionalism.

Sociologists began to do the same under the rubric of economic sociology. (See in particular the works of Granovetter (1990), Powell and DiMaggio (1991), Swedberg (1987), and Trigilia (1998).) More recently, Becattini and Burroni (2004) have argued cogently how a particular branch of economic study, that of specialized territorial clusters, serves as a valuable entry point for the reintegration of economics, sociology, political science, and geography. One cannot claim that social scientists in general are now talking fully across the boundaries, and that the epoch of specialization and differentiation has been superseded by one of recombination, because mainstream neoclassical economists as such remain aloof from the re-engagement. Still measuring their achievements and their prestige by the sophistication of their mathematical work, they risk losing reputation if they address broadly defined issues that require an extension rather than an intensification of analysis. However, among political scientists, sociologists, and geographers, one finds both those who seek recombination through the use of economics techniques in the study of social questions (rational choice theorists) and those who seek to bring the perspectives of their own disciplines to bear on economic questions.

Thanks largely to the neo-institutionalists, intellectual recombination is therefore occurring. The starting point of the analysis has been the observation that the mechanisms of a market economy cannot be taken for granted. Contrary to the assumptions of philosophers like Hayek (1973: 35–54), the market is not how human beings 'naturally' conduct themselves if only the state does not prevent them from so doing. The word 'natural' is deeply problematic when applied to human beings, as strictly speaking it relates only to those behavioural characteristics that we share with other animals. Those all-important characteristics that distinguish humans from other animals are not 'natural', but social, produced by interaction and the imposition of various kinds of rules, including the internalization of rules by the individual, intended to suppress the frequently disruptive, violent and antisocial exercise of natural impulses. The sources of such rules are very diverse; to define all or most of them as 'natural' with the exception of the state is curious. As North (1990a) showed in relation to US and British history, the market economy requires political construction. The point was vividly demonstrated after the fall of the Soviet Union, when, to the surprise of Hayekians (Hodgson 2002), sudden removal of the state and law did not liberate market-conforming capitalism but, as Hobbes (1651)—who famously described life in the state of nature as 'solitary, poor, nasty, brutish, and short'—would have predicted, gangster capitalism.

Not only are markets constructed; they need repeated reconstruction. Here Hobbes, or at least the residue of his influence on neoclassical economics, is less useful. In his thought experiment, men wanted so much to escape the state of nature that they agreed to establish an external authority (Leviathan, the sovereign) that would, through the rule of law, regulate their interactions with each other. Only by obeying this authority could they live in peace. This moment of founding the social contract was a one-off event, a unique moment of political action. After that, the common law of contract, enforced by the sovereign, would regulate affairs with no further need for politics. This is where the view of Hobbes and theorists of English common law is not a useful guide to the regulation of economic affairs in a modern society. Changes in technology, in economic processes, in accountancy practices, in financial arrangements, all require constant exogenous adjustment of the law by government and parliament, sometimes with radical consequences.

For example, changes in laws of patents and intellectual copyright in the USA had profound effects on the commercial exploitation of biotechnological research during the 1980s and 1990s. The liberalization of financial markets in the same period shaped the globalizing economy. The financial scandals that affected some of the most important corporations in the USA and elsewhere at the start of the twenty-first century followed directly from aspects of that liberalization and in turn generated a new wave of legislative control. Further, this process of constant re-regulation of markets does not follow some predictable evolutionary process. Nor is it something that judges can work out, following the myth of how common law operates, by applying some elementary principles of justice to new situations. Law creation by governments is always mediated through political action, with its conflicts of interest, mobilizations of coalitions, and arbitrary trade-offs. Economic institution building is essentially political and social. Take, for example, patent law. This has to balance the need to give inventors incentives by protecting their inventions from copying by those who have not invested in their creation against the need to avoid monopoly and to ensure competition. There is no one answer to how long a patent should be protected, or for exactly what should be permitted to count as invention. The answer has to be found at a political level, and while the political judgement can be informed by expert opinion, this is a field where distinguishing between disinterested experts and partisan lobbyists can be very difficult.

The market itself is one of the biggest instances of the necessarily socially created nature of human institutions. The market defines the rules that govern the mass of transactions which take place among buyers and sellers, such that prices are established that indicate for everyone the relative costs of all goods and services being produced and offered for sale. Fundamental to the concept of the market is the idea that no one actor is big enough or strong enough to affect a price by its own actions; and individual actors are not permitted to combine to act strategically. Prices, and the patterns of supply and demand that they produce, must emerge from a very large number of individually small actions. If this condition exists across all factors of production, then the outcome will be one that produces an optimal situation for all participants. As soon as one actor acquires enough power to act strategically and shape a market outcome in its own favour, it begins to raise prices and act in other ways to acquire privileges. If the market is pure, barriers to the entry of new producers to combat this dominance are so low that soon new entrants enter and compete, leading to a fall in prices and erosion of the privileges acquired by the potential monopolist.

Markets defined with this degree of strictness do not exist in a state of nature, but only when certain very sophisticated rules have been established and then enforced. First, people have to accept that they use only the mechanisms of buying and selling (rather than just taking and giving) to allocate resources. Next, there is the question of how much of the activity that is required for markets to function is itself to be within the market. The pure answer would be that everything should be within the market, otherwise a full comparison of costs and alternative uses of factors of production cannot be made. But in practice this is never done. People are at least partly educated outside the market; they live in families that sustain them emotionally outside the market; they acquire tastes and preferences outside the market. The supply of human labour itself, the basis of the economy, depends on decisions made by people whether they will produce children or not, which in virtually every society is seen as a decision which must remain outside the market.

Further still, the pure market with low entry barriers and a very large number of producers and consumers is in practice often impossible to achieve, and in many sectors of an economy there are either monopolies or competition among a very restricted number of strategically located producers. Buyers are similarly not always the mass of anonymous purchasers envisaged in theory, but may be a small number of large organizations, or a single government. This then raises an important point: Should concentration and limited competition be permitted, producing distortions in the market? Or should political intervention in the market be used to break up large firms in order to enforce the conditions of a pure market? Such a decision will not be made in some kind of pure technical space: the interests of powerful groups will be affected by the way in which the decision turns, and they can be expected to try to influence the outcome. This dilemma draws our attention to two different problems. First, what is more true to the idea of the market: imposing market competition by measures, which are themselves not market measures, to ensure the participation of large numbers of units? Or leaving the market alone until the process of concentration, which usually results from competition, destroys the conditions of a true market? Second, who is the decision-maker in such situations? Since actors within a market cannot by definition interfere with the rules of the market, there has to be some idea of a non-market actor, the behaviour of which cannot therefore be explained by the market. The market and its associated science, neo-classical economics, cannot therefore be autonomous.

The neo-institutionalist revival has brought all these concerns to the forefront of academic attention and has challenged disciplinary segregation. Some broad consensus points have emerged, as well as some where dispute continues. A rich literature has now developed, and the sociologists and political scientists who have grouped themselves around it are usually known as 'neo-institutionalists'. The 'old' institutionalists from whom the 'neo-' is intended to distinguish them are not the classical sociologists who first developed the study of the economy as a set of institutions, but are from an earlier tradition within economics itself, the so-called institutionalist economists. These included such figures as Gustav Schmoller, Joseph Schumpeter, Werner Sombart, Thorsten Veblen, Alfred Weber, and John Commons. They worked at a time when there was considerable interaction among economists and other social scientists. Their approach was very descriptive, and they were eventually eclipsed by the stronger mathematical skills of the neoclassicists who came to prominence as the subject cut its links to other social sciences and excavated deeply into its specialisms.

Neo-institutionalists try to remedy the deficiencies at the level of theory that eventually led to the decline of the old institutionalist economics. In so doing they have themselves sometimes gone different ways, with rational-choice neo-institutionalists staying closer to standard economics and taking different approaches from the so-called historical, sociological, and organizational neo-institutionalists. Recently some authors have begun to label these as different schools within institutionalism (e.g. Campbell 2001; Campbell and Pedersen 2001*a*: 10). Such labelling can be very helpful to students trying to find their way around a bewildering variety of approaches, but it can result in blocking off from authors in some schools approaches that are available to others. These differences should not be taken too seriously, as authors can easily move away from the obvious limits identifiable for each of these 'schools' (as ironically do virtually all contributors to the Campbell and Pedersen collection that insists on the divisions (Campbell and Pedersen 2001*b*)). Little use will be made of these distinctions in this study, which is after all engaging in an exercise of recombination, not intensifying specialisms.

Institutions and their Governance

Two ideas central to the discussion have been the launching point for the re-entry of sociology and political science into analysis of the market and the economy:

- that the pure market is just one of a number of forms which might be assumed by patterns of economic behaviour;
- and that some kinds of mechanism are likely to be in place, that devise, enforce, and revise these patterns.

The first of this leads us to the concept of the *institution*—which is of course fundamental to the whole idea of institutionalism; the second to that of the *governance* of institutions.

Institutions

Institutions will be defined here as: *patterns of human action and relationships that persist and reproduce themselves over time, independently of the identity of the biological individuals performing within them.* Sociologists have long understood such a concept, but much of this earlier history has been ignored by recent political scientists and others who have come autonomously to the idea of the institution as they have sought to convey the idea of behaviour being shaped and routinized, fitting into patterns, which are not necessarily those that would be freely chosen by a rational actor needing to decide what to do. Thus, North (1990*a*), an economic historian, defines institutions as 'humanly devised constraints imposed on human interaction'.

Most rational-choice accounts of why institutions exist follow Hobbes in assuming (sometimes only implicitly) some founding moment, at which actors realize that they need the institution to avoid the chaos that might follow if they follow pure individual free choice (e.g. Knight 1992, 1995; Calvert 1995). Often the founding moment is only a heuristic device; it is not located in historical time, but takes the form: 'It is as if actors did this.' But even in this form the idea is not helpful to modelling how most human beings, including institutional entrepreneurs, encounter institutions in their daily lives, which is as pre-existing, taken for granted, constraining.

Theorists differ on how institutional origins should be depicted. Only Knight sees the possibility of unintended development, but even he minimizes this because he wants to concentrate on power. For Calvert, institutions are the equilibria that result from repeated interactions among actors. A multitude of equilibria are possible in this way, which ignores the fundamental point, that individual instances of a particular type of institution exhibit some similarities, implying that there is some external regulation of them and not just a convenient agreement among unconstrained individuals. Rational choice theorists also tend to ignore the accidental elements in even the apparently purposive founding moments of institutions.

But this is not the approach of all observers. North and Thomas (1973) describe the rather accidental way in which England and the Netherlands developed market-friendly commercial rules in the seventeenth century. For Amable (2003), institutions represent compromises resulting from social conflict originating in the heterogeneity of interests among agents. Even within the rational choice tradition it is possible to take a more realistic view. For Hechter (1990: 14), a rational-choice sociologist, 'the existence of a social institution is revealed by the appearance of some regularity in collective behaviour'. He continues:

Collective behaviour may be said to occur if different individuals behave similarly when placed in the same social situation... *[R]egularity* ... indicates that this collective behaviour endures over some long but indefinite period of time.

He shares the starting point of most rational choice theorists by stressing the origin of institutions in individuals' desire for instruments that will help them achieve their goals: 'The demand for co-operative institutions arises from individuals' desires to consume jointly produced private goods... that cannot be obtained by following individual strategies' (ibid.: 16). However, he goes on to accept (ibid.: 20) that once established the institutionalized group might go on to produce quite different goods from those providing its initial rationale (see also Thelen 2003: 214 for a similar argument). Hechter then makes a further highly important point: Because the group has the comparative advantage over its constituent individuals of being organized, it might then go on, as a collectivity, to provide public goods and not just joint ones. By this point he has managed to take us, through an ostensibly economistic form of reasoning, to a completely sociological view of institutions as external and constraining in relation to individuals, capable of focusing on working for ends not foreseen by the sum of those individuals.

Key points in this approach to institutions are the predictability that follows from the reproduction of behaviour (the process of institutionalization as such), and the relative autonomy that an institution has from the individuals comprising it. In real life, reproduction is never perfect, and individuals nearly always bring some idiosyncrasy, some independence and novelty to how they perform their role. These points are particularly important to institutional innovation. It is impossible to say at what point an observer must conclude that reproduction has become so unreliable, and the variety of individual behaviour so dominant, that the phenomenon being observed is so fragmented that it cannot count as an institution.

As already noted, it is important to distinguish an institution as a generic type from instances of it. For example, we can define 'the family' as a human grouping comprising certain expected reproducible regularities of behaviour. It can then be broken down into many subtypes, by geography, history, social category, which will embody different regularities within the basic frame. If we then identify a particular group of people as constituting an instance of 'family' (the Jones family, my wife's family, a family with whom I stayed in Mongolia, etc.), we imply that it conforms to the behavioural and relational regularities understood to be typical of 'the family', or a designated subtype of family. For example, if I tell you that a certain group constitute 'members of my wife's family', you will expect them to behave towards each other within a certain range of potential behaviours. If I add that they are Mongolians, you would expect this range to be different from what you had expected if they had been western Europeans. The range will be different again from that which you would expect if I had identified the group as 'members of my wife's firm', as opposed to family.

From this follows an important point: If different instances of an institution share certain behavioural and relational regularities, there must be something *external* to these instances that somehow maintains their conformity. In the most obvious cases this conformity is maintained by something clear and formal, often the law. For example, all instances of the institution called 'the firm' within a particular jurisdiction must have a system for keeping accounts that can be externally inspected; this is a legal requirement. If we encounter something that has all the other characteristics that we associate with 'firm' but keeps no accounts, we suspect illegality. But external regulation can be far more diffuse and informal. For example, we would be surprised to find that members of a group that we have regarded to be an instance of 'the family' conduct all their relations with each other as financial exchanges, with formal payment to each other for cooking meals, repairing each other's bicycles, having sexual relationships. There is nothing in the law that says that families should not do this, but there are strong normative pressures and expectations that they will not do so.

According to Stinchcombe (1968), who first fully formulated the idea that institutions need to be exogenously regulated, it is third-party enforcement that indicates whether a rule has legitimacy. This, Streeck and Thelen (2005*l*) have more recently argued, distinguishes institutionalists from, on the one side rational choice theorists, and on the other extreme constructivists. For the former (unless they follow Hechter's reasoning cited above), an institution always needs to be useful to the specific actors who choose to have it, otherwise they would reject it. For the latter, institutions are defined entirely according to the subjective perceptions of those concerned. Mutually antagonistic though rational choice and constructivism frequently are, they come together in overlooking something that, for most neo-institutionalists, is fundamental about an institution: its constraining nature. An institution, argue Streeck and Thelen, is thus a regime, a set of externally imposed rules. This then enables them to make a point that will be extremely important to the argument of subsequent chapters: a regime is always subject to pressure for change, as there is always friction between a general rule and its application to individual cases (see also Scott 2001: 188).

There is some disagreement among the disciplines over the relative weight to be placed on clear and formal regulation of institutions and more diffuse mechanisms. Jurists and political scientists are inclined to look for the former, while sociologists are more likely to point, not only to the latter, but to the way in which institutional regularities are maintained by actors' internalized subjective perceptions. Indeed, the so-called sub-school of 'sociological neo-institutionalists' denotes those scholars who stress these aspects. One institutional theorist, Philip Selznick (1957: 16–17), actually defined 'to institutionalize' as meaning 'to infuse with values'. He also traced what he described as the growth from organization to institution as groups moved beyond their formal, mechanistic character to become organic, incorporating unanticipated aspects. Aoki (2001), unusually for an economist, mixed elements of this with game theory when he defined an institution as 'a self-sustaining system of shared beliefs about a salient way in which the game is repeatedly played'. But elevating the role of beliefs to definitional status pre-empts the range of the governance of institutions, study of which absolutely needs to consider both formal and informal external rules as well as internalized ones.

Sewell (1992: 8–9) takes a similar approach to that adopted here. He follows Giddens (1976) and Lévi-Strauss (1962) in seeing the rules that govern social action (what he calls schemas) as generalizable procedures for the reproduction and enactment of social life. They make up structures, but have a dual existence, being both material and virtual, intersubjective, operating at widely varying levels. Similar too is Bourdieu's idea (Bourdieu et al. 1973) of a mutually sustaining relationship between mental structures and the world of objects. Also on the same lines, Scott (2001: 51 ff.) sees institutions as comprised of three 'pillars': the regulative, normative and cultural cognitive systems of institutions. These provide different bases of compliance, mechanisms, indicators, and bases of legitimacy. He sees neo-institutionalist economics as dealing with the regulative. Sociologists go further and deal with subjective reference (hence the normative), and to see actors as essentially in relation to others. Finally, cultural-cognitive theorists see knowledge as *prior*-constructed and codified. This is useful, for example in showing how the state is not just about coercion, and how norms and culture-cognition are multifaceted, durable, made up of symbolic elements, social activities and material resources (ibid.: 128–9). Rules, norms, and actual behaviour all need to be maintained within the concept. I am, however, reluctant to follow Scott and some other authors in relegating the sociological approach to the study of norms, since sociology also contributes considerably to the study of external interaction.

For sociologists, one concept that has helped to model institutions that are neither individualistic in the neoclassical sense nor determinist is that of social embeddedness. This derives originally from Polanyi's critique (1944) of then mainstream accounts of how markets transformed traditional society. Markets are always influenced by the structures of the societies within which they emerge, he argued. This idea was returned to and developed further by US scholars remaking economic sociology in the 1980s (e.g. Granovetter 1985). They have in particular specified the different kinds of context in which markets may be embedded: cognitive, cultural, social, structural, political (Granovetter 1990; Zukin and DiMaggio 2000). From these differences will emerge differences in the structure of the markets themselves.

Streeck (2001) applies this general idea specifically to the study of capitalist diversity. He regards an economy as socially embedded in so far as the transactions by which it is made up either (i) are supposed to serve other than economic purposes or (ii) are supported by non-economic social ties. The former conveys the central idea of institutions inhibiting maximizing activity, but the latter is important in that it envisages the possibility that economic transactions might be *supported* and not just inhibited by a constraint on individual maximization.

The social ties are, however, still seen as primarily overriding or distorting the market. North (1990a) takes the claims of institutionalism in a different direction, and shows how non-market institutions make the market possible. Institutional analysis of the economy does not require that institutions be set *against* markets. In contrast, it requires that markets themselves be seen *as* institutions. They are not the only means of action available to actors, and they may not even be the only means whereby actors can realize economic goals. The conflict with neoclassical analysis comes only at a rather precise point, where the latter insists that in the long run only the conditions of the perfect market will provide perfect efficiency, and that any apparent superior performance achieved by other institutions will in that long run be seen as delusory.

Let us assume, for example, that a firm has found an efficient way of doing business by using workforce-training resources made available to it by a local business association that provides services to local firms in order to strengthen the competitiveness of its geographical area. According to a neo-institutionalist account, the fact that the firm is embedded in the local context enables it to acquire services that would be difficult and expensive to find in the market, but which, once acquired, enable it to compete more effectively within the market. But a strict neoclassicist would argue that these apparent efficiency gains are at best temporary. At some point the market will change, such that really efficient firms will no longer use the skills or training methods being provided by the association; but the association, not being in the market, will be slow to change. Firms using its services will go on doing so, because they are cheap, and they will therefore miss out on necessary moves out of the methods concerned to new ones. And firms that have bought their training services in the market, while they may have had to pay more for training during the initial period, will have responded quickly to the change, and will therefore have moved on to more efficient methods. It is important to note that a neoclassical economist is not forced to this conclusion. He may build into his account assumptions of high costs of acquiring information about changing training requirements through the market, and even conclude that a business association might find answers to these problems faster than the market. But the simple model is used very frequently in political discourse to undermine attempts at institution creation. Alternatively, if institutions are conceded, they are frequently dismantled and changed. (This has, for example, been the practice of UK governments for the past quarter century.) This approach proceeds from a view that the attainment of adequate knowledge for performing tasks is entirely unproblematic, while established institutions present major problems of rigidity and path dependence.

Several studies have made use of this ambiguity of embeddedness, showing how institutions that afforded a group of actors' advantages

during stable times suddenly became disadvantages at a time of change
(e.g. Grabher 1993*b*; Herrigel 1993). A highly useful means of analysing
the question has been established by Granovetter (1973), who distinguished between strong and weak ties in embeddedness: the latter
could be used by actors when helpful, but they could be broken at
relatively low cost when they became hindrances. (There is of course
some cost—weak ties are not 'no ties'.) Strong ties on the other hand,
while enabling higher levels of trust, could continue to constrain long
after they had ceased to be useful. The concept of embeddedness as such
does not necessarily lead neo-institutionalists either to establish a contradiction with market relations or to exclude the possibility of change; it is
just a useful concept and does not constitute a theory.

Institutions and Change

When we describe the way in which institutions constrain the actions of
individuals, we stress continuity, fixity, prevention of change, especially
that produced by individuals' wayward actions. This is fundamental to
the purpose of institutional analysis, and is important to the task of
explaining why so much human action is repetitive, predictable, routine.
However, as Streeck and Thelen (2005*l*) remind us, change and innovation do occur. If our theories of action and structure are heavily deterministic, social science will always be taken by surprise by change and
will have to regard it as something exogenous and mysterious: Explanation has to stop while innovation takes place, and then start again when
things have settled down and new routines have been established.

To quote an old social science joke: Economics explains how people
make choices; sociology explains how they don't have any choices to
make. However, while neoclassical economics is good at explaining
choices, it is also poorly equipped to describe the way in which actors
make *innovations*. In the market change happens as entrepreneurs keep
seeking ways of producing new goods and services. In a pure market,
with very large numbers of producers, some will hit on developments
that succeed in winning consumers' attention; their market share will
increase; other producers will start to imitate them. If the number of
producers tends towards infinity (as in the theory it does), then eventually
every possible innovation will be made, and every innovation that is
attractive to consumers will succeed. This is considerably more dynamic
than the standard idea of an institution, which cannot anticipate innovation at all. However, it relies for its account of innovation on there being
very large numbers of entrepreneurs, some of whom, if they try hard

enough, will hit on the right idea. The processes that they will use to try to innovate are beyond the reach of economic theory.

As a result, economics has given up developing a theory of innovation and entrepreneurship as such. Paradoxically, innovation being built into the pure model of the market, economics sees no need to examine it specifically (see Barreto 1989 for a good account of how the entrepreneur became excluded from neoclassical economics). The heterodox branch of economics called 'evolutionary economics' tries explicitly to deal with these issues, in an approach similar to that which will be adopted here. Nelson (1993, 2000), one of the main founding fathers of this subdiscipline, points out that systems of scientific and other know-how evolve in planned ways. Real advances cannot be planned by definition; if something can already be provided for, then it is already known. Technological advance is therefore a permanent evolutionary process during which winners and losers are determined by an *ex post* selection process. This limits the role for perfectly rational calculating behaviour of the kind modelled by standard economic theory. For example, Nelson (2000) cites a study of aeronautical engineers, that shows how technological advance has to reach beyond what is known, so that at a certain point its practitioners themselves are 'blind'.

This leads us back to the central problem announced at the outset: how can we retain all the insights of neo-institutionalism concerning the constrained nature of human action while also being able to account for innovation? How can we sustain theoretical rigour in such accounts, rather than lapse into narrative description? And can we develop models of the kinds of operations that social actors perform when they innovate, avoiding reliance on the assumption that innovation will necessarily flow if the numbers of actors are large enough, as economic theory does?

In a much cited phrase, Hall (1986: 19) defined institutions as 'the formal rules, compliance procedures, and standard operating practices that structure the relationship between individuals in various units of the polity and economy'. It is necessary to ask what is understood by 'individuals' here. In much economics literature 'individuals' are firms, not individual biological human persons. And in many contexts the individuals that are designated in economic theory are what sociologists call roles rather than persons: An individual 'warm-blooded' role-holder might move away, retire or die without many of the predictions made about performance of the role being affected. It may even be questioned whether warm-blooded human beings have anything at all to do with the neoclassical individual, which can be relied upon to concentrate on the maximization of its economic interests without interference by sexual or other appetites, emotions, moods, or psychological states. All these characteristics, which are fundamental to the study of human biological individuals, are excluded from the model of methodological individualism (Pizzorno 1983). March and Simon (1958) asserted that rational action was possible only within an organizational or institutional framework; individual human actors lacked the capacity for true, fully calculating rationality.

As we have seen, part of the power of neo-institutionalism is that it challenges the concept of the maximizing actor (whether collective or individual) with the idea of structures, expectations, and various other constraints, which together constitute the institutions that prevent actors from seeking immediate maximization. Not only are institutions likely to constitute part of a pre-existing, taken-for-granted world for any given generation of actors, but it is also important to avoid even the assumption of a myth of a founding contract as the starting point for an institution. Institutions exist; their origins may have nothing to do with the uses to which current social actors are trying to put them. Individuals and groups inherit them, not necessarily willingly or even consciously; they encounter them and have to shape their lives and projects in relation to them. These institutions both constrain and facilitate; they can often be adjusted; but they should not be expected to be fully subject to human will. They certainly should not be expected to be coherent, unless certain evolutionary assumptions, which will be examined below, can be made.

A genuinely individualistic (in the sense of human individualistic) approach to the study of institutions is paradoxically more likely to emerge from a structural model of institutions and society than from methodological individualism. Structuralists can locate limited, perplexed, myopic human persons within structures that they have inherited willy-nilly, and that partly help and partly thwart them. They can then ask how, given various different assumed goals, they are likely to respond. These actors can then be seen, not just as following the rules of the institutions in which they find themselves, but as trying to innovate, cheat, bend the rules, or escape from them in various ways. It will also be possible to distinguish those structures that impose rigid constraints, such that innovation within them requires radical new departures, and those that are flexible enough to permit frequent incremental change, which of course may over time result in radical departures from the initial conditions (as Thelen (2004) has brilliantly argued in an historical study of changes in vocational education in a number of societies).

As Sewell (1992: 16–19) puts it, we need a conceptual vocabulary that shows how the operation of structures can generate transformations: the multiplicity of structures, the transposability of schemas, the unpredictability of resource accumulation, the polysemy of resources, the intersection of structures. Ironically, neoclassical theory and neo-institutionalist determinism come together in trying to reduce the need to discover these fascinating creatures, real human individuals. This can be easily illustrated by considering the metatheoretical status of game theory, currently one of the most popular means for extending the rationale of economic analysis throughout the social sciences. At one level, game theory provides for pure neoclassical experiment. Actors are attributed with a clear maximizing objective ('winning' the game) and are required to use prescribed means (the rules of the game) to reach it. They are assumed to be maximizers who will compete with each other individualistically. But the environment defined by the game is a totally determined structure; the participants have no chance to change it; and it is assumed that there is a gamemaster who is able to tell them what to do and be obeyed. It requires an approach of a totally different kind to ask: What if the participants refuse to play the game? Or say they don't care about the goals set for them? Or try to find means of getting the prizes other than those prescribed by the gamemaster? Or combine together to demand a change in the rules?

In this book human individuals are assumed to operate in a permanent dilemma between following the rules of the institution within which they operate and challenging, breaking, innovating against, those rules. The chances that they will engage in non-conforming behaviour of various kinds will depend partly on the flexibility allowed them by the institution, partly on the external positive and negative sanctions that will be likely to follow non-conformist behaviour, and partly on norms that they have internalized about the ranges of conduct that are compatible with their sense of themselves. There is similar diversity in the goals that people might be maximizing when they make whatever choices they do in relation to the rules. Are they maximizing monetary reward? Or approval and prestige from one or other significant others? Or the satisfaction of doing a job well? Or having a quiet life? If we study particular individuals, we can try to build some knowledge about their positions on these variables, but at the level of theory we can only make assumptions. Unless we do this, we cannot make progress in our knowledge of how institutions and individuals will behave; but as soon as we make one set of assumptions, we ignore others which might have given us important information. Similarly, as a starting point for analysis we have to assume some consistency in actors' preferences over time, though in reality we know that human individuals are not fully consistent and act in contradictory ways. Somehow theory has to both make assumptions and be aware for these being falsified from time to time. Conventional economics and game theory make the single assumption of the maximization of gain as a goal, and take for granted consistency. This enables these approaches to make extraordinary progress at the level of theory-construction, but at the expense of becoming remote from reality. This was a choice made by the majority of practitioners of the discipline; it is not a necessary implication of adopting an economic model.

Innovative economists are able to return to the fundamentals of their discipline and amend their assumptions. It is important that sociologists and others concerned to produce more realistic accounts of human action than those of conventional economics build on these new developments within that discipline. If we simply assert complexity without being willing to submit it to rigorous analysis, the new institutionalism will go the same way as the old. Jaccoby (1990) has pointed to four issues in the old institutionalist versus classicist debates, from which the latter emerged triumphant because of their capacity to clarify. Institutionalists confronted determinacy with indeterminacy; posed endogenous against exogenous determination of preferences; behavioural realism against simplifying assumptions; diachronic against synchronic analysis. It was always the latter of these pairs that proved more amenable to analytical rigour. For Scott (2001), neo-institutionalist economics stands a chance of challenging the neoclassical paradigm in three ways especially if it incorporates the evolutionary approach of Nelson and Winter (1982): (1) it has a broader concept of the agent, replacing the idea of simple maximization with that of doing so within a list of known alternatives; (2) it focuses on processes rather than on equilibrium analysis, and therefore accommodates learning and other *changes* over time; (3) it accepts the role of institutions other than the market in coordinating economic activity. The second in particular captures the idea that Giddens (1976) has developed within sociology with his insistence on structuration (a process resulting from human action, which is knowledgeable and enabled) rather than structure (fixed and already determined).

Governance

The concept of governance will be central to the analysis in later chapters, as it has a fundamental role in the idea of an institution. It will be defined here as: *those mechanisms by which the behavioural regularities that constitute institutions are maintained and enforced*. A similar approach is taken by Scott (2001: 140), who sees governance as all arrangements by which organizational field level power and authority are exercised, involving formal and informal, public and private, regulatory and normative mechanisms. This provides for potential huge variety. Campbell (2004) also insists on the importance of 'mechanisms', the processes that account for causal relationships among variables, following Elster (1989: 3) who sees mechanisms as the nuts, bolts, etc. that link causes with effects.

Many observers object to the use of governance, as it seems to be a pretentious synonym for government. But this is not the case. As will be demonstrated later (Chapter 5), government is a subset (the most important subset) of governance, and a subset cannot be a synonym for the set of which it is a part. Government refers to a particularly formal and explicit form of governance, but less formal, more implicit mechanisms can also be used to sustain institutions and maintain conformity. There are, for example, what Luhmann (1980) calls codes, values or *Weltbilder*. As Rosenau (1992: 4) puts it, governance is more encompassing than government. It includes government, but also non-governmental mechanisms whereby 'those persons and organizations within its purview move ahead, satisfy their needs and fulfil their wants'. Kooiman (1993: 4) similarly uses governance to stress the multi-actor nature of governing; no actor, public or private, has enough knowledge to solve all problems or enough overview or action potential.

In this book I shall largely follow the approach to governance first developed by Campbell, Hollingsworth, and Lindberg (1991) in a study of the US economy, and developed further in a comparative context by Hollingsworth, Schmitter, and Streeck (1994). This distinguishes, in addition to government or the state, the market, corporate hierarchies, associations, communities, clans, networks, and formal law (as distinct from government) as the major governance forms. This approach has some similarities to what a group of French scholars had identified as *régulation* (Boyer and Saillard 1995), the two perspectives being brought together in Hollingsworth and Boyer (1997).

There is an alternative and different approach, found particularly among some British authors. These use 'governance' instead to identify a kind of soft and flexible *alternative* to government (e.g. Greenwood, Pyper, and Wilson 2002; Leach and Percy-Smith 2001; Rhodes 1997). Thus, regulation by private firms, or pre-eminently by the market (Le Grand 2003), is seen as necessarily gentler and more favourable to individuals than that by government.

This is an unfortunate and unwelcome development, as it incorporates a normative, even ideological approach where we need analysis. Some political scientists are turning away from use of the concept of governance as a result, and we are in danger of losing an idea very useful to institutional analysis. Governance mechanisms of various kinds may be strong and powerful, or fragile and crescive, depending on the encounter between the actions of maximizing agents and the rules that are framed both to facilitate and to restrain their maximizing search. For example, it must be remembered that governance by the market is not only a device for ensuring that individuals achieve their choices, but for ensuring that their choices take a certain form. As we have already seen, the concept of the human individual or self embedded in the market's highly structured actors is problematic. It is a form of constraint, a highly complex set of mechanisms designed to ensure that actors achieve their aims in a competitive way and through a process of exchange. Actors may themselves prefer the greater security and ease of fixed, shared arrangements rather than a competitive process. Or they may prefer some other form of distribution than exchange. This may be the case with the poor, who have little to offer within exchanges; or with those possessing superior strength or power of some kind, who might achieve superior returns without making exchanges.

Firms, systems of research and education, families, all institutions, have governance mechanisms. If the governance mechanism of an institution collapses, the institution will collapse; if the governance mechanism changes, it is likely that the institution itself will change, as different regularities will be established. Institutional entrepreneurs therefore work at the manipulation of governance—just as scientific and technological entrepreneurs work at the manipulation of materials and techniques, and economic entrepreneurs at the manipulation of products and markets. At moments of major innovation and change, they recombine elements, even fragments, of various governance forms that they find available, in an attempt to increase the range of capacities available to actors within fields of interest to them.

Governance rules may be very informal and implicit, as can be sanctions, as well as 'compliance procedures and standard operating practices'. All this starts to give us a purchase on the idea that institutions may take diverse forms, their forms of governance being major potential sources of variety. And where there is diversity there is potentially the possibility of recombination and, therefore, change and innovation. It is for this reason that governance will be a central concept in the later stages of our analysis.

The Argument in Brief

The initial problematic having been set out and central definitional issues having been tackled, it is possible to outline the argument of the rest of this book. Initially there will be a closer look at how neo-institutionalist approaches to the diversity of capitalism are falling into the trap of oversimplification and determinism. In Chapter 2 we shall see how over-simplification often results from confusion between ideal types and cases, with the latter being seen as exemplifiers of the former, rather than the former being seen as constituents of the latter. This is combined with excessive concern with identifying national, rather than more micro level, patterns of institutions. Characteristics of economies have been bundled together as coherent wholes with inadequate attention being paid to the forces which produce the bundles, and this has often been done through an account of types that has been too closely linked to the polemic between neoliberalism and social democracy.

Some important concepts like *Gestalt* (the general, congruent shape of a set of institutions), *Wahlverwandschaft* (a hypothesized tendency for insti-tutions with similar features to be found together), and complementarity are being inappropriately used in all this. In Chapter 3, I shall try to assert the importance of establishing the micro foundations of institutions if we are to treat actors as potentially creative and innovative. Weber's concept of ideal types as one-sided accentuations of idealized forms of reality, possibly operating alongside *Wahlverwandschaft*, needs to be rediscovered and its implications for theory building recognized. There will also be a discussion of the often unrecognized functionalism of much neo-institutionalism, which will be checked by giving an adequate role in the theory to power relations, social compromises and other contingent results of social interaction. These considerations lead to an important hypothesis: that institutional heterogeneity will facilitate innovation, both by presenting actors with alternative strategies when existing paths seem blocked and by making it possible for them to make new combinations among elements of various paths. Finally, the problematic nature of taking for granted that the boundaries of nation states are the boundaries of institutions and systems of action will be considered, and the import-ance of regarding endogeneity and exogeneity as a continuum addressed.

The position of the actor and the scope left to the actor by strong assumptions of structural determinism will be discussed in Chapter 4. This will be done within the framework of about the most heavily deter-ministic sets of arguments found in neo-institutionalism: path depend-ence theory. A model of what is known as a Bayesian decision-maker will be established, more accurately to model the relationship between actors and their environments. It will then be shown how such actors who are institutional entrepreneurs seeking ways out of increasingly un-successful but still constraining paths might behave. They might carry out costed searches into alternative paths concealed within their own past experience; or they might seek to transfer experience from different action spaces; or from other agents through networks of structured relationships. This last also helps break down the rigid dichotomy between endogeneity and exogeneity as sources of actors' responses. Finally, I introduce the possibility of several viable alternatives, only one of which is likely to be discovered, to model how ideas of 'one best way' solutions become established. The overall conclusions here are similar to those of Garud and Karnøe (2001*a*: xiii) in their model of entrepreneurs as: 'embedded path creators—not as completely original, even exogenous, forces. [Institutional] entrepreneurs develop along the paths provided by history, but attempt mindfully to depart from it, usually by recombining existing elements in unusual ways.' Such an account does not contest the currently dominant forms of neo-institutionalism with a series of anti-theoretical empirical objections along the lines of classic English historiography, but is theoretically grounded.

To change an institution requires changing its governance. For a similar approach, which also considers the implications of changes in governance for path dependence theory, see Magnusson (2001). Chapter 5 models how this can be done. First, in order to provide the scope within which institutional entrepreneurs operate, the standard forms of governance on which most analysts (including this author) rely have to be deconstructed into smaller component units; entrepreneurs cannot be expected to take fixed structures for granted. For example, if told that market governance involves certain types of behaviour, some of which they find convenient but others not so, they must be assumed to try to dispose of the latter while retaining the former. Whether they can actually do this is a matter for research, but the initial important point is that theory must be able to anticipate their trying to do so. The importance of compound rather than ideal-typical forms of governance in empirical cases is then stressed, as it further establishes the possibility of recombining governance modes, and the hypothesis that institutional heterogeneity will facilitate innovation.

Chapter 6 presents some examples of compound and recombinant governance in action. The former is depicted through an account of the institutions that govern the high-tech sectors (biopharmaceuticals and information technology) of southern California; recombinant governance is seen in the neoliberal turn in the UK at the end of the 1970s. Finally, Chapter 7 resumes the argument and sets out a research approach for the next stage of neo-institutional analysis.

2

Typologies of Capitalism

That capitalist economies might take diverse forms has been long recognized by some scholars. Sometimes this diversity has been seen as a matter of evolutionary development. This was true of Max Weber's ideal type approach, that of the advocates of post-war modernization theory, and of those who followed Antonio Gramsci's identification of a Fordist phase of capitalism that was deemed to succeed the classic free-market form. This last idea flourished particularly in the French *régulationiste* school (Boyer and Saillard 1995). These approaches, different from each other though they are, all see some forms of capitalism superseding, and as therefore in some sense superior to, earlier modes. Hence these are not theories of a true diversity in the sense of a continuing multiplicity of forms, the historical superiority of any of which might never come to an issue.

Analysts willing to adopt this latter, less grand approach have been rarer. The modern *locus classicus* was Shonfield's work (1964), which examined the role of various institutions surrounding the economy—various branches of the state, banks, stock exchanges—in a number of western European countries, the USA, and Japan. Although he thought some were more efficient than others—in particular he was impressed by those that inserted some elements of planning into otherwise free markets—he did not talk in terms of historical transcendence.

When more theoretically inclined political scientists and sociologists returned to considering economic questions in the 1980s, they resumed Shonfield's concern with national politico-economic systems and hence national varieties of capitalism. Occasionally subtypes would be recognized within a national economy (mainly with regard to Italy and Spain), but these themselves have nearly always been geographically subdivided, so the concept of territorially based economies has been retained. This does not mean that each nation state has been seen as embodying its own unique form of capitalism; rather, national cases are grouped together under a small number of contrasted types.

This literature has many achievements. It has provided an intellectual counterweight to easy arguments about globalization, which predict an inevitable trend towards similarity among the world's economies. Whether globalization theorists predict a convergence based on US hegemony or an endogenous and voluntary aspiration towards a prosperous and rational new world, or whether they do not distinguish between these two, they have little time for arguments which insist on the viability of continuing differences. Neo-institutionalist accounts of diversity have provided both theoretical arguments and some empirical demonstrations to suggest that these may be great oversimplifications. However, I argued in Chapter 1 that, if we are to model the diversity of economic institutions more scientifically, and particularly if we are to study institutional change and innovation, we need to deconstruct the taken-for-granted wholes of contemporary neo-institutionalism and discover their constituent elements—elements which are able to survive in combinations other than those identified in the taken-for-granted wholes.

The fundamental point is: *Empirical cases must be studied, not to determine to which (singular) of a number of theoretical types they should each be allocated, but to determine which (plural) of these types are to be found within them, in roughly what proportions, and with what change over time.* This alternative is less ambitious than the current fashion, in that it does not enable us to map the economic world with a few parsimonious categories. But it is also more ambitious, partly because it corresponds more closely to the requirements of scientific analysis, but also because it is able to accommodate and account for change taking place within empirical cases. This is something which most of the neo-institutionalist literature on capitalist diversity finds difficult to do, leading to the functionalism and determinism of much of its analysis.

More specifically, we can identify certain methodological flaws of the neo-institutionalist approach. Whatever else they do, schemes for analysing the diversity of capitalism usually answer two fundamental questions: How many types of capitalism do they perceive? And how extensive is the range of institutions their model covers? In answering the first, many theories derive their types in a dubious way. In tackling the second, they often make a flawed use of the concepts of elective affinity and complementarity. From these defects follow: an oversimple relationship between types and cases; and a reluctance fully to accept empirical heterogeneity. These further combine with an uncritical application of theories of path dependence to culminate in an inability to anticipate endogenous change and hence the emergence of a less static range of capitalist forms.

In this chapter we shall concentrate on the first of the two initial flaws—deduction of the number of types. In Chapter 3, we shall consider problems of elective affinity and complementarity and their further consequences.

Pitfalls in the Formulation of Types

The smallest number of theoretical types consistent with the idea of diversity is two. For almost all authors, one is always the free-market model of neoclassical economics. This constitutes the principal intellectual antagonist for neo-institutionalists, even when they argue that it accounts for only a highly specific form of capitalism (Boyer 1997). There must be at least one other form to make a theory of diversity: hence dichotomies. At the other extreme there is no theoretical limit to the number of forms that might be identified, but theories rarely propose more than five or six. Given the relatively small number of empirical cases of advanced capitalism for those tied to a national case approach (currently around twenty-five), it is difficult to sustain more than a handful of types without lapsing into empiricism.

The work of Albert (1991), who made the original contribution to dualistic analysis, is typical. He modelled two types of capitalism, which were seen in an antagonistic relationship. They are labelled in geo-cultural terms as Anglo-Saxon and *rhénan* (Rhenish). The former defines free-market capitalism, considered to be embodied in the Anglophone countries.[1] The second takes its name from certain characteristics considered to be common to the riparian countries of the Rhine: Germany, the Netherlands, Switzerland, more problematically France. However, not only is the author uncertain whether France's institutions fully belong to this type (an anxiety which was one of his main motives in writing the book), but Japan and Scandinavia are considered to be part of it. More disconcerting (at least from our perspective) than an image of the Rhine rising under Mount Fuji and entering the sea at Saltsjöbaden is the broad institutional range being gathered together to form this second type. The essential idea is a capacity to make long-term decisions that maximize certain collective rather than individual goods. But this means ignoring differences among the very diverse forms of collectivism found.

It is important to note that this dualism in the identification of types of economy parallels the debate between political philosophies—neoliberalism and social democracy—which lies behind the analysis and behind most contemporary political debate (Campbell and Pedersen 2001c). This has created some confusion over whether neo-institutionalism's confrontation is with neoclassical economics, and therefore at the analytical level only; or with neoliberal politics, implying an ideological confrontation; or with all political practices associated with the anti-Keynesian and pro-capitalist forces which came to prominence during the period.

Neoclassical analysis considers how economic actors would behave if a world of perfect markets existed. It usually but not necessarily incorporates the normative assumption that both economy and society would be improved were institutions to take this form, but neoclassical economists are at liberty to consider that this may not always constitute a practical proposition. They are not bound to by their analytical approach to any particular policy conclusions, or to consider that the world in reality takes a certain form. It is neoliberalism which, as a political creed rather than a form of analysis, not only definitely adopts a positive normative evaluation of markets, but also believes that they could always be introduced in practice.

But in practice not even neoliberals do this. A by-product of the ideological dominance of neoliberalism since the 1980s, and in particular its association with the most powerful nation-state on earth—the USA—has produced a tendency among even serious analysts to assume that certain practices and institutions constitute part of the neoliberal paradigm just because they are found in the USA. The characteristics of the neoliberal model are derived from empirical observation of what is thought to be its main empirical example. But it is logically impossible to derive the characteristics of a theoretical category from the characteristics of an example of it, as the theoretical characteristics have to be known before a case can be considered to be such an example.

For example, an extremely powerful, scientifically oriented military sector, tying a number of contracting firms into close and necessarily secretive relations with central government departments, is a fundamental attribute of the US economy, and central to much of its innovative capacity in such sectors as aerospace and computing (as we shall see in Chapter 6). The operation of such a military sector has nothing to do with the principles of either neoclassical economics or neoliberal politics. Analysts respond to this in two ways. Some just ignore the existence of this sector and its special characteristics in their account of the US economy. For example, the OECD (1994) felt able to describe the USA as a country lacking any close support from government for industry. Alternatively they argue that the defence sector is somehow part of the US 'liberal' model, without noting the difficulties of such an assumption (e.g. Amable (2000)). At the level of US political ideology, it is significant that neoconservatism is replacing neoliberalism as the dominant force. The former has no difficulties with a dominant state-supported military sector.

As Campbell and Pedersen (2001c) argue, at the practical level neo-liberalism has not been the monolith that both its advocates and opponents set it up to be. Within it have been contained a diversity of practices, some not particularly coherent with others. Kjær and Pedersen (2001) point to clear differences from the normally presented model in the form taken by so-called neoliberalism in Denmark. King and Wood (1999) have even demonstrated clear differences between the neoliberalisms of 1980s UK and USA, two cases normally seen as joint paradigms.

As noted in Chapter 1, the collection of studies edited by Hall and Soskice (2001b) under the name *Varieties of Capitalism* represents the most ambitious and significant contribution to date of the dualist approach. It draws much from Albert, though it barely acknowledges his contribution. Their book has become the emblematic citation for all studies of diversity in capitalist economies. It is also an example of the preoccupation of many neo-institutionalists with coming to terms with and, in this case, eventually becoming absorbed by, an idealized version of neoliberalism. It seeks, not only to allocate every developed capitalist economy to one or other of two categories, but derives from this account a theory of comparative advantage and a list of the kind of products in which the country will specialize (Hall and Soskice 2001a: 36–44). This is achieved with the aid of certain assumptions concerning what constitutes radical and what incremental innovation—a characteristic which is considered to differentiate whole classes of goods and services. It is this factor, combined with its use of this sectoral analysis to account for certain important developments in different national economies during the 1990s, which has made the account so appealing.

Despite some ambiguity about a possible third model, these authors work with an essentially dualist approach along the rationale outlined above. They specify (Hall and Soskice 2001a), first, a liberal market economy (LME) identified with neoliberal policies, radical innovation, new sectors of the economy, and the Anglophone countries (Australia, Canada, Ireland, New Zealand, the UK, but primarily the USA). Germany is at the centre of a second type, called a coordinated market economy (CME), where social and political institutions engage directly in shaping economic action. This form is linked to social democracy, incremental innovation, declining economic sectors, and non-Anglophone countries.

It is odd that the core linguistic uniting characteristic of the LMEs, the only generalization that really works, is never actually discussed as such. More aware of Irish sensitivities than most authors, Hall and Soskice always talk of 'Anglo-Saxon and Irish' economies. But, perhaps because like others they resist the far simpler and more accurate 'Anglophone',

they miss some serious potential implications of this. For example, one of
the most impressive pieces of evidence cited by them to support their
contention that radical innovation is concentrated in LME countries and
only incremental innovation in CMEs is work carried out for them on
patent citations (Estevez-Abe, Iversen and Soskice 2001: 174–5). This
reveals a strong statistical tendency for patents taken out in Anglophone
countries to cite scientific sources, while those taken out in continental
Europe and Japan tend to cite previous patents or non-scientific sources.
The six leading countries out of eighteen studied are all Anglophone
(headed by Ireland). Prima facie, the distinction between radical and
incremental innovation does seem to be well proxied by that between
academic and product citations, and one can see this being related to the
character of research in firms, research centres and universities. But it is
also possible that firms in Anglophone countries are more likely to cite
articles in the overwhelmingly Anglophone literature of global science
than those in other countries. Further, liberal market economies are
largely defined by their having characteristics determined by common
law traditions; these also encourage the use of patenting of innovations to
a greater extent than civil law systems. Therefore, higher levels of patenting—as a legal device, not necessary a reflection of actual innovation—
will be most widespread in common-law, and hence liberal market,
systems. This distortion may help explain why, according to Estevez-
Abe, Iversen and Soskice (2001: 175), New Zealand has more radical
technological innovative capacity than Germany, Sweden, or Switzerland.

The LME type of economy depends on labour markets that set wages
through pure competition and permit very little regulation to protect
employees from insecurity, and on a primary role for stock markets and
the maximization of shareholder value in achieving economic goals. Such
an economy is considered by the authors to be poor at making minor
adaptive innovations, because employers make inadequate investment in
employee skills which might produce such innovations; but it excels at
radical innovations, because the combination of free labour markets and
external shareholders makes it relatively easy to switch resources rapidly
to new and profitable firms and areas of activity. A CME, featuring
corporatist wage-setting, strongly regulated labour markets and corporate financing through long-term commitments by banks, follows exactly
the reverse logic.

The authors stress strongly that they are depicting two *enduring* forms
of capitalism, because each has different comparative advantages. However, those of the CME form are located solely in minor adaptations
within traditional and declining industries, while LMEs have assigned

to them all future-oriented industries and services sectors. In the end therefore this is a neo-institutionalism that fully accepts the logic of neo-classicism set out above: in the long run all institutions other than the pure market fail to cope with the future. Since these different forms of capitalism are considered to have been the products of historical *longues durées*, it also means that the German economy *never was* radically innovative in the past, which requires explaining away many past events in the economic history of such German industries as chemicals, machinery, steel, motor vehicles, when these sectors were at the forefront of technological advance.

This brings us to a further fundamental point: Typologies of this kind are fixed over time; they make no provision for changes in characteristics. As Zeitlin (2003) puts it, approaches like that of Hall and Soskice render learning almost impossible. Or, as Bertoldi (2003) says, they ignore any impact of change in the world economy and make no allowance for evolutionary development (see also Regini 2003; Lütz 2003). As Hay (2002) has it, this literature tends to take either a spatializing approach (the elaboration of models, as in the cases we are discussing here) or a temporalizing ones (identifying historical phases, and therefore probably giving more scope to actors' capacity to change, but ignoring synchronic diversity). It is not necessary for neo-institutionalist analysis to be as rigid as this.

Hall and Soskice also assume automatically that all innovation within new industries represents radical innovation, while all within old ones can represent only incremental innovation. This is because they use different sectors as proxies for different types of innovation. According to such an approach, when Microsoft launches another mildly changed version of Windows it still represents radical innovation, because information technology is seen as a radical innovation industry; but when some firms eventually launch the hydrogen-fuelled motor engine, this will only be an incremental innovation, because the motor industry is an old industry. Further, the authors do not confront the leading position of two clearly CMEs (Finland and Sweden) in new telecommunications technologies and the Nordic countries generally in medical technologies (Amable 2003: ch. 5; Berggren and Laestadius 2000). Boyer (2004*a*, 2004*b*) has shown that the institutional pattern found in the Nordic countries can favour high-technology growth in information and communication technologies as much as the Anglo-American one. This is completely lost in accounts that insist on dualism and an a priori allocation of institutional patterns. Instead of the a priori paradigm case methodology, Boyer (ibid.) and Amable (2003), who reaches similar conclusions, used Ragin's Booleian techniques (Ragin 2000) to derive institutional patterns empirically.

A further serious flaw in the Varieties of Capitalism approach is that it misunderstands the work of individual innovative companies. While engaging in radical innovation, firms usually also need to bring out products with minor improvements in order to sustain their position in markets while they wait for a radical innovation to bear fruit; but according to the Hall–Soskice model it is not possible for firms within an LME to succeed at incremental innovation. It is a major advance of the approach that they focus on the firm as an actor, rather than take a macroeconomic approach to the study of economic success. However, many of the advantages of this are vitiated by the fact that their model allows the firm virtually no autonomy outside its national macroeconomic context. This problem will be further considered in Chapter 3.

These authors further follow conventional wisdom in arguing that the superiority of American (or Anglophone) firms over German ones results from the fact that in the Anglophone countries all managerial power is concentrated in the hands of a chief executive (CEO) who is required to maximize shareholder value, with employees engaged on a hire-and-fire basis with no representative channels available to them. Here they are failing to distinguish between the firm as an organization and as a market-place. By seeing the CEO's power as being solely to maximize share values by the use of a hire-and-fire approach to management, they are able to present the firm in an LME as solely the latter and not as an organization. They can therefore dispense with the knowledge accumulated in the theory of the firm, which distinguishes between market and organization, and presents at least the large firm as an organization with personnel policies, and with management having a wider range of discretion and possibilities than just maximizing share values.

This is significant. In reality firms differ considerably in the extent to which they construct organizational systems, internal labour markets, and distinctive ways of working, even developing specific corporate cultures, rather than simply establishing themselves as spaces where a number of markets intersect. For example, a firm that develops a distinctive approach to work among its workforce as part of its competitive strategy cannot depend on a hire and fire personnel policy. Employees need to be inducted into the firm's approach, and are likely to demand some understandings about security if they are to commit themselves in the way that management wants. Rapid hire and fire meets neither of these needs. This fundamental difference in corporate strategy has nothing at all to do with differences between LMEs and CMEs; both can exist within either, particularly the former. Neglect of the firm as an organization is a weakness of much neo-institutionalist analysis. It is caused by the obsession already noted with a dichotomy between two mutually incompatible politico-economic ideologies, a dichotomy in which the distinction between firm and market is not at issue. At times Hall and Soskice (2001*a*: 9) seem to regard the organizational structure of the firm (or corporate hierarchy) as a characteristic of both LMEs and CMEs, and therefore an irrelevant variable—though the relevant passage is worded ambiguously:

All capitalist economies also contain the hierarchies that firms construct to resolve problems that markets do not address adequately (Williamson 1985). In liberal market economies, these are the institutions on which firms rely to develop the relations on which their core competences depend.

They seem here to be building into their model a functionalist balancing item, implying that hierarchy will exist to the extent that it can 'resolve problems'. In that case, why does their theory not build into the features of both LMEs and CMEs those that they would respectively need in order to have them cope with the kinds of innovation that their theory says is impossible for them? At the level of type-building one should not pick and choose which institutional features automatically receive compensation and which do not. As Weber originally formulated the concept, ideal types are 'one-sided accentuations', pressing home the logical implications of a particular kind of structure. The aim is not to provide an accurate empirical description, but a theoretical category, to be used in the construction of hypotheses. Again, the authors are not building their theory deductively, but are reading back empirical detail from what they want to be their paradigm case of an LME—the USA—into their formulation of the type. It is simply not possible within their methodological approach to ask the question: 'Is everything important that occurs in the US economy the embodiment of free markets?'

One contributor to the Hall and Soskice volume, Tate (2001), provides an analysis of standard setting in a number of countries which, because of its acute empirical observation, completely breaks the bounds of the master framework: Differences between France, Germany, the UK, and the USA simply cannot be contained within the LME/CME dichotomy. He points out the tendency to monopoly power embedded in the lack of authoritative public standards in the USA and subsequent need for regulation, and the strong role of the military arm of the state in establishing US standards. When he then tries to fit his subtle analysis to the dichotomy, he is forced to strange conclusions. For example, he labels as 'liberal' the tendency of the British Standards Institution to develop member-only services (ibid.: 448), while the tendency of the German standards institution (DIN) to develop universal standards is seen as a non-market characteristic (ibid.: 453–5). One could attribute the labels in the opposite way with at least equal plausibility.

Similarly, Tate (ibid.: 467–8) cites the current US approach to standardization, whereby the standards of individual corporations become national or even global, as an example of a liberal market process. But it is a defining characteristic of a liberal market that no one firm is able to impose conditions on others. If a single firm is able to impose such a thing as a standard on an entire market, there is not perfect competition, and that firm has been able to impose entry barriers. This is not regulation by the free market, but, again, by corporate hierarchy. An important aspect of the economic history of the initial triumph of the market model in the USA concerned the way in which many basic standards were imposed, usually by law, in a *neutral* manner that ensured a level playing field across a vast country and made market entry relatively easy. This did secure the true conditions of a competitive market. The establishment of national or super-national standards for electrical voltage and fittings, gas pressures, sizes of paper and a myriad other things by public authorities or business associations enabled new firms to enter a market and consumers to choose their products without adapting a mass of other non-compatible equipment. This was true market making by public infrastructures. The contemporary trend in, for example, computing and telecommunications for individual giant firms to use their market dominance to impose private standards and thereby erect large entry barriers against rivals is a mark of the rise of corporate hierarchy over both the market and public authority.

The path dependence literature has demonstrated how successful early standardization establishes the increasing returns that prevent the emergence of neoclassical equilibria (Arthur 1990; 1994). Much of the success of US firms in the new information economy of the 1990s consisted of such combinations of first-mover advantage with the large scale and international political weight of the country. This does demonstrate an important characteristic of the US variety of capitalism and helps explain its success in many new economy sectors, but it is misdescribed if it is defined as 'liberal market'. It *could* certainly be described as a strong instance of 'coordination' by corporate hierarchy and state leadership— qualities lacking *per definitionem* in an LME.

In practice the number of countries discussed at any length in the empirical chapters of Hall and Soskice's collection is very small—though a wider range appears in statistical tests. The UK (in eight chapters) and USA (four chapters) are the only LMEs subjected to any detailed analysis. As cases of CMEs there are: Germany (eleven chapters), Italy (one chapter), Sweden (one chapter). France appears in four chapters, always with serious question marks about its relation to the theory, and Japan similarly in two. In reality, therefore, this is a comparison between the UK/USA and Germany. But Germany is at times a problematic paradigm CME. It is the only large country among what the authors see as unambiguous European CMEs, and one with a very high degree of federalism. As Schmidt (2002: ch. 4) notes, because of its federalism, German network relations and the German state's enabling relations with economic actors are considerably less closely integrated and less influential than in most of the smaller countries. So the paradigm case is an outlier on a crucial aspect of the coordination variable. Another characteristic of the German economy is its tough anticartel law—one of many examples of how the post-war German economic constitution explicitly balanced the system's use of associative devices with mechanisms to ensure that these did not interfere with free competition. This is ignored by the authors of *Varieties of Capitalism*. Instead, antitrust law designed to prevent companies from colluding to control prices or markets is seen as typical of an LME model, and contrasted with the corporatist inter-firm relations of CMEs (Hall and Soskice 2001a: 31).

These authors do briefly consider diversity within the CME form. Apart from Germany, they also see Japan, Switzerland, the Netherlands, Belgium, Sweden, Norway, Denmark, Finland, and Austria as unproblematic—though differences between what they call 'industry-based' coordination of the German type and 'group-based' coordination found in Japan and Korea (ibid.: 34) are recognized. In an earlier work Soskice (1999) fully recognized these two distinct forms of CME: a northern European model, and the 'group-coordinated' East Asian economies. ('Northern Europe' is here defined by Soskice to include Italy but not France.) But not much is made of the distinction in the full development of theory or cases.

A 'Mediterranean' group (France, Italy, Spain, Portugal, Greece, and Turkey) is also given some recognition by Hall and Soskice. Like Albert (1991) before them, they accept that France is somehow different (Hall and Soskice 2001a: 35), and consider that a so-called southern European group (including France) probably constitutes a third, state-led, post-agrarian model. This at least makes matters more differentiated, though it produces a type curiously unable to distinguish between the French state and the Italian or Greek ones. Sometimes this 'Mediterranean' group is seen as being empirically poised somewhere between the LME and CME model, which enables the authors to insist that LME and CME remain the only points which require theoretical definition. But elsewhere the Mediterranean countries are treated as examples of CMEs; Thelen (2001), for example, treats Italy as almost unambiguously a 'German-type' 'coordinated' economy. One of the starting points of the Hall–Soskice model was an earlier paper by Soskice (1990) criticizing the Calmfors and Driffill (1988) model of wage bargaining. This model had contrasted economies with centralized and decentralized collective bargaining arrangements, classing the French, Italian and Japanese among the latter. Soskice pointed out that although these three countries were not as coordinated as Germany or Sweden, one could identify within them various mechanisms that ensured some coordination of wage bargaining. He found (within the sample of countries being considered) that only the UK and the USA lacked such mechanisms; therefore all other cases were classified as CMEs. Both here and in Hall and Soskice, the basic drive of the dichotomy is to confront the neoclassical model with a single rival type.

Beyond Dichotomies

Some contributors to the study of capitalist diversity have gone beyond dichotomies. Schmidt (2002) has three models of European capitalism: 'market' (very similar to the LME model); 'managed' (with an 'enabling' state that encourages economic actors to co-operate, more or less the CME model); and 'state' (an interventionist state of the French kind). The last is designed to remedy the neglect of this form by Hall and Soskice. Acknowledging that the role of the state has declined considerably in France in recent years, she points out that its background role and historical legacy remain of considerable importance in enhancing national economic capacity. But indeed much the same could be said of the US state, whose role in the vast defence-related sector could well be defined as 'state enhancement' of economic capacity.

Schmidt (ibid.: ch. 2) also manages to be sensitive both to change and to its *timing*—an unusual attribute among institutionalists. She studies how countries embodying each of these types respond to the challenges of globalization and Europeanization. A central hypothesis is that these challenges do not lead to simple convergence. Governments of the various countries have responded in complex ways, producing new forms of diversity. If there is any overall convergence it is mainly towards a loss of extreme characteristics and thus some sharing of attributes from the various models. And these diversities are full of interesting paradoxes: The UK, having had in many respects the weakest economy of the three, was thus the earliest to be forced to come to terms with the pressures of globalization. As a result, it now appears better prepared to face that challenge than Germany which, being initially the strongest economically, could delay adjustment.

A second hypothesis fundamental to her study is that political discourse has been particularly important in shaping national responses to the challenge. By this Schmidt means not just that different substantive discourses were adopted, but that these took different forms. She distinguishes between 'communicative' and 'coordinating' discourse forms. The former, more suited to centralized systems like the British and French, inform the public of what needs to be done; the latter, more typical of Germany, is used to develop consensus among powerful actors who cannot be controlled from the centre.

This work therefore marks a refreshing shift towards an actor-centred and non-determinist account. Schmidt by no means discounts the existence of very strong structures, within which her actors need to operate. But these are malleable by innovative actors, in particular by politics. She criticizes particularly effectively the oversimplified accounts that characterize much rational choice work in international political economy. This, she argues, is a curiously depoliticized form of study of politics, assuming as it does that the interests of nation states can be modelled in a straightforward way, with fixed, consciously held preferences. She demonstrates effectively how governments in the three countries of concern to her study developed very varied positions in relation to Europeanization: For example, the UK was quickest to respond to many of the single market initiatives, but slowest to the single currency. This can all be explained, and she provides good explanations, but these require tactical and historically contingent political actors.

But Schmidt still follows the practice of identifying empirical cases as standing for ideal types. This is unfortunate, because her own actual practice is well able to cope with the implications of seeing cases as amalgams of types: her actors are creative political schemers, looking for chances to change and innovate, not automata acting out the parts the theorist has set for them. And, as noted, she succeeds in showing how over time individual countries have moved around the triangular space which her particular model of types of capitalism allows them.

Several other authors present three or more forms of capitalism, or of elements of capitalism, nearly always retaining a geo-cultural approach. Esping-Andersen's analysis (1990) of different types of welfare state embodies variables relating to the outcomes of political struggle, or dominant political traditions, which avoids some of the functionalist implications of the Varieties of Capitalism model (a theme that will be considered in Chapter 3). Again, one starting point is free-market or liberal capitalism associated with the Anglophone group of countries, and another is Germany, producing a conservative, 'continental European' model. There is however a third, social-democratic pole, geographically associated with Scandinavia.

Critics of Esping-Andersen's model have concentrated: on identifying mixed cases (Castles and Mitchell 1991); on stressing how the treatment of women in different systems does not seem to correspond to the simple typology (Daly 2000); or on breaking up the overextended 'conservative continental' category. A fourth type has now been clearly established, separating southern European welfare states from this one on the basis of their particularly large role for the family (Naldini 1999) and other informal institutions (Ferrera 1997). Ebbinghaus (2001), concentrating on policies for combating early exit from the labour market, which he sees as deeply related to the form of the overall welfare regime, adds a fifth type based on Japan. All these works continue to depend on the characteristics of paradigm cases, which can be highly misleading. Viebrock (2004), in a study of different forms of unemployment benefit systems, has shown how Sweden—usually the absolute paradigm case of social democracy—has for reasons of political history retained a role for voluntary associations alongside the state in the organization of its unemployment insurance system.

A strong move away from dualism, which neither starts from nor privileges the free-market model, is the scheme of Whitley (1999). He builds up a set of fully sociological models of capitalism based on six types of business system (fragmented, coordinated industrial district, compartmentalized, state organized, collaborative, and highly coordinated), related to a number of different behavioural characteristics (ibid.: 42). He also presents five different ideal types of firms (opportunist, artisan, isolated hierarchy, collaborative hierarchy, allied hierarchy) (ibid.: 75), and a diversity of links between these types and certain fundamental institutional contexts (the state, financial system, skill development and control, trust and authority relations) (ibid.: 84). Significantly, Whitley's main fields of study are Japan, Korea, Taiwan, and other far-eastern economies, rather than either the US or the German cases, and he is therefore further removed from the obsession with neoliberalism and a contrast between it and a model of 'organized capitalism' that sometimes distorts the analysis of those who concentrate on western Europe and North America.

By far the best and most sophisticated approach to a 'post-dualist' typology of capitalism to date is that established by Amable (2003). He collected quantitative data on a vast range of characteristics of the national economies of most OECD countries: product markets, labour markets, financial systems, social protection. He uses literally dozens of individual indicators to assess each. He then allows a typology of groups of countries to be formed empirically by these data; he does not start from paradigm cases. This procedure gives him five groups, which, as with other authors, fall into familiar geo-cultural patterns: market-based (primarily Anglophone), social democratic (Nordic), Asian (Japan and Korea), Mediterranean (southern European), and Continental European (continental western European less the Nordic and Mediterranean countries). He further finds (as have others, e.g. Crouch 1999) that this last group does not show much internal coherence, and for some purposes splits it further into two subgroups, one comprising the Netherlands and Switzerland, the other Austria, Belgium, France, and Germany. Further, Amable is not afraid to draw attention to further diversity for some of the characteristics, with the result that countries do not always figure within their normal group.

At times Amable lapses from his finely nuanced stance. For example, the book ends (2003: ch. 6) with a future- and policy-oriented dialectic between the market-based and a simplified and generalized Continental European model. It seems that engaging in the rhetoric of debate about the future course of capitalism leads always to dualism, even when, as in Amable's case, the best strength of the author's position lies precisely in the demonstration of a far more differentiated world. He also depends necessarily for his data on sources like the OECD which are often constructed with in-built biases. For example, although at one point Amable (2003: 200) acknowledges the importance of military-related research and production in many of the high-tech sectors of the US economy, he follows the OECD in excluding all consideration of this from the indicators of the role of the state in the economy and of the regulation of external trade.

These minor criticisms apart, Amable has demonstrated that a genuinely scientific approach, using very extensive and diverse kinds of data, produces a useful and coherent typology comprising five or six types, at the same time enabling clear recognition of exceptions within types.

Dichotomizers will argue that they are applying the principle of parsimony and Occam's razor to complex schemes of Amable's or Whitley's kind. They will claim that, while there is clearly a loss of information if one collapses Whitley's 'coordinated industrial district, compartmentalized, state-organized, collaborative, and highly coordinated' mechanisms into the single idea of a CME, that idea seizes on the essential point that divides all these forms from the pure market one: coordination. But, as

Scott (2001: ch. 9) and Hay (2002) have separately argued, parsimony must not become an excuse for inaccuracy and ignoring important diversity. Is coordination the fundamental attribute of all the types in Whitley's list? On what grounds could this quality be regarded as more fundamental than the other characteristics which divide them, especially since the co-ordination takes place at very different levels? Recent developments in the governance approach (Crouch et al. 2004) draw attention to the role of collective competition goods provided by various governance modes in local economies, without demonstrating anything remotely strong enough to be called national 'coordination'. This suggests the possibility of analyses more moderate than those addressed at the whole macroeconomy.

Meanwhile, Hage and Alter (1997) have convincingly demonstrated analytical distinctions among several institutional forms. In that case, to apply Occam's razor to reduce them all to one idea of coordination is to cut into serious theoretical and empirical flesh. An explanation becomes more parsimonious than another when it uses a smaller number of explanatory variables *while explaining at least as much* as its opponent. For example, it is more parsimonious to model the solar system as heliocentric than terracentric, because the former uses far simpler mathematics to account for at least as many planetary movements as the latter. We should be far less impressed with the heliocentrist if she had to say: 'Forget about the outer planets; this theory is more parsimonious because it just looks at the inner ones.' But contemporary social science often makes use of precisely this kind of argument, using the idea of parsimony as meaning a kind of rough, tough macho theory that concentrates on the big picture and ignores detail.

One explanation of this tendency is a technical methodological one. In the social sciences (outside psychology) it is rarely possible to achieve very high levels of accuracy in explanations. The variables are so diffuse; the number of cases so few (at least for cross-national comparativists); and our means of observation are so less precise than those available to natural scientists. We are therefore very happy to achieve coefficients of correlation (R^2) with values like 0.65, which means that we have explained about one-third of the variance. Natural scientists, for example chemists, are likely to insist on (and can in practice achieve) correlations of 0.99. A theory that claims parsimony when it has achieved an R^2 of 0.65 has a very different stature than one that claims it at 0.99.

As Whitley's formulations demonstrate, the relationships between different forms and different behavioural characteristics present a varied patchwork of similarities and differences, not a set of polar contrasts. This suggests in turn the fundamental point: *that individual empirical cases might well comprise more complex amalgams still of elements from two or more theoretical types.* Whitley (1999) himself treats a fragmented market model of economic organization separately from one dominated by large firms, and is therefore able to see the USA itself as a hybrid of two different forms of capitalism rather than a pure case (see also Jackson: forthcoming).

This question has considerable practical implications, as will be noted at several moments in the subsequent discussion, particularly in Chapter 5. It is often recognized by authors who speak of 'hybrid' forms. For example, Schmidt (2002: ch. 4) suggests strongly that some changes in French institutions are making that case increasingly a hybrid, with borrowing from Germany as well as from neoliberal sources. Jackson (forthcoming) suggests that hybridization, as opposed to simple imitation of the exogenous, is the usual outcome of attempts at 'borrowing' institutions, even under extreme periods of transition, such as Germany or Japan under post-war occupation. Other researches (Ferrera, Hemerijck, and Rhodes (2000); Hemerijck, and Schludi (2000)) have shown the power of hybrid cases in achieving important reforms in welfare state organization—for example in recent changes in the Danish, Dutch and Irish cases (Ferrera and Hemerijck 2003). Zeitlin (2003) discusses various national cases that have become exceptions to their 'types' as the result of mixing institutional forms at the initiative of what I would call institutional entrepreneurs. Considering an earlier period, Windolf (2002: 85) discusses how French family capitalism played an important part in the country's post-war modernization, merging with advanced financial means of control and the strong state to produce a dynamic new model.

As we shall discus in a later chapter, 'hybridization' deals with only one way in which cases may deviate from types, and it is still very close to the idea of clear, macro-level types, because it sees these as the source of the hybridization. However, it does constitute an important challenge to simple equations of cases and types.

Questioning the Centrality of the Nation-State

The centrality of the nation state in most typologies of capitalist diversity also needs to be questioned. This centrality is found in most neo-institutionalist studies, including those on 'social [i.e. national] systems of innovation and production' (Amable 2000; Boyer and Didier 1998). It is also central to work from the parallel but distinct literature on 'national systems of innovation' (Freeman 1995; Lundvall 1992; Nelson 1993). At one level the case is well made. Very extensive elements of governance in the industrial and post-industrial societies of which we have knowledge do operate at the level of the nation-state: states have been the main sources of law, and most associations and organizations target themselves at the state (Crouch 2001). Given that markets are framed by law, this means that of the modes of governance usually discussed in governance theory, the state itself (obviously), markets, and various levels of associations are all heavily defined at national level, while community and informal association exist at a lower geographical level. Even research that explicitly works at comparisons between regional or other substate geographical levels often has to acknowledge the importance of the nation state as a major instance for the determination of socio-economic variables (Cotts Watkins 1991; Rodriguez-Pose 1998, 1999).

But many macro-level neo-institutionalists go further than this and postulate virtually hermetically sealed national institutions—often because they are concerned to address debates about economic and social policy, and these are mainly conducted at national levels. Radice (2000) argues that this has perhaps been particularly the case for left-of-centre analysts desiring to 'bring the state back in', leading to an exaggeration of the importance of national policy. More generally neo-institutionalists are led to stress the nation state by their functionalist assumptions, which model discrete, autonomous systems, each equipped with their sets of institutions, like a body with its organs. There are also methodological advantages in being able to treat nation states as discrete units of analysis, as many economic data are produced at national levels. Theorists of the diversity of capitalism are therefore eager to play down the implications of globalization, and argue intelligently and forcefully against the naive assumptions of much other literature that globalization somehow abolishes the significance of national differences (Hall and Soskice 2001a: 54–60; Whitley 1999: ch. 5; Hirst and Thompson 1997).

However, the position of the nation-state as the definer of the boundaries of cases is not so fixed that it should be taken for granted *per definitionem*. This is particularly obvious with respect to multinational corporations. As Beyer (2001) shows, large firms draw on resources from a range of different national bases; it is very difficult to identify them with particular national types and to see their institutional possibilities as being constrained by their country(ies) of location (see also Grant 1997). As Jackson (forthcoming) puts it, national models of capitalism are becoming 'institutionally incomplete'. This seems particularly true where international corporations are concerned, but even firms that are nationally owned and operate primarily within one nation state have access to knowledge, links and practices existing outside the national borders. Radice (1998: 278) similarly criticizes the national innovation system literature for a kind of mercantilism, arguing that it does not take adequate account of the fact that technology is always a public/ private collaboration, and that the private actors are usually global firms. Something always 'leaks' abroad from national programmes; innovation is at once global and national. He also points out (ibid.: 274–5) the falsity of the dichotomy between the so-called globalizing and national forces, as though one could identify them and then establish their relative importance. The phenomena associated with globalization are brought about at the behest of domestic actors working to influence national governments. Keune (forthcoming) has demonstrated this in relation to the former communist countries of central Europe. So the idea of national versus global collapses. As Helleiner (1994) earlier made the point: Internationalization is not an independent variable, because it is an outcome of state policy.

Radice (1998: 273–4) demonstrates a different weakness of nation-state based analysis by pointing out that all states are not equal as units. The USA is able to borrow to fund its deficits in a way not available to others, which means that comparing the 'performance' of that economy with others is not a true comparison of institutional capacities. One can move from that observation to point out that nation states cannot always be treated as a series of unit instances of the same phenomenon; they are also linked together in a hierarchical way to form an overall system, as Wallerstein and other world system analysts showed (Hopkins and Wallerstein 1982). For example, the units 'Portugal' and 'France' cannot be treated as equal units within which the effects of various independent variables can be independently and comparatively assessed, because they are partly defined by their relationship to each other. Scott (2001: 83 ff.) stresses the need to consider a range of levels: world system, society (nation-state), organizational field, organizational population, organization, and organizational subsystem. As he points out, different disciplines tend to look at different components of this. Hollingsworth and Boyer (1997: 4) are helpfully explicit that their scheme can be used at subnational and transnational, as well as national, levels (see also Coleman 1997).

We need always to be able to ask: Are arguments about the characteristics of national economies limited to specific economic sectors and industrial branches, or do they claim to apply to all? And how far beyond the heartland of the economy does the theory claim to range? If the nation state is at the heart of the analysis, are political institutions also to be covered by the characterization? Or does the theory apply even further, to structures like the welfare state, family or religion, for example? As we develop thinking of this kind, we soon come to see that the clear division between endogenous and exogenous that is so fundamental to nation-state-based theories becomes replaced by *a continuum of accessibility*—an idea which will be explored in more detail in a later chapter.

Conclusion

The governance approach to institutional analysis both builds on socio-logical and political science concepts of action and departs strongly from dualism—though it is often still tied to the analysis of national systems. Because it looks principally at the way in which economic action is governed or regulated, the focus of this body of theory is on action rather than structures. Structures emerge from the encounter between the actions of maximizing agents and the rules that are framed both to facilitate and to restrain the maximizing search. It is important to note that, just because this approach deals with rule-making, it is not necessarily concerned solely with either formal rules or the restraint of economic actors. As the *régulationistes* have shown us, rules are more a means by which economic actors attain their goals than just constraints over them.

The action-centred as opposed to functionalist orientation of governance theorists enables them to deal with greater complexity at the theoretical level. The market is present as a type and often remains a starting point or even a limiting case, but contrasts between it and other forms are not the sole focus of the account; these latter can be compared with each other without necessarily relating back to the market. Significantly, and in contrast with the Varieties of Capitalism school, the governance approach identifies corporate hierarchy as a form distinct from that of the free market. This and other elements of the approach will be fully developed in detail in Chapter 5. Meanwhile, on the basis of the present chapter we have estab-lished the following unsatisfactory characteristics of much, though by no means all, neo-institutionalist analyses of capitalism:

1. There is confusion between ideal types and cases, with the latter being seen as exemplifiers of the former, rather than the former being seen as constituents of the latter.
2. Despite the claim to be firm-centred, the approach has been too con-cerned with the macro-level picture of whole economies, and the account of types has been too closely linked to the polemic between neoliberalism and social democracy.

3. Characteristics of economies have been bundled together as coherent wholes with inadequate attention being paid to the forces that produce the bundles.

The next stage in the development of neo-institutional theory has to be an attempt to surmount these defects.

Note

1. It has become routine to use the term 'Anglo-Saxon' here, but it is problematic. It was developed originally to group together the collection of peoples of English, German, and Scandinavian origin who inhabited England on the eve of the Norman invasion of 1066; it served to contrast them with both the French-speaking (though originally Scandinavian) invaders and the Celtic inhabitants of other parts of the British Isles. Such a term became useful over 800 years later to distinguish the British and other northern European (and by now primarily Protestant) inhabitants of the late nineteenth-century USA from more recent Latin-language-speaking and Irish immigrants, and by extension also from Poles and other Catholics as well as from Blacks and Jews. Its contemporary use by academic social scientists as well as international organizations like the OECD seems not only blithely ignorant of these connotations, but also commits the solipsism of using it mainly as a contrast with Germany—which includes the Saxon half of the mythical Anglo-Saxon identity. Its contemporary use also normally includes Ireland—a people explicitly excluded from both the original and subsequent US terms. It is in fact used entirely consistently to identify that group of countries where English is the dominant language and the majority population is white-skinned: the UK, Ireland, the USA, Canada, Australia, and New Zealand. The correct, unambiguous term, which precisely identifies this group of countries is 'Anglophone', and one wonders why this clear and accurate term is not used instead of the more popular, exotic but highly dubious alternative. To insist on this point is not pedantry, but draws our attention to certain possible implications of the fact that the economics litera-ture which finds it far easier to make sense of the Anglophone economies than others is itself almost solely Anglophone.

3

Wahlverwandschaft, Complementarity, and the Theoretical Utility of Institutional Untidiness[1]

Neo-institutionalists vary considerably in the institutional range of their theories and models. At the narrow end, researchers concentrate on one theme: The set of extra-economic rules which (for rational-choice institutionalists) have been constructed or (for historical institutionalists) have emerged to guide economic behaviour, albeit within a context of other relevant institutions. At the broad end, authors will try to demonstrate how a wide range of social institutions, not all directly part of the economy, may be pulled into a common *Gestalt* compatible with and contributing to its form.

Welfare regime theory (as discussed in Chapter 2) is an example of a single-institution theory. It directs our attention at forms of income maintenance outside the labour market. Governance theory is in a midway position. It addresses a single institutional point: rule formulation and enforcement within the economy. But this single point is one capable of considerable generality, if it can be shown that the governance mechanism has the relevant institutional reach. For example, *régulationiste* theory links governance to social systems of production (Hollingsworth and Boyer 1997). Some versions of such theory make even larger claims about, for example, the implications of economic regime for political system or family structure. Whitley's model (1999) similarly extends further than governance of the economy to include major elements of its structure, and also observes links to the family and other ostensibly non-economic institutions.

Creators of single-institution models may try to increase their scope by developing hypotheses about links between the core institution and others. Sometimes they go beyond this point and build the hypothesized links into the model. Multi-institutional theories of this kind are potentially very powerful explanatory devices, if they can demonstrate how the inter-institutional links that they require are forged. But doing this can prove very difficult. As Scharpf (1997: 29–30) observes, social scientists usually lack the knowledge of enough variables to construct full explanations and predictions; it is therefore better that we work with small and medium-sized mechanisms that render things plausible, rather than general theories. We might then try to extend to more ambitious levels, step by step.

Excessive weight is often placed on industrial relations institutions in neo-institutionalist macroeconomic accounts, with sometimes distorting consequences. As the most obviously sociological and political component of the economy, industrial relations was the focus of much early neo-institutionalist work (Trigilia 1998: ch. X), but the centre of gravity of the theory often does not shift enough when attention turns to modelling whole economies. This explains some of the oddities of case allocation in neo-institutionalist studies. For example, Kitschelt et al. (1999a) divide one of their categories of whole economies—the 'industry-coordinated' group—into those with primarily national concertation (Scandinavia) and those where concertation is primarily sectoral (Belgium, Germany, Switzerland). It is difficult to make this industrial relations-derived scheme work for other economic institutions. Similarly, Italian industrial relations might just about be claimed as a case on its way to collective bargaining coordination (Thelen 2001), but this does not mean that the whole Italian *economy* is 'coordinated'. Indeed, the Italian economy *embodies* no single model, but several *are found within it*. Analysts usually distinguish three Italian political economies (Bagnasco 1977): that in the north-west based on large-scale Fordist industry; that of the centre and north-east based on areas of specialized small firms nested in local communities; and that of the south, dependent on state subsidies to large-scale industry. But even this can today be broken down further: the service-oriented economy of Milan is not the same as the industrial one of Turin and other parts of the north-west; clear differences have emerged between the structure of the small-firm economies of the north-east and those of the centre (Burroni and Trigilia 2001). This internal diversity is a characteristic that Italy exhibits particularly strongly, but the point applies with different degrees of strength to most other countries; the USA is probably the most extreme case.

Similarity and Complementarity

More important than empirical difficulties with particular extensions of institutional range used by various authors are difficulties in the identification of the logic of coherence that is considered to impart some kind of *Gestalt*, which might enable the observer to say that a characteristic of one institution is somehow related to that of another. To achieve this two totally opposed potential logics are used: similarity and complementarity.

The Logic of Similarity

This has been strongly asserted by Goodin et al. (1999: 6):

These clusters [of different forms of welfare capitalism] ... represent intellectually and pragmatically unified packages of programmes and policies, values and institutions. It is between these whole packages—these welfare regimes as a whole—the social engineers are obliged to choose. It is the performance of these welfare regimes, taken as a whole, that we ought to try to compare.

For Hall (1999), similarity emerges from the way in which a given set of national, regional or sectoral institutions tends to create equilibrium forms of firm behaviour, combined with a broader set of factors that include the presence of specific public policies, social coalitions and socio-economic conditions. Hall and Gingerich (2004) take this further to argue that systems mixing institutions of different fundamental types (specifically, mixing CME and LME characteristics) will underperform pure types. In other words, pedigree dogs will outperform mongrels. Their theoretical argument is supported by impressive quantitative evidence on national economic performances. It belongs in the class of 'U-curve' theories which, disconcertingly for most policymakers, predict that extreme cases will outperform compromises and hybrids. As Hay (2002) has pointed out, having derived theoretical reasons for producing a set of types, authors tend to regard as somehow 'incoherent' those cases whose histories have happened not to place them in the theorist's boxes. He cites the instance of Garrett (2000), who, having set up Scandinavia and the so-called Anglo-Saxon model as his theoretically 'pure' cases of different forms of welfare state and political economy, has to insist that Germany and the Netherlands are 'incoherent'.

The idea of *Wahlverwandschaft*—elective affinity, a concept that Weber developed from Goethe who developed it from eighteenth-century chemistry—is often used to describe this process whereby institutions across many different parts of a society find some kind of fit together, mainly through cognitive processes and social learning (Powell and DiMaggio 1991: 63–82). Both formal and informal sources, regulation and cultural cognitive processes might induce this isomorphism. Kitschelt et al. (1999b: 3), for example, see *Wahlverwandschaft* linking types of production regime, patterns of socio-economic inequality and protection through welfare states, and the constitution of corporate political actors in parties and interest groups. Whitley (1997) does not use the term elective affinity, but describes the same phenomenon, when he argues that patterns link the training system and the role of employers and workers' organizations in running it, the academic stratification of the labour market, the strengths and policies of the state concerning the integration of the pre-industrial training system, the extent to which owners are locked into the fate of the firms into which they invest, their trust in the formal institutions governing property rights and other economic issues, and systemic trust in general, which is in turn linked to types of financial markets, and the nature and form of legitimation of authority relations.

Streeck (2001) proposes that German and Japanese capitalism are distinguished from the Anglo-American variety by their financial systems, corporate governance, worker citizenship, approaches to employment, welfare states, industrial relations, training, and wage distribution. He does not extend his range beyond these strictly economic institutions. For Hall and Soskice (2001*a*), however, the political system in an LME should also function like a market, with a large number of actors pursuing their goals in a system which achieves balance through the sheer number of transactions and the incapacity of any one group to dominate. This is the model of pluralism embodied in US political theory and regarded as replicating in the polity the conditions of the market economy. It is not only analogous to the economic system, but it helps sustain the market economy by preventing accumulations of political power.

As Hall and Soskice (ibid.: 17–21) put it, particular institutions develop similar capacities in neighbouring spheres, such as corporate governance, vocational training, and collective bargaining. Such assumptions have, for example, enabled proponents of neoliberal labour market reform in Europe to argue that intensified product-market competition will be a spur to such reform because, if firms are competing intensively in product markets, they will find it difficult to cooperate in labour markets (Blanchard 2004). But often authors achieve their generalizations about such links by looking at a few components of an institution and falsely assuming that all others are isomorphic with it. For example, in examining types of welfare state, Goodin et al. (1999) consider only their tax transfer aspects. As a result they are not required to confront such apparent anomalies as the major role of public investment and public institutions in the US education system, or the universalist national health service that endured in the UK from the 1940s until very recently. Some studies have taken a more careful approach and have therefore revealed greater complexity. Zysman's pioneering study (1983) of comparative financial institutions, while as normal linking the USA and UK (capital-market systems), also put together Germany and Sweden (relatively autonomous banks with some state role), distinguished from each other in the Esping-Andersen model of welfare states; and France and Japan (state control of investment), contradicting most typologies. Viebrock (2004), in a study of different forms of unemployment benefit systems, has shown how Sweden—usually the absolute paradigm case of the social democratic welfare state—has for reasons of political history retained a role for voluntary associations alongside the state in the organization of its unemployment insurance system. And Kristensen (1997), comparing the development of management systems in England, Germany, and Denmark, finds the last to be dominated by a 'personal reputational' system, which does not feature in any of the usual stereotypes of Scandinavian countries. The scope of *Wahlverwandschaft* has therefore not been fully established. Many authors are rushing to conclusions about the scope for generalization without absorbing the more differentiated results of detailed inquiries.

The Logic of Complementarity[2]

Strictly speaking, complementarity should be seen as the opposite principle to that of similarity. In the everyday sense of the word two things are 'complementary' when one 'completes', or *makes up for the deficiencies* of the other. Complementary items are therefore contrasting, and in a precise way. Unfortunately, use of the term by neo-institutionalists has been much less precise than this everyday usage. At least three different meanings of it can be discerned, ranked in descending levels of clarity and rigour.

   1. *Complementarity where components of a whole mutually compensate for each other's deficiencies in constituting the whole.* This is the meaning noted above: the strictest even if the everyday sense. It defines two phenomena (in our case institutions) as complementary when each can be defined in terms of what is lacked by the other in order to produce a defined whole. Höpner (2003b) cites the computer scientist's sense of complementary binary numerical series as an instance. Two hemispheres that together form a sphere are a further good example. Another is Nils Bohr's discovery that the transmission of light requires both point-like and linear characteristics—features that earlier scientists had considered to be mutually incompatible. For Bohr it was precisely the contrast afforded by such incompatible principles that made the phenomenon possible.[3]

   When such cases are encountered in institutional analysis it is worth noting them, as they are rich in information and predictive possibilities. But they are rare, as they depend on the identification of perfect matchings of a kind that can usually only be found in mathematics and physics. There are temptations to functionalism if we search for 'necessary' complementarities of this type among social structures. Even then, the analysis depends on defining the institution in question solely in terms of these matching characteristics. We might get close to the idea with, for example, non-transferable company pension schemes in US corporations, which offset the tendency towards high labour mobility of many other US labour market institutions. Another might be the highly portable skill qualifications of the German vocational training system, which offset the tendency towards low labour mobility of many other German labour market institutions. A third would be the role of big institutional investors in the US economy, whose individual impact on a firm or whole sector can be so large that they cannot behave as in a pure market, but need to act strategically, often engaging in dialogue with firms' managements. They thereby offset the bias towards spot markets of some other US financial institutions, and make possible a supply of patient capital. In each case we have to assume that the 'deficiency' is widely recognized to be such.

A further instance would be those arguments that show how establishment and maintenance of the free market require a strong state that provides uncompromised support for the maintenance of market institutions, keeping at bay sectional demands for special interventions—though centralized state strength is the opposite of the characteristics of the free market itself (Gamble 1988). For example, Carruthers, Babb, and Halliday (2001) have shown how central bank rules have become stricter while bankruptcy laws have become softer, the former being consistent with strict neoliberalism while the other is not. The authors conclude:

[Bankruptcy law] is the institution that constitutes the legal preconditions for market pressure! Indeed, bankruptcy laws are being altered so as to ameliorate the market pressures that distressed corporations face. This does not invalidate the idea of institutional efficiency, but it casts doubt on the idea that market pressures drive institutions in the direction of ever-greater efficiency. (ibid.: 119–20)

Similarly, a family pattern complementary to a free-market economy might be one that provides resources of emotional support and maintenance of the worker to offset the rigours and insecurities of the labour market (Parsons and Bales 1955). Whitley (2005) talks of how in the Netherlands the links between the corporate governance system, state policies, and the organization of business groups are so strong as to outweigh the relatively arm's-length bank-firm relationships. He also points out (ibid.) how there are likely to be contradiction between dominant institutional arrangements with respect to firm governance, strategies, authority sharing, and employer–employee commitments, these contradictions giving managers the chance to develop idiosyncratic strategies and capabilities. To turn to an institution of a very different kind, Renate Mayntz (2004) has drawn attention to the combination of hierarchy and network as modes of governance within terrorist organizations. These were not 'designed' as complements to each other, but coexist as coincidental diversity. In a hostile environment the capacity to switch from one to the other becomes a complementarity. This is typical of the unpredictable and non-designed character of complementarity in institutions. A difference becomes a complementarity when it 'works'. But this requires specification of a goal; for terrorist organizations trying to survive under pressure, goals are clear. But one of the ways in which normal life institutions differ from terrorist organizations is that they have multiple, contested, and uncertain goals.

2. *Complementarity in the economist's sense*. Economists have a concept of complementarity as part of the production function. It is defined clearly in terms of two goods, a fall in the price of one of which will lead to a rise in the demand for the other. Aoki (1994) extends this concept to institutions, defining institutions as complementary when the enhancement of one will assist provision of the other. Hall and Soskice (2001a: 17) follow Aoki in defining complementarity as when 'the presence (or efficiency) of one [institution] increases the returns (or efficiency of) the other'. (Deeg (2005) prefers to use 'coherence' for this concept, and would also include in coherence the logic of synergy.) Amable (2003: 6, 58–66) uses complementarity well in the economist's sense, to mean items that are empirically found together, without using either the idea of 'completion' or of affinity or isomorphism. This works well as a *post hoc* discovery by research, but it is necessary to recognize that the ensembles thereby discovered might not be the only viable ones, as Amable (ibid.: 73) himself points out. They might also be changed by innovative action by social actors. They do not imply necessities. Further, unlike the previous definition, they do not imply that the two items identified are necessarily enough to produce some kind of whole when combined.

A good example of the original concept in relation to goods is the hypothesis that, if the price of flour falls, there will be a rise in demand for tomatoes. This happens because the fall in the price of flour causes a reduction in the price of pizza, leading to a rise in demand for tomatoes, flour and tomatoes (with some other ingredients) being complementary parts to the whole pizza. This carries something of the idea of completion—one item somehow 'needs' to be accompanied by the other to make a final product, though of course both flour and tomatoes can be used without each other to make other products. But the concept can easily slip into the far weaker idea of things that just happen to 'go' together, without much knowledge of the mechanisms that are linking them. Unlike cases falling under 1, there is no logical relationship between flour and tomatoes, such that one is defined as the characteristics lacking in the other (as in the two hemispheres). They are linked by a purely empirical phenomenon, the pizza. This is itself the fortuitous consequence of human creativity, certain human tastes, the coincidental existence of large numbers of tomatoes in the region where pizza dough was first developed, and then a large quantity of tradition. This complementarity depends on certain strong *ceteris paribus* clauses. A change of taste (such as a growing popularity, consequent on the rise of tomato allergies, of *pizze bianche*— *pizze* made without tomatoes) could destroy the relationship altogether.

If we bear in mind the role of human creativity in their construction, we shall find that many institutions display this contingent form of complementarity. For example, the studies by Streeck and Yamamura (2001; Yamamura and Streeck 2003) of German and Japanese historical development shows how the bundle of characteristics of those economies came together because actors worked creatively to make them do so. Over a long period they then adjusted them to make them fit better. Later observers then erroneously think that they had been strategically planned. If we bear in mind the role of human creativity in forging these complementarities, we shall be aware that entrepreneurial actors may intervene at points of change and produce surprising new combinations that unsettle the *ceteris paribus*.

The economist's concept of complementarity is purely empirical; the associated goods are not bound together through necessity, but as a result of a large number of consumer choices expressed in the market. The Coasian firm as an organization may also be at work alongside this market. Assume that there is a pizza-making monopoly, which firm is also trying to break into the mobile phone business. It therefore uses a fall in the price of flour, not to reduce the price of its pizza, but to cross-subsidize its mobile phones. We therefore observe that a fall in the price of flour leads to a rise in the demand for mobile phones. This is certainly a complementarity in the strict economics sense, but it exists at a different level from that of the consumer-driven market case of the pizza. Many of the institutional complementarities observed in the literature that can be related back to a public policy take this form. Government (or the policy elite more widely defined) is a policy monopolist, and it acts across a range of areas. There is no real market for institutions: there are too few producers and too few consumers of institutions. The observation that two institutions tend to be found together therefore tells us little in itself; the same producer might have made them all; there might be simple imitation among a small number of institutional producers and consumers. The links produced by all these processes are real enough and can be highly significant, but they are *constructed* complementarities; they do not imply relationships of necessity. As such, they are more useful than those discussed as type 1 complementarities, partly because they are found more frequently, and partly because they do not lead us into functionalist traps. When they can be defined as rigorously as in the economists' production function, they meet high scientific standards. Outside that frame, however, there is a danger of them weakening to become merely observed associations, as in 3, which we now consider.

3. *Complementarity as mutual effects.* Pierson (2000a: 78) refers to configurations of complementary institutions as being those 'in which the performance of each is affected by the existence of others'. This is similar to 'reciprocal reinforcement', but is much weaker, as it specifies only 'affected by'. It also loses the tension that was present in the idea of goods that required ingredients making different contributions to the whole. But many authors use complementarity in this weak sense. There is some notion that institutions go together, but how is not specified; it could mean similarity, elective affinity, leading us to the very opposite of complementarity in its strongest sense. For example, Amable uses the concept to support the assumption that national systems must possess an overall internal congruence, or different components will give contradictory signals to agents (Amable 2000: 6, 57). His idea is deeply interesting, and we shall return to it; but it is best not to see it as complementarity. The same applies to Whitley (2005), when he defines complementarity as the degree to which social institutions encourage similar kinds of economic actors to behave in similar ways and reinforce each other's effects. This refers to situations where the existence of one institution provokes that of another, which in turn strengthens the first, and so on. This is a powerful concept, as it can demonstrate how certain kinds of path dependence might be created, but it obscures the necessary element of difference needed to distinguish complementarity from similarity.

Of these three approaches to complementarity, the first makes the strongest and most theoretically based claims. If it really can be demonstrated that one institution completes, in the sense of making up for the deficiencies of, another, then something important has been learned about the association of these institutions. But it will be only rarely that our theories are strong enough to support such claims. The second, the economist's, meaning points to an empirical association, but outside the realm of the production function it is difficult to specify the association. The third approach is very weak, identifies only a weak association, and should probably not be dignified with the name of complementarity at all.

Similarity and Complementarity: A Conclusion

The logic of strict complementarity is that certain efficiencies are achieved when balancing or contrasting characteristics are found alongside each other: the advantages of the mongrel over the pedigree animal. The latter has heavily reinforced characteristics, which means that vulnerabilities are exaggerated, while the mongrel avoids such reinforcement and may therefore appear more 'balanced'. At the same time, of course, the pedigree animal, because it does have exaggerated characteristics, does some things particularly well. Both types of animal offer advantages, but they are different types of advantage. The same may be true of ensembles of institutions. Those based on balanced complementarities may be adept at certain activities; those based on similarities at others. This leads us to interesting research questions about when which type is appropriate.

For Goethe, *Wahlverwandschaft* helped express the subtle and paradoxical mix of similarity and contrast that constitutes the mutual attraction between two persons. Similar complexities apply to institutions.[4] We seek similarity in our institutions because we operate more easily in contexts where everything is familiar to us, even if there is no objective advantage to such similarity in itself. We seek difference in order to take advantage of the compensation and balance offered by complementarity in the first, strongest, sense. A particular institutional ensemble will comprise a complex mass of these opposed principles. For example, the actors who constructed the contemporary Japanese economy took a series of pragmatic opportunities, sometimes aiming at increasing competition, at other moments seeking coordination. In the end it is impossible to classify Japanese institutions in terms of competition or coordination, similarity or difference. They are all of these things.

But using this idea scientifically to construct a logically derived model of how social institutions are connected together presents a severe methodological challenge. The logic of similarity argues that institutions with similar properties will be found together; that of complementarity that those with balancing, even sometimes opposed properties will do so. Theories of similarity are likely to reflect a model of societies as having been shaped by more or less conscious design, at least of the fictional social contract kind, as one might expect powerful shaping forces to seek some degree of homogeneity in the structures they produce. Theories of complementarity, however, reflect a functionalist logic, as they assume that evolutionary survival has privileged those social forms in which different institutions operate together in a way that balances the whole.

Examples of both approaches can be found in the literature. For example, there is widespread agreement among economic historians that the common law system of Anglophone countries was more favourable to the growth of the free-market economy than the civil codes of most of Continental Europe. This is an example of similarity: The common law approach does not permit a central authority to frame an a priori comprehensive code, but it evolves gradually in synchrony with, and in the same manner as, developments in the market economy itself. Possession of a common law tradition and being Anglophone have a virtual one-to-one correspondence, as both derive from having been part of the British Empire.

However, when it comes to more specifically political institutions where Anglophone countries (or at least the only two which are systematically studied in the comparative literature, the UK and the USA) differ sharply, observers find themselves drawn towards contractarian or functionalist approaches depending on the country they are regarding as paradigmatic. As already noted, those focusing on the USA draw attention to the similarities between the mode of operation of the highly fragmented, strongly decentralized political system and the market economy. Those focusing on the UK stress how the strongly majoritarian and centralized character of its politics reduces the role of lobbies and pressure groups, enabling government to maintain the rules necessary to a market economy (Wood 2001: 254–6). Indeed, Wood has elsewhere (King and Wood 1999) explicitly contrasted the political economy of neoliberalism in the UK with that of the USA during the 1980s. Wood is here using complementarity in the best sense: by itself the market cannot produce the kind of external, monopolistic, non-competitive power source required if the rules that the market itself requires are to be devised, enforced and revised. Drago (1998) has similarly demonstrated at length how the quality of aloofness from organized interests often seen as characteristic of British government applied even more strongly to the Chilean dictatorship of Auguste Pinochet, a regime which introduced a free-market level playing field because, having liquidated all opponents, it did not have to pay any attention to special lobbies on behalf of particular producer groups. This seems to refute Knight's assertion (2001: 30) that neoliberalism in Latin America was associated with the rise of democracy; rather, it shows a good example of complementarity.

It is interesting to note that Fioretos (2001: 234), dealing with a rare period (the early 1990s) when the German government could rely on its parliamentary majority far more confidently than the British, manages to give the argument a startling new twist: *Precisely because* of its parliamentary stability, he claims, the German government was more worried about its relations with non-parliamentary interest organizations; British government, worried about parliament, had no attention to spare for such interests. Most comparisons of the British and German political systems characterize them in exactly the opposite way, with the majoritarian British government having a free hand, while German governments are subject to complex pluralistic lobbying. Fioretos is not wrong, as he accurately describes what he observed. What we must learn from his account, and perhaps the others, is that system characteristics are not always consistent and persistent; and the familiar lesson that there are few mechanical relations between cause and effect, because of the inter-mediating, creative capacities of human actors. Butzbach (2005), in his study of changes in French and Italian savings banks, argues similarly that national systems are characterized by contradictions and discontinuous equilibria, with non-teleological evolutionary configurations rather than convergence or divergence as the process.

The problem is that theory-builders, rather than recognize the coexistence of the two processes, will move between opposite logics—similarity and complementarity—as makes theory seem more convincing, presenting an overall account which looks plausible but which is not vulnerable to counter-factual test. This usually happens because, as noted in Chapter 2, they construct their models by working from a small number of empirical cases which they regard as paradigmatic, and embed their characteristics—which contain a complex mass of similarities, complementarities and mere accidents—into the theoretical type. But, as was stressed in a different context in Chapter 2, Weber argued that a type should be developed as a 'one-sided accentuation' of logically implied characteristics, representing that is the imposition of a single rationale, *from which of course it is fully expected that empirical cases will diverge*. This does not permit mixing the logics of similarity and complementarity, but makes the matching of cases to the types a rewarding exercise.

This becomes important, for example, when considering the phenomenon of neoliberalism, which we have already seen can take diverse forms. As Campbell and Pedersen (2001c: 257) argue, in a good statement of complementarity as compensation:

[T]he development of neoliberal institutions in one area was compensated for by institutions based on different principles in other areas ...; the adoption of neo-liberalism was heavily mediated by other institutional principles.

Theory can be permitted to combine contrasting rationales if it posits either a central group of actors who can be considered to have skilfully fashioned major elements of the society after their interests, or a compromise between identified major actors engaged in power struggle. For example, the *régulationiste* literature was able to propose a homogenization of coherent Fordist principles across a wide range of institutions, because it was fundamentally related to Marxist theory, which in turn sustains a thesis that all the institutions of a social formation will reflect the interests of a dominant class. (There is of course considerable diversity and ambiguity in Marxist theory whether an actor-centred or a functionalist account should be given of how this domination comes to be expressed.) Esping-Andersen's (1990) model of welfare-state formation is an example of a logic of stylized compromises between opposed social and political forces, as the designation of his types in terms of political models implies. (See also Korpi 1983 for a general formulation of this power-relations approach to social analysis; for an application aimed specifically at the study of capitalist diversity while also bringing power into a game-theoretic approach, see Amable 2003: 9–10, 46, 66–73.) It is also possible to depict the establishment of particular kinds of governance as an outcome of socio-political struggle. Similar again is North's account (1990a) of the emergence of the Anglophone model of capitalism: a liberal but non-democratic political settlement that favoured the interests of bourgeois property owners over both aristocratic elites and the propertyless masses. Steinmo, Thelen, and Longstreth (1992), Thelen (1999), Kristensen (1997), and Streeck and Yamamura (2001) and other 'historical institutionalists' (Campbell and Pedersen 2001a) have similarly looked at the role of conflict and contention in the establishment of particular national sets of institutions. Teubner (2001) has drawn attention to the way in which incompatibilities between different legal principles in a complex system provide useful 'irritants' from which innovation can result. From a different theoretical perspective, Bourdieu also considered 'fields' of action as *both* arenas of purpose and of conflict (Bourdieu, Chamboredon, and Passeron 1973). Therefore the organizational field becomes an important source of constraints and patterns, denying simple rational choice models (Scott 2001: 140).

If we do not adopt a functionalist approach we shall want to postpone the search for such links to the empirical application of a theory rather than its initial formulation (Streeck 2001). For example, it is possible to show how South African and Northern Irish capitalism took advantage respectively of racial and religious segregation to segment and maintain dominance over the labour force, even though such segregation in itself contradicts market principles—cases of complementarity rather than *Wahlverwandschaft*. It would however be an error to move from that observation to the thesis that segregation was functionally necessary to capitalism—though South African and Irish Marxists used to make such an analysis. Capitalists were certainly able to *make use* of racial and religious discrimination and to bind it into their economic system, but this was the result of skilful action, not system requirements. And eventually they were able to shed their dependence on these forms of labour control when their negative features outweighed their (for them) positive ones.

Distinguishing Unhelpful Incompatibility from Complementarity

This discussion seems to lead to the conclusion that mixed institutions are always likely to be more useful for change and innovation, and more resilient, than those that reproduce similar characteristics over a wide institutional range. However, some empirical studies seem to demonstrate exactly the opposite: that 'pure' cases perform more highly than mixed ones. As already noted, Hall and Gingerich (2004) found that pure CME and LME economies performed better than those with mixed character-istics. Calmfors and Driffill (1988) found that inflation was lower in coun-tries with either highly centralized collective bargaining or completely unorganized labour markets. These studies present 'U-curve findings': performance is higher at extremes than at midpoints. They are claiming that a certain critical mass of a specific pattern must be found across fields and/or subfields before a given capacity can be usefully present at all. If there is heterogeneity among relevant fields and subfields, actors within the institutional context will be able to achieve nothing.

This is fully plausible. But it does not refute the argument concern-ing complementarities. Arguments concerning isomorphism can defeat those concerning complementarity only when it can be shown empiric-ally that a particular activity tends to do better with an isomorphic pattern—and, of course, vice versa. Clearly, some incongruent patterns will provide useless sets of capacities, but others will not do so. Micro-analysis, rather than a *grosso modo* methodology, heavily dependent on simplifying assumptions and proxies, is essential if we are to discover this.

The research methods used in such studies as Hall and Gingereich (2004), Calmfors and Driffill (1988), or Garrett (1998, 2000) cannot discover the presence of complementarities. They start with broad generalizations about the logically coherent characteristics of systems; they cannot notice crucial exceptions that might constitute complementarities (like venture capital angels within an otherwise neoclassical financial system), because they exclude the possibility of their relevance a priori. To discover such phenomena we need a research strategy such as that of Ragin's Comparative Qualitative Analysis (2000). This uses Boolean algebra to discover relative possibilities that a number of phenomena—for example, a governance mode and a set of capacities—will be found together. This can tell us how often some phenomena rather than others are found together; and what never seems to be found at all. Being based on small n research or even single case studies, the results of such work can never be conclusive. Also, Boolean approaches cannot show linkages, only associations; therefore they do not reveal how complementarities might be operating. But they can gradually establish knowledge of a more painstakingly thorough and detailed kind, from which hypotheses can be derived.

A further interesting implication of 'U-curve' findings is that, though they are usually based on cross-sectional research (i.e. comparing a number of cases at one time), they are sometimes used to derive strong and negative predictions for possibilities of change. Let us assume that cross-sectional analysis of a number of cases has demonstrated a U-curve relationship between characteristics of the two hypothesized types of economy and economic performance found in Calmfors and Driffill's analysis. Let A represent a national case with suboptimal performance, lying closer to the coordinated than to the free market pole. If strategic actors in A want to improve their performance, Calmfors and Driffill (1988) have two forms of advice to offer them: Either become a purer example of the former, or transform into the latter, accepting in that case that for a considerable period this will bring worsening performance. This follows because, with the possible exception of revolutionary situations, all institutions cannot be rapidly and simultaneously transformed. There is likely to be a lengthy transition process, during the course of which A gradually loses coordinated characteristics and acquires free-market ones. The U-curve implies that this will necessarily bring a deteriorating performance in the short and medium run. However, when we are dealing with *change over time* within cases rather than comparing separate instances we must take account of reflexive, creative actors, able to perceive what is happening to their institutions and possessing (limited) ability to try to interact with the lessons of their experience, to learn, and then to innovate. Synchronic analyses cannot be seen as simple proxies for diachronic ones.

Problems of Functionalism

There are certainly cases of societies that have been centrally and effect-ively designed by very powerful rulers with a taste for institutional congruence; it is notable that many accounts of institutional development emphasize the role of centralized elites and rule-makers (e.g. Streeck 2001). But these are rare in complex societies. Normally a theory of macro-societal coherence whereby emergent rather than planned empir-ical cases correspond closely to theoretical types requires assumptions of evolutionary functionalism, which 'rewards' a limited number of success-ful types and 'punishes' odd, incoherent cases. As in biological evolution, the exigencies of the struggle for survival can be considered to favour certain social forms over others, and the number of these will be consid-erably less than the possible combinations of empirical characteristics that might in principle exist. But to apply this to macro-level developments among advanced societies begs certain questions.

First, biological evolutionary theory, similarly to economic theory, de-pends on very large numbers—verging on infinity—of individual units. Those which survive will be those which happen to have found successful formulae. But when the universe of study is nation states undergoing advanced industrialization and post-industrialization, we have far too few cases. Also, these are not discrete, autonomous individual examples of a phenomenon; they are bound together as part of an overall system, related to each other by comparative advantage, interdependence, and also combinations of economic and politico-military dependence. These relations may themselves be outcomes of historical accident or military conquest unrelated to the issue of economic performance. National eco-nomic history in no way provides us with a universe resembling that of biological evolution. We have no idea where the forms of capitalist econ-omy known to us stand on a continuum of an infinity of possibilities (Sabel and Zeitlin 1997).

As Knight (2001: 37) argues, for economic institutions competitive selec-tion is normally invoked as the primary causal mechanism, because markets with vast numbers of transactions are assumed. On the other hand, for political institutions the intentions of actors serve as the basis for the explanation of change, since the number of actors involved is normally far smaller and the condition of anonymity is not respected. We therefore need to watch closely if political institutional theories make use of arguments concerning evolution through competition that they cannot sustain.

A second problem is that we have no clear indicators of 'survival success' societies or economies. Societies and economies do not have aims or goals; external observers can impose these on them, and evaluate the relative success of their different institutions at achieving economic growth, or quality of life, or social equality, or anything else in which the observers are interested and for which they can construct more or less plausible indicators. (See Quack and Morgan 2000 for a good discussion of the endogenous definition of 'performance'.) But these are external impositions of the observer, and we have no idea how these might relate to some idea of evolutionary success.

Now, a focus on governance or rule-making assumes that purposive human action lies behind the sources of difference. This might also lead straight to acceptance of the contractarian frame of reference criticized in Chapter 1, but not if the theorist accepts that social compromises often take the form of permitting contradictions to rest unchallenged, or of some interests achieving their ends in one institutional sphere while others secure theirs in another, rather than the all-considered positive-sum deal of social contracts (Knight 1992). Approaches which acknowledge this are more likely to accept an accumulating complexity of structures in empirical cases, though this need not prevent them from producing sound theoretical schemes which rationalize and schematize certain typical outcomes of compromise (e.g. Esping-Andersen 1990).

Neo-institutionalist theory here needs the arguments developed by Mayntz and Scharpf (1995) in their concept of actor-centred institutionalism. This depicts actors who might have a variety of goals, acting within contexts that constrain them in various ways, but with the actors having some capacity to change the constraints. This provides a balanced approach. On the one hand it does not follow neoclassical economics into elaborate but abstract theories in which institutional constraints and particularities are simply assumed away. At the same time it does not reify institutional constraints to the point where they would deny the role of maximizing, if boundedly rational and imperfectly knowledgeable, collective and individual agents. The Mayntz/Scharpf model 'gives equal weight to strategic actions and interactions of purposeful and resourceful individual and corporate actors and to the enabling, constraining, and shaping effects of given (but variable) institutional structures and institutionalized forms' (Scharpf 1997: 34). Scharpf's concept of 'actor' usefully includes corporate and collective actors as much as human individuals (ibid.: ch. 3). There are of course problems of coordination for collective actors, but that should be incorporated in the theory of the institution concerned (ibid.: 59).

As he later developed it in detail, Scharpf's core model is that familiar from two-actor, non-cooperative game theory (ibid.: 31). By sketching in for his actors some realistic assumptions and goals framed by their institutional context, he is able to achieve considerable explanatory and some predictive power in a way which remains analytically rigorous but also more empirically comprehensible than much pure theory in this field.

The particular game-theory model used by Scharpf is not directly relevant to our current purposes. The main theory underpinning much contemporary institutionalism is that of path dependence (Hollingsworth 1997), which concerns actors making choices within a range of parameters, past choices increasingly constraining the range left to subsequent ones (technically, parametric decision-making modelled through Polyaurn processes (Arthur 1994)). As we shall see in Chapter 4, this requires modelling a 'game against nature' rather than the game against other strategic players for which game theory was devised, though it can be developed in a manner generally analogous to Scharpf's. Central to the argument is the theoretical possibility—though certainly not the probability—that active and entrepreneurial social agents may succeed in innovating and making radical changes that refute the logic of their path dependence. But only some forms of institutional analyses of contemporary capitalism can be used for this purpose.

If a theory is constructed according to evolutionary functionalist principles or classical social contracts, it will produce models embodying heavily determined logics of action and path dependences. Change then always has to come from outside, to be exogenous. If, however, theory is based on active human agents, whether of a single dominant interest or of conflicting ones producing compromises, it always contains within itself the possibility that the identity or interests of dominant actors or parties to the compromise may change. This change may take place within the polity or some other sphere of society, outside the logic of economic performance, and may thus disrupt the economy's path dependence. An important recent example would be the implications for labour markets in many nation-states of autonomous changes in women's expectations and self-perceptions. Similarly, Streeck (2001), while insisting on long-term characteristics of the German and Japanese economies, acknowledges that major changes took place in those societies at certain points during the twentieth century, when, at 'extraordinary political moments', national state elites took 'strategic, autonomous and authoritative action'.

Models which incorporate complex social compromises rather than either functionalist or purposive logic are likely to describe societies containing much internal diversity and unresolved contradictions and tensions. These may possibly—but only possibly—produce complementarities. For example, the compromise between capitalist and religious elites in most European countries in the late nineteenth and early twentieth centuries left the family with certain guarantees of autonomy from capitalism and therefore enabled it to survive as a source of certain kinds of stability and non-market collective goods (Crouch 1999: chs. 2, 7). The capitalist economy may have subsequently benefited from this. However, it could not itself have created this situation, it was in several respects hostile to its premises, and capitalist elites were probably totally unaware of the relationship. But compromises may simply result in certain contradictory components being left 'lying around' within the society, possibly but not necessarily subsequently becoming forms of serendipitous redundant capacity (Streeck 1997: 205 ff.).

Institutional 'redundancy' is a term that we shall meet again in Chapters 4 and 5. It derives from engineering science, but has widespread applications. For example, an aeroplane contains many thousands of rivets, large numbers of which never bear any strain at all. They are inserted because, under certain extreme conditions, or in the event of failure of other strain-bearing rivets, they will be needed. From the point of view of the perfectly efficient functioning of the aeroplane they are surplus to requirements, redundant; but they have to be there, just in case. More simply, we can take the idea of 'belt and braces'. Either of these items will sustain a pair of trousers, but what if one has only belt and it breaks? Whether one decides to wear both will depend on a trade-off between the perceived risk that the belt will break and the cost of wearing both (which will include the cost of being laughed at for so doing.)

A simple social example of the same principle would be the following. A railway operator needs a certain number of qualified engine drivers at work at any one time. But there is always a risk that some will be indisposed. To avoid having to cancel trains, the operator has to maintain (and pay) some additional drivers to be available to step in, just in case. Redundancy has to be designed into systems to provide against the untoward and the unexpected. The problem is: How much redundancy should be provided, since it is expensive? Should the railway operator provide one spare driver for every one on actual duty? One in a hundred? Or in a thousand? Systems designers, like the man with the belt and braces dilemma, have to establish a trade-off between the amount of cost to be borne providing redundant capacity and the degree of acceptable risk to be taken in not providing it.

So far we have discussed designed redundancy in the face of known parameters. Serendipitous redundancy concerns things that might possibly be useful at a future time, but which are of no use at present. I no longer need that strip of leather, but would it come in handy in the event that my trouser belt should break? The railway operator has in a warehouse somewhere several kilometres of a type of cable which is no longer produced and for which there is no present use, but which might just possibly be wanted following some future unpredictable change in railway operation. Should it be kept, just in case? The answer will depend on the cost of storing the cable, but because its future possible use is totally unpredictable, this cost cannot have any estimable risk factor offset against it. Serendipitous redundant social institutions, or social capacities, are like the cable. For example, let us assume that mass factory production of bread is found to be (by some combination of the market and the evaluation criteria adopted by governing elites) to be more efficient than small-batch production by skilled craft bakers. Small bakeries and the skills of baking become redundant; maintaining the bakeries in existence and continuing to train new bakers become expensive. Will they nevertheless be maintained, in case one day there is, say, an unpredicted health problem relating to factory-produced bread? It is unlikely. Redundant social institutions are likely to be maintained only if there are no costs (including opportunity costs) in allowing them to survive, or if no one notices them, or if there is some disagreement, and a minority interest somehow keeps them going.

A major cause of institutions becoming redundant is the belief, which occurs from time to time, that there is 'one best way', one best institutional solution, to a particular problem. Alternative means that had been thriving or at least surviving then become defined as redundant, and their survival is placed in jeopardy. Contending against this idea is that of functional equivalents, that there are alternative ways of producing similar outcomes. This can heavily offset the determinism and functional reliability of the *Gestalt* which theorists assume (Whitley 1997: 10–11). As Scharpf (1997: 42) puts much the same point:

Institutions . . . cannot influence choices and outcomes in a deterministic sense. Institutionalized rules, even if they are completely effective, will rarely prescribe one and only one course of action. Instead, by proscribing some and permitting other actions, they will define repertoires of more or less acceptable courses of action that will leave considerable scope for the strategic and tactical choices of purposeful actors.

Instead, he argues, we should start with the institutional explanation, moving beyond it and losing its parsimony when explanation requires us too. Or, as Jackson (forthcoming) argues:

The changes that prove to 'fit' with an existing configuration may be surprisingly diverse, since different functionally equivalent means might be found to produce similar results.... Moreover, it is difficult to judge the 'coherence' of institutions by their economic performance, because *fortuna* of external circumstances may prevail and compensate for underlying institutional mismatch.

Jackson (2001) has himself shown how, although Germany and Japan have broadly similar patterns of ownership and employee-involvement, they achieve the integration of stakeholders through quite different but functionally equivalent institutional mechanisms. To offer another example, it has been argued that successfully innovative machinery industries will need a vocational training system of the German apprenticeship form (Soskice 1995). Regini (1996) however, using the idea of functional equivalence, has demonstrated how the Italian machinery industry found quite different but also effective solutions to the problem.

It follows from the above arguments that models of capitalism (or any other institution) are more likely to be favourable to an action-centred approach, the larger the number of types they identify and the smaller their institutional range. Theories which identify a higher number of types are naturally more likely to produce analyses which see more than one model at work in a given empirical case, and therefore envisage the possibility of creative actors combining and recombining elements of these models as they confront new challenges. As for the second dimension, the more ambitious that theories are in their institutional scope, the more they require functionalist assumptions, and these are inimical to actor-centredness.

As noted in Chapter 2, Hall and Soskice (2001a), who have been used here as the main exemplar of dualist and multifunctional theory, claim very prominently that their theory is 'firm-centred', and therefore presumably actor-centred rather than systemic and 'top-down'. They claim to construct their model in terms of the possibilities facing an individual firm within the institution set of a given type of economy. (They take for granted an Anglo-American concept of a firm capable of being an unproblematic unitary actor—a model that does not easily transfer to, say, East Asian economies (Whitley 1999: 32).) Nevertheless, they see firms as totally trapped within the institutional resources and confines of their nation-state. Even if one assumes that that this is simply a theory which cannot be applied to transnational firms—critical weakness though this is for a theory claiming to explain the early twenty-first century economy—there remains a puzzle: If successful firms are entrepreneurial and profit-maximizing, should they not be expected to try to change elements of their national context that inhibit them, or to seek to construct through other means institutions which their nation-state does not provide? A firm-centred theory should provide space for the *institutionally* entrepreneurial firm. In other words there is a difference between Schumpeterian and neoclassical institutional theory similar to that in economic theory.

The problem is rooted in the dominance of rational expectations theory, which makes entrepreneurialism unnecessary to neoclassical economics, as was noted in Chapter 1 and has been set out at length by Barreto (1989). As Eliasson (2003; Carlsson and Eliasson 2003) has repeatedly pointed out, it is not possible for the rational expectations model to accept entrepreneurial activity, as entrepreneurialism involves a constant searching, which in fact changes the definition of the pursued optimum itself. Error and mistakes are essential to the process of business (and, one might add, scientific and technological) innovation (see also Grebel, Pyka, and Hanusch 2003).

In neo-institutionalist theory that accepts many neoclassical assumptions, firms are passive 'institution-takers' in the same way that in neoclassical economics they are price-takers. (Firms seem in this model to be constrained by both sociological and hierarchical embeddedness (Baumann 2002). The former is more obvious: Firms' actions are determined by what they know to do, based on past experience in a state of general ignorance. But the fact that it is the state and a national, ultimately law-based, set of institutions that constrains them implies a hierarchical model too.) For example, Casper (2001) assumes firms bound to accept given rules of a game-theory context, never seeking functional equivalents, ways round the rules or innovations in them. Scharpf (1997: 46) says that the study of policy needs to recognize, in addition to the formal rules of game theory, 'anarchic fields with minimal institutions'. The study of the overlapping field of the scope for institutional entrepreneurship has similar requirements.

Behind this argument lies a far more general point. As noted in Chapter 1, game theory is itself an example of the dependence of rational-action and market-oriented models of human behaviour on institutional frameworks that lie beyond the theory's own reach. In a theorized game it is taken for granted that someone devises the rules, and the participants, although they are seen as aggressively maximizing actors within the game, dutifully accept these rules. What if, for example, in a prisoner's dilemma game, one of the participants should say: 'Look, we are not really in prison; we are just accepting these constraints because the social theorist has designed the game that way. Let's refuse to play until he changes the rules to make them more reasonable.' In other words, what happens when the game itself is endogenized and brought within the fields of social action? Conventions of social science theory building prevent this from happening. But in real life, aggressively maximizing, entrepreneurial actors must be expected to challenge all conventions and rules that shape their opportunities and environment. They will try constantly to endogenize Leviathan.

Cases and Types

As noted at the outset, most contributions to the literature on the diversity of capitalism conflate theoretical models and empirical cases through a research strategy that seeks the unique theoretical box to which an individual case must be assigned. For example, Goodin et al. (1999), while arguing that the USA constitutes a pure type of 'market' welfare regime, acknowledge that 80 per cent of US social protection expenditure goes to social insurance schemes of a corporatist nature and not to the means-tested schemes associated with the market model. However, because they consider that this is a smaller proportion than goes to such schemes in other cases, they claim that they are justified in regarding the USA as a paradigm of the 'pure' market model. They do not consider the possibility that the corporatist elements of the welfare system might act complementarily to the market process in the US case, and that the US system might operate differently if it really was a pure market one.

In fact, the differences that have been identified among neo-institutionalist theories have major implications for how they relate theoretical models and empirical cases. There are broadly two ways of doing this: the labelling method and the analytical method. The two approaches are analogous to the two different forms of categorization found on bottles of mineral water: First, the water is labelled as either still or sparkling—the water 'is', unambiguously, one or other of these types; second, the detailed chemical analysis of the elements and compounds, traces of which can be found in the water—the water 'contains' these chemicals.

The neo-institutionalist researcher following the labelling strategy inspects the characteristics of an empirical case and decides which of a limited number of theoretical models (ideally two) it most closely resembles. The case is then considered to be 'an example' of that model and labelled accordingly, all features of it which do not fit the model being considered as noise and disregarded. A clear example is again the study by Goodin et al. (1999), which takes three national cases as examples of three models, then reads back empirical features of these cases into the models. In defence of such procedures Hollingsworth (1997: 268) claims that, even if an individual society has more than one social system of production, one will dominate. This is possibly true, but, not only should it remain an hypothesis worth testing rather than an a priori methodological assumption, but the role of 'minor' or hidden institutional forms can have major importance, as we shall see in the following chapters.

The researcher following the analytical approach considers to what extent traces of each of a series of models can be found within the case; there may be no conclusion as to which form it most closely resembles. Even if there is, that information remains framed in the context of the wider knowledge of its attributes. But it is also necessary to recognize weaknesses of the analytical approach in enabling us to identify potential innovation. We rarely have in macro sociology or political economy measuring instruments of the kind at the disposal of the chemist analysing the mineral water. If we could say: 'The Californian economy comprises x per cent pure market governance, y per cent basic state support, and z per cent immigrant community dynamic effects'—we would be saying something very significant. But we cannot; we can only say: 'The impact of immigrant communities may be important as catalysts for innovation...'. The analytical approach thus runs the risk of being wrong-footed as less 'scientific' by an alternative presenting a false scientific precision.

Labelling works best when there is only a limited number of models to which cases can be assigned, but these models embrace a wide range of institutions without worrying about excessive complexity. Conversely, the analytical method is most likely to be found among theories that accept a larger number of types but are less ambitious in their institutional coverage. These theories can best demonstrate their richness when showing how complex an individual case can be, and for that require a large number of models, but therefore are only really feasible when a limited number of institutions is being considered.

Each form of categorization has its advantages and limits. The strongest point of the labelling approach is its clarity. The designation of still or sparkling is always far more prominent on the water bottle than the detailed chemical analysis, and it is the only information in which most consumers are interested. Likewise, policymakers, investors and other users of social research into forms of capitalism probably want to know simply, 'Is this economy like the USA or like Germany?' The labelling model is also of particular value when measuring instruments are crude. We do not have finely tuned ways of measuring elements within a national economy; but we might be able to say what an economy is more or less 'like'—in other words, which simple model does it most resemble?

Authors often make elisions of this type in order to be able to carry out statistical tests using the typology they develop, despite having only a small number of cases; as Jackson (forthcoming) points out:

Using three or four or five 'types' for each institutional variable generates more combinations of variables than observable national cases, given that the Varieties of Capitalism approach might usefully be applied to only some 25 existing advanced capitalist economies.

Is unemployment higher in liberal, conservative or social democratic welfare states? Are exports higher in liberal or coordinated market economies? Chi-squared and other simple tests can be used to answer such questions among the very small *n* of all-EU or all-OECD countries, provided cases can be seen as unproblematic examples of models, and provided there is only a limited number of categories, ideally two. This point enables us to understand the reluctance of researchers to accept hybrid cases, otherwise the obvious bolthole for those wishing to reconcile labelling and analytical approaches. If the researcher is trying to apply a chi-squared test cases have to be put in one or another box—or they must be excluded altogether, thereby reducing *n*. For example, the Dutch and British welfare states which were part of the study by Goodin et al. (1999) are almost certainly mixed examples of, respectively, continental and socio-democratic, and liberal and social democratic welfare states. Goodin et al., and some other authors, treat the Dutch case as 'social democratic'; but in the original analysis of Esping-Andersen on which this typology is based, the Netherlands was treated as a 'conservative corporatist' case—a pattern also widely followed (e.g. Scharpf and Schmidt 2000*a*, 2000*b*).

An analytical approach, in contrast, is able to depict the actors within its cases as confronting an empirical complexity made up of elements of a number of models. If these actors are institutional entrepreneurs, then, unlike the actors within a game theory, they can be presented as having the capacity to try to combine these elements in new ways, making use of serendipitous redundancies embedded in the empirical incongruences of their situation. As theorist and real-world actors interact, the former may be able to develop new theoretical cases out of the recombinant institutions produced by the more successful of these attempts. The two approaches present opposed logics of research. What is noise for the labelling approach becomes grist for the mill of explaining what actors can do for the analytical approach. A high degree of diversity within a case, a problem for labelling theory, becomes for an analytical theory a crucial independent variable for explaining innovative capacity.

Conclusion: The Importance of Heterogeneity and Change

These considerations lead to an important hypothesis, which takes us back to the start of this book and the alternative pilgrim routes of the Via Francigena: *that institutional heterogeneity will facilitate innovation, both by presenting actors with alternative strategies when existing paths seem blocked and by making it possible for them to make new combinations among elements of various paths.*

This point can be argued more formally. Let us assume an actor-centred approach that accepts that knowledge is problematic for the actors. They will have easier access to knowledge that already exists in practical form close to them than that which is remotely or only theoretically available. 'Closeness' here means principally institutional closeness on the scale running from the endogenous to the exogenous: the capacity of the actors to have easy access to the institution in which the relevant knowledge is embedded. Institutional distance will be zero when the actors concerned are already working directly with the relevant knowledge, and that distance increases as they need to cross institutional boundaries to gain that access. (For a formal demonstration of the importance of institutional proximity for agents solving learning problems by observing others, see Anderlini and Ianni 1993.) Arguments of this kind lie behind most neo-institutionalist assumptions of path dependence or, at least, embeddedness.

But from the same arguments we can derive the conclusion that, the more heterogeneous the context within which actors operate, the more opportunity they will have of encountering practical knowledge which they have not used before in the immediate context, but which is part of the more general repertoire they have acquired or which is relatively accessible to them. Stark (2001) similarly argues that while tensions emerging from institutions with 'conflicting principles of rationality' (Lepsius 1990) may have destabilizing effects on a particular organizational configuration, they may also be a source of necessary variety and make possible recombinations of practices. This point has profound real implications; we shall return to it in Chapter 5.

It will by now be clear that the disadvantages of the labelling approach to capitalist diversity are not limited to its obvious crudeness, but also— and this is here our fundamental concern—its incapacity to help us account for or anticipate change and innovation. Hemerijck, Unger, and

Visser (2000), discussing some of the most tightly structured societies in western Europe—Austria, Belgium, and the Netherlands—show how these have become increasingly differentiated despite initial institutional similarities in the post-war years. Deeg (2001*a*) and Lütz (2000) have shown how German bank-firm relationships became far more market-oriented during the 1990s; they did not simply become 'Americanized', but produced interesting hybrid forms. Both Dore (2000), and Streeck and Yamamura (2001) describe change in several German and Japanese institutions in similar ways. Schmidt (2002: ch. 4) shows how far the post-war British industrial relations system departed from the market capitalism stereotype, possessing as it did a strong level of state intervention and high level of collective action (ibid.: ch. 5). These instances all come from essentially neo-institutionalist authors, and they can be multiplied many times. Clearly neo-institutionalism needs to find its own means of accounting for such changes which make use of rather than ignore the assumptions of path dependence and embeddedness which have been major props to its analytical achievements.

Unfortunately, as we have seen, some developments in the capitalist diversity literature make it impossible by definition to carry out such a programme—though this stricture certainly does not apply to Amable's study (2003). They are virtually bound to consider all evidence of modes of action which do not fit their overall characterization of a given national or super-national system as so much untheorized, empirical 'noise', which needs to be disregarded in the interests of an elegant and sharply profiled account. In contrast, it is precisely on incongruities, incoherence, and within-system diversities that we depend for an attempt to build—not a series of *ad hoc* empirical objections—but a theory of crisis resolution and Schumpeterian change that does not depend on either exogeneity or prediction of inevitable failure (see also Hage and Hollingsworth 2000: 983). Theories that provide clear and strong predictions are by that very characteristic inappropriate for a research programme in which an escape from path dependences and embeddedness can be modelled in entrepreneurial discovery of concealed, unacknowledged or surprising potentialities of the available institutional repertoire.

In this chapter we have established:

- The importance of establishing the micro foundations of institutions if we are to treat actors as potentially creative and innovative.
- The need to return to Weber's concept of ideal types as one-sided accentuations of idealized forms of reality, possibly operating alongside

Wahlverwandschaft. Relations of complementarity should then be identified at a second, empirical stage of analysis of institutions.
- The possibility of adding social compromises and other contingent
  results of social interaction as a third stage.
- That institutional heterogeneity may facilitate innovation, both by presenting actors with alternative strategies when existing paths seem
  blocked and by making it possible for them to make new combinations
  among elements of various paths.
- The problematic nature of taking for granted that the boundaries of
  nation states are the boundaries of institutions and systems of action,
  and the importance of regarding endogeneity and exogeneity as a
  continuum.

In Chapters 4 and 5 we shall move from criticism of existing literature to
an attempt at constructing an approach to analysis that respects these
conclusions and those from Chapter 2.

Notes

1. This chapter benefited considerably from collaboration with Maarten Keune.
2. The following discussion benefited considerably from discussions in the 'Complementarities' group (see Acknowledgement and Crouch et al. 2005), and in
   particular from an unpublished paper presented to the group by Martin
   Höpner (2003*b*).
3. I am indebted to Rogers Hollingsworth for drawing my attention to Bohr's
   work on this.
4. I am indebted to Wolfgang Streeck for the observations in this paragraph.

4

Innovation and Path Dependence[1]

It has been noted at several points in the previous chapters that path dependence is a major instrument of neo-institutionalist theory. It is the means by which institutions often achieve continuity over time and constrain the scope for individual maximization of actors—even to the point of preventing change that might be in all actors' long-term best interests (e.g. North 1990b; Putnam 1993; Thelen 1999, 2003; Pierson 2000a, 2000b; Deeg 2001a, 2001b). It thus serves explicitly as a counter to those forms of economic theory which posit that interactions between economically rational actors will lead to efficient outcomes (North 1990b; Pierson 2000b), and argues instead that inefficient equilibria may be stable. It also presents a major challenge to attempts at modelling institutional entrepreneurs, making it necessary to demonstrate how innovative possibilities may be made available by those same institutional contexts which constrain. Otherwise, all change has to be seen as exogenous and outside the scope of the theory.

Three types of response to this may be seen in the literature. First, less sophisticated approaches misunderstand path dependence, arguing that paths are set at a given point in time, so that actors are ineluctably condemned to follow out a specific trajectory without possibility of change or exit (e.g. the account of Italian regional development in Putnam 1993). While Putnam suggests in his conclusions that change is possible, he does not seek to integrate this suggestion with the main body of his argument, which emphasizes how the dead hand of path dependence weighs on current political outcomes (for a similar criticism of Putnam, see Levi 1996). Under such accounts, paths of development exercise an influence so compelling that outcomes are more or less completely determined.

Second, more sophisticated applications of the theory (North 1990a; Pierson 2000a) acknowledge the difficulty. They seek to avoid determinism, arguing that short periods of wide-ranging change are likely to be succeeded by much longer periods in which change continues, though relatively closely bounded (Pierson 2000a); but they fail to advance arguments about what such wide-ranging change involves, and how actors will respond to it. Pierson (2000a: 265) limits himself to observing that change is bounded 'until something erodes or swamps the mechanisms of reproduction that generates continuity.'

Third, and most usefully, some authors have started to consider how endogenous change can be modelled within a context of path dependence. One example is the theory of cumulative change by gradual accretion developed by Thelen (2003; 2004). Mahoney (2000: 1) stresses the need for path dependence theories to postulate initial contingent events that set in train patterns with deterministic properties, with thus a strong distinction between critical juncture moments and long periods of stasis (Streeck and Thelen 2005b). But as Pempel (1998) points out, this entails a model of occasional radical shifts. Streeck and Thelen want to look at more permanent change processes, because they do not accept the rigid distinction between stability and change. Indeed, major change can happen through an accumulation of little changes, that is, incremental change with transformative potential.

The central point from which we can make a departure is that the path that eventually emerges as dominant is always one of a number of possibilities (Arthur 1994). A series of small, random events privileges the emergent path, and the fact of this repetition in itself brings the increasing returns to scale, which establish the path. (Arrow (2000) casts doubt on the necessity for increasing returns, and suggests that the crucial point is irreversibility. Even with constant returns and competitive equilibrium path dependence may occur.) In principle, a different arrangement might have been viable, but the particular form that appeared acquired the advantages of first mover. Our first theoretical challenge is to model how actors might get back to a situation resembling that which existed before events began to favour one outcome.

Path dependence theory works in the following way. Probability theory asserts that, if each of two possible outcomes of an action is equally likely to occur, the frequency of their occurrence will tend towards equality the larger the number of occasions on which the action is taken. When the action is taken only a small number of times, there may well be considerable imbalance in their respective occurrences. Such inequality is random and is compatible with the long-run chances of the two outcomes being equal. Path dependence theory then considers what would occur if, every time that one of the two outcomes occurred, the chances of its reappearance on the next iteration were *increased*. In the classic example used in the literature, one of two balls of two different colours is drawn blind from an urn in a long series of iterations. Whenever a ball of one colour is drawn, an additional ball of that colour is added to those in the urn (Arthur, Ermoliev, and Kaniovski 1987). This increases the chance that a ball of this colour will be chosen. In contrast to the tendency to equality of the case where chances of each outcome are equal, the colour initially randomly favoured will become increasingly dominant. Its dominance continues to increase, and eventually the second colour will be drawn only rarely. Formally, the ensuing pattern takes the form technically known as a random walk on a convex surface (Arthur 1990).[2] This is the establishment of a path dependence.

Arthur and others (David 1992a, 1992b, 2000) argue that many economic situations are better modelled using these increasing returns assumptions rather than those of diminishing returns anticipated by standard economic theory. An example often cited in the literature concerns industrial location. Imagine that firms in a particular new industry have a choice of locating themselves in either of two regions, each initially equally attractive for the activity concerned. Standard economics would predict that in the long run there should be an equal amount of activity of the industry in the two regions. If it so happens that random chance leads to one becoming initially more popular, the laws of supply and demand would ensure that costs within it became higher than in the other, creating diminishing returns, and shifting location to the second region. Path dependence theorists would, however, point to self-reinforcing aspects of these initially random choices of one region. As this region acquires its initial advantage, specialized services for the industry, supplier and customer firms, and also skilled labour gravitate there. It increasingly attracts more and more firms from the industry, and the other region hardly attracts any; there are increasing returns. This helps explain, for example, why Silicon Valley remains more or less unique and has not been imitated by many other regions throughout the USA, despite many attempts to do so. Orthodox economists can point out that in the long run diminishing returns set in—for example, as transport networks in Silicon Valley become blocked, housing costly, and labour expensive. But path dependence theory is very useful for explaining why the onset of such returns is very slow, and why there is considerable growth in the region's increasing returns before that point is reached.

Very important in all this is the idea of chance or contingency in the events that start the path, chances which eventually disappear, leaving the path to develop under its own logic:

Fluctuations dominate motions at the outset; hence, they make limit points reachable from any initial conditions. But they die away, leaving the process directed by the equivalent deterministic system and hence convergent to identifiable attractors. (Arthur 1994: 123)

North (1990*a*) argues that institutions too are subject to the forces of increasing returns. In what is perhaps the most influential application of path dependence theory, he seeks to explain a near-inexplicable puzzle for efficiency based approaches to economics; why it is that countries in the developing world have not converged on the more efficient set of institutions offered by the developed world. He argues that the divergences in the economic histories of South and North America may in large part be explained by the differing initial institutional matrices they inherited from Spain and Britain respectively. Most recently, Pierson (2000*a*, 2000*b*) has sought to build upon this by offering a more general set of insights into institution-building as a path-dependent process. In Pierson's argument, initial institutional steps may have a strong conditioning effect on later ones. Insofar as institutions generate learning effects, co-ordination effects and adaptive expectations, they may substantially affect trajectories of institutional development, so that later institutions reflect these earlier steps. Positive feedback may in turn lead to a single equilibrium that is likely to be resistant to change.

Djelic (1999) points out how conventional organization theory links determinism with rational decision-makers. The latter act as the selection mechanisms for a Darwinian process of change, institutions being merely obstacles in their path. She claims that only historical neo-institutionalists grasp the specificities of institutions, but that unlike old institutionalists, they have dropped the idea of the institutional entrepreneur. Rational choice neo-institutionalists, she argues, turn outcomes and consequences into causes in the manner of classical efficiency theory, and they are not interested in process. Overall she prefers a mix of phenomenological (which can account for structural convergence through diffusion mechanisms) and historical neo-institutionalism, the latter looking at the constraints that shape institutional development.

Self-reinforcing Mechanisms in Social Action

It must be pointed out that path dependence should not be seen as necessarily characterizing all institutions. In many cases increasing returns simply do not arise. In others, the very structure of an institution permits gradual changes within it, which can eventually culminate in radical transformation. Nothing is gained by claiming universal application of a specific theory. Within these confines, the concept of path dependence is very useful in sociological analysis, because there are many examples of self-reinforcing social mechanisms. Mahoney (2000) points out the need to understand the different specific mechanisms that produce self-reinforcement, because different mechanisms will be reversible in different ways. He also distinguishes usefully between self-reinforcing and reactive sequences in path dependence. These themes will not be developed in detail here, but two mechanisms that are particularly important are the learning curve and power relations among actors.

The Institutional Learning Curve

The learning curve can be a very clear source of path dependence. Assume that an actor has a choice of a number of procedures to tackle a problem, each of which may be (as far as the actor knows in a state of ignorance) equally able to achieve the goal. By chance the inexperienced actor tends to use one of these more often than the others. While these others remain potentially effective, the actor will be increasingly likely to keep returning to the initially only randomly preferred one, solely because she now has experience of how to use this one more than others; she is becoming more confident, and more expert, at it. In time this becomes *in fact* the more effective approach for this particular actor, because she is more likely to practise it expertly. We can illustrate this with a simple example. Imagine a young person, who has never cooked bacon before and who is indifferent whether his bacon is grilled or fried, suddenly being confronted with the need to cook bacon every day, with both a grill and a frying pan being available. Each morning he randomly selects one of these two cooking methods. As the days pass his expertise slowly increases, as he ascends the learning curve that enables one not to burn, and not to undercook, the bacon. However, it so happens, purely by chance, that on most days he cannot find the frying pan, and therefore more often than not grills the bacon. He climbs the grilling learning curve far more rapidly than the frying one, and gradually comes to prefer the results of the former method. Irrespective of whether the frying pan is available, he now starts consciously to prefer grilling, and a path dependence with increasing returns has established itself.

This result of the learning curve may even operate if, in principle, another approach might have been overall more effective had it been initially randomly favoured. If he only knew it, our young person would have preferred perfectly fried bacon over perfectly grilled; but he does not persist with frying long enough to achieve this perfection. In time, therefore, such rejected approaches become seen as anomalies and are discarded from the actor's repertoire. If, at some future point, the chosen path loses its effectiveness (the grill breaks down), while one of the discarded alternatives becomes the only effective solution, the actor is unable to change, because all competence at the discarded approach has been lost. Even if the actor comes to perceive this, she is unable to do anything about it, but knows only how to keep repeating the now failing path. It is for precisely this kind of analysis that path dependence theory has become useful to neo-institutionalism. In particular, it enables us to predict and explain the otherwise irrational behaviour of an actor, who perceives that the path she is using no longer achieves her ends, wants to change it, but is unable to do so.

However, the theory achieves this effectiveness by making some very strong assumptions: that social actors operate in monotonic environments, in which the same approach is used across the whole range of an actor's scope; and that all other actors known to and sharing interests with the first actor, and who might therefore have been expected to help and teach different approaches, are trapped within the same monotonic environment. It is to provide support for these strong assumptions that most neo-institutionalist theories assume mechanisms of the kind discussed in Chapter 3—such as complementarities, *Wahlverwandschaft*, a tendency to institutional congruence or a strain towards institutional consistency—which anticipate the existence of precisely such environments. However, particularly in the analysis of complex situations, we must be ready to suspend that assumption. Actors may be forced to operate in more than one action space, with different approaches needing to be used in different spaces. Or they may have easy access to other actors who operate in different spaces, enabling them to 'borrow' from them.

In comparison with the single path, these forms of diversity initially constitute inefficiencies, what were described in Chapter 3 as redundant capacities. An actor able to use only one approach in all situations has far lighter learning and expertise requirements than one who has to learn several different approaches, most of which lay around redundant for most of the time. And borrowing approaches from others involves various transaction costs. We should expect rational but myopic actors positively to *seek* monotonic environments. Sometimes, however, enduring institutional rigidities do not enable them to do this, but require them to keep cultivating, and bearing the cost of, redundant capacities. These actors are required to have diversified repertoires, or may have to work alongside 'neighbours' who operate with different knowledge bases and are therefore unable to assist them at moments of need. But these actors, inefficient in the short-term, may in the long run be able to escape from a doomed path dependence

and adopt a new approach—provided of course that the alternatives
which happen to be available to them do constitute viable solutions to the
changed situation the actor faces in the original action space.

The Role of Power Relations

But social situations are rarely 'innocent' spaces where all we need to
understand are actors acquiring and using knowledge to achieve goals.
As we have noted in earlier chapters, differential power among actors,
which they deploy in zero-sum ways, is an ever-present possibility.
Considerations of power are not part of the logic of path dependence
theory, because that theory does not deal explicitly with interaction
among actors. And power relations are often ignored in applications of
the concept: North's account of institutional development in South America may be criticized for this (see Knight 1992; Solokoff and Engerman
2000. However, it is quite possible to model power relations as one of the
means by which increasing returns—a fundamental characteristic of
path-dependent situations—become established (see Mahoney 2000: 521
for a similar discussion).

Even where actors start with initial equality endowments, randomly
chosen but self-reinforcing actions can favour the interests of some rather
than others. Assume that among a group of actors, with initially equal votes
to participate in decision-making, there is a number of equally valid alternative approaches to solving a collective problem. Each actor supports a
different one of these alternatives, and the group repeatedly has to decide
together which one to pursue in an indefinite number of iterations. Once a
particular approach has been chosen, the actor associated with it is allocated
an additional vote. In the initial rounds the group has to have recourse to
random selection of an alternative, as no actor is willing to depart from
advocacy of her preference. We now make the assumption fundamental to
path-dependent situations: quite by chance the random selection process of
the early rounds favour the choice associated with one actor, who as a result
acquires increasing votes. In time he is able to dominate the decision-
making in a self-reinforcing way, and a path dependence is established.

Modelling Change in Knowledge Patterns and Power Relations

Learning curve and power imbalance work together to produce overde-
termined path dependence: all actors become more expert at pursuing the
courses of action which favour powerful interests, and this process in
itself further advances the position of those interests. Potential rivals to

the dominant group not only lack the power to make a challenge, but lack expertise and the possibility of convincing others that alternative actions are practically viable. This is a theoretical account of the strength of conservatism. 'Workers of the world unite: you have nothing to lose but your painfully acquired knowledge of how to survive' is not a rousing slogan, as Przeworski (1985) has demonstrated at length in his study of the problem of working-class political mobilization. Interests and experience alike develop around existing systems and seek to maintain and strengthen them and block possible changes, even if the existing system is failing to deliver results.

A path may therefore continue to be followed by rational actors even if it no longer produces general positive returns, because it does produce insider rewards for powerful interests. We can here use the example of a scientific research institute dominated by a hierarchy of ageing scientists. Initially their work had produced great results, from which their power derived and reinforced itself. Gradually, however, it becomes clear that new theories and methods, associated with a younger generation of scientists, are achieving more success. It is in the rational interest of the institute to replace the older generation. However, if they hold power, they may prefer to retain their positions at the expense of the institute's achievements.

If a path depends solely on power balances of this kind, then the eventual failure of the path to produce these insider returns would enable the powerful actors to change a path—provided they also had adequate knowledge of how to follow an alternative. Alternatively, innovation may be triggered by a change in the identity of the most powerful interests. Such a change is exogenous to the particular set of practices around the established path dependence, but it may be endogenous to the wider context. Again, however, to the extent that issues of learning are involved, even such actors may be unable to force a change. As in the 'innocent' case, the chances of achieving a change in a failed path will depend on actors' access to alternatives, through other practices or a capacity to borrow from neighbours. In the case of a change in the identity of the powerful group, the newcomers may bring with them access to approaches perfected within other, 'their' institutional arenas, which are then transferred to the one in question.

Adjusting Path Dependence Theory for Innovative Actors

The core of path dependence theory is the simple model of the actor drawing balls from an urn as described above. It is not provided that the actor can ever examine her pattern of choices and decide whether she likes them or not. These actors are therefore denied the fundamental human characteristic of being able to reflect on the outcomes of their actions and to consider adjusting them. This is a weakness of the theory when applied to the realm of human decision-making as opposed to pure mathematical processes, especially when we are dealing with institutional entrepreneurs. To address this problem I shall make a major change in the form of the theory. The classical account folds the individual agent and her reaction to the action of others into the sequence itself (though some formulations (e.g. North 1990*a*) seek, as we do, to take account of the cognitive effects of institutions). A firm makes a location decision that may reflect the previous location decisions of other firms, and may in turn affect the future decisions of other firms still. Path dependence theory thus models the action of the agent as itself a single step in the mathematical process. It is necessary instead to treat the agent's own action sequence in isolation from its effects on the environment, but allowing her to update her behaviour in order to respond to environmental path dependences.[3] Path dependence assumes a process in which balls are taken from an urn, and replaced according to a specific logic. My model differs in that it posits an agent that seeks to match developments in her environment by drawing from a separate urn.

Assume an agent (A), and an environment (E). Each round, A incurs some small fixed cost, K, regardless of her action. Further, assume that both the agent and the environment draw balls from separate urns. Balls in each urn may be either red or white. As in Arthur's original example (1994), when a ball of either colour is drawn from either urn, it is replaced, and a new ball of the same colour is added to that urn. Both A and E draw balls unsighted from the urn; however, A, unlike E, may ascertain her ball's colour after it has been drawn, but before she has seen E's ball. For a cost, C, which is additional to K, she may replace it and draw a new one, and may repeat this procedure until she has drawn a ball with which she is satisfied. E then draws its ball. Only A's final choice of ball will be returned to the urn along with another one of the same colour. If the final choice matches the colour then drawn by E, A receives a reward, R. The exercise is repeated infinitely. Under these circumstances A will seek to maximize the sum of rewards, subject to some discount factor, ∂, so that future rounds of the game are not valued as much as the current round.

Assume further that A has knowledge of the basic parameters of the game (in particular that both her urn and that of the environment E are subject to increasing returns). She possesses a set of beliefs about the world and interprets what happens in the light of those beliefs, only challenging them if they prove manifestly unsound. For example, if she believes in praying for rain in a drought, she will interpret every instance where it rained some time after she prayed as evidence confirming the belief. It would require prolonged continued drought for her to start to examine the belief. This is different from the pure type of a scientific actor, who in principle continually challenges all her beliefs and submits them to thorough testing. It is probable that the former type is more common than the latter in everyday life, if only because the constant challenging of beliefs and submitting them to scientific test is highly expensive and impracticable. In statistical theory such actors are known as 'Bayesian', after the statistical theorist who first tried to model such behaviour. Bayesian statistics are based on the probability that a particular event will occur, but not in the purely statistical sense of mainstream probability theory. Instead, they make the probability expectation contingent on a particular belief about the relationship between causes and consequences being true. If the belief changes at a certain point, the future probability expectation also changes. The theory is therefore useful where actors occasionally revise their normally very fixed views of situations. In the first instance, it applies to the beliefs of the theorist herself, but it can be adapted to relate to social actors. (For the application of Bayesian principles to social situations, see Breen 2000; Western 2000.)

If A wishes to maximize the sum of her rewards, she will need to solve a problem: given her information about which balls have been drawn, are the draws from E's urn on a path P_r, in which red balls predominate, or P_w, in which white balls do? Bayesian calculation allows her to update her beliefs in each round, given the ball that E has played.

In the first round, A will know that there is a 50:50 chance of either red or white being drawn by E, and will not wish to incur the cost C, so she will simply present the ball that she has drawn at random. Let us assume that E establishes a path P_r soon thereafter, in which red balls predominate. A will conclude at some point that E has begun to establish this path, and, if her expected rewards for so doing outweigh her expected costs, will begin to invest in search costs in order to present red balls. The speed of A's adaptation to red path dominance will be a function of the variables: C, R, ∂, plus a random element dependent on the 'luck of the draw'. In most circumstances, one may expect the dominant colour to become more quickly established thereafter for A than for E—insofar as A is capable of forming beliefs about the environment and its future course of development, and guiding her own institutional path so as to match that of the environment. It must be remembered that red does not achieve 100 per cent dominance; white balls remain in both urns and, until the number of red balls approaches infinity, stand a small but finite chance of occasionally being drawn.

This provides a simple model of how behavioural routines or institutions may become matched to their environment. But what happens if the environment changes? Let us assume that for some exogenous reason E's urn is switched for a new one, containing again a single red and a single white ball, under the same conditions as for the original urn. In this instance, however, draws from the urn become dominated by P_w, so that white becomes established as the dominant colour.

In Breen's Bayesian terms (2000), the agent perceives the change from the perspective of her existing beliefs, and cannot immediately move to new, more appropriate ones. Depending on her precise beliefs, it is likely that A will at first consider the sudden appearance of white balls as examples of the occasional appearance of this colour, which she has always experienced and has learned to disregard. Guided by this belief, A will persist with her path-dependent behaviour, and will continue to present red balls. After a time however it will become clear to her that there has been a true change of probabilities, and that her earnings are seriously declining. The length of this time period will depend partly on the strength of her beliefs. There will come a point where A realizes that she needs to locate white balls and may deem it rational to incur considerable search costs if necessary. A's willingness to switch to the new white path when she realizes this is appropriate will depend on three factors: (i) the relationship between costs (C, K) and rewards (R); (ii) the ratio of red to white balls in A's urn; and (iii) ∂, the extent to which A discounts the future.

Clearly these parameters permit a wide range of variation; for purposes of illustration let us examine two extreme cases. First, take that where costs are high relative to rewards, where A's urn has a strong preponderance of red to white (so that it is difficult to switch over), and where ∂ is high, so that A discounts future rewards heavily. Under such parameter values, A is unlikely to incur the costs necessary to change the path in her own urn, so that she may consistently find white balls to match those of E. Given the cost K incurred each round, A will expect to incur losses if she seeks to remain in the game for the rare occasions when E presents a red ball given white ball dominance. A's expected future earnings from the game will very likely be outweighed by her costs. This is the classic path dependence situation. The agent is left indefinitely unable to change paths. Our example of the research institute dominated by the hierarchy of old scientists is an instance of this. Not only do they refuse to give up their power, but the younger staff have neither means, nor knowledge of how, to challenge them; they have so rarely been invited to offer their own opinions, and because of the institute's reputation, it is unable to recruit scientists from outside with a different approach.

Alternatively, if rewards are high relative to costs, there is a relatively low preponderance of red to white balls in A's urn, and ∂ is low so that A places a relatively high value on future rewards, one may expect A to seek to respond to the change in the environment by changing the path dependence of her own urn. She will accept search costs in order to find white balls, and may thus come to establish white ball dominance. Search costs will then decline and earnings rise. Clearly this may involve a lengthy transition period. In our example of the research institute this might be the case where the hierarchy has been established for a shorter period, and where the views of younger staff have been sought less rarely. (Consultation is the white ball.)

At the level of generality which my arguments involve, it is impossible to specify more precisely the relationship between the parameter values and the extent to which mid-range outcomes (in which some parameters point in one direction and others in another) will tend to leave A trapped in her path dependence, or incurring the necessary costs to find a new path. However, by specifically incorporating learning and adaptation costs, my model provides some basic insights into what change is likely to involve. A is capable of drawing both red and white balls from her urn in order to respond to a given environment. These may serve as a simple proxy in my argument for different possible patterns of behaviour, or even more generally different paths of institutional development, which respond to different varieties of increasing returns in the environment, and themselves involve increasing returns (Pierson 2000a). Even when A has established red-ball dominance in her urn, she will occasionally draw white balls, which, insofar as they do not match the red balls typically produced by E, will be viewed as examples of institutional misfit and inefficiency. However, in situations where the environment has changed (E's red-ball dominance switches to white), such apparent examples of maladaptation change their significance, so that they become 'dormant resources', which actors will seek to draw upon, in order to respond better to changed circumstances. (White balls had, in fact, been cases of potentially useful redundancy during the period of red domination.)

This first model draws our attention to the existence of dormant resources, present but inaccessible in the pure path dependence case, but potentially accessible to an agent capable of search into her discarded past repertoire. It also indicates in an abstract way the kinds of circumstances in which an agent might succeed in such a search. For example, the longer that an existing path has been in operation, or the more costly the search, the more difficult it will be to go back to the dormant resources.

These abstract ideas can be developed to provide hypotheses about when search might be successful in specific contexts. For example, the 'costliness' of a search for a dormant resource by a policymaker would be affected by such factors as the difficulty of renewing practice of the dormant policy resource (a function of the re-learning curve and the cost of re-establishing support resources), confrontation with powerful interests hostile to its policy implications, the embarrassment of making a major change, and its degree of difference from, or even contradiction of, the dominant path which is to be rejected. Ebbinghaus and Manow (2001a) consider how change may occur in these situations through a process of 'layering', showing how institutions within some European welfare states have defied the predictions of path dependence analysts and have been reformed. As institutions develop over long periods of time, they argue, they cease to embody a simple logic, but a complex bundle, dormant elements of which may open up possibilities for change at difficult moments (see also Quack and Djelic 2005). A good example is found in the account of changes in Dutch social policy by Visser and Hemerijck (1997). They show how some existing but neglected and almost forgotten policy mechanisms were used to enable policy actors to solve what had seemed to be some apparently intractable emerging problems. My model helps explain both how the path dependence trap was sprung, and also why it was an existing, neglected mechanism rather than total novelty or piece of external imitation that was used to do so.

Thelen (2004) similarly uses layering to describe how reformers sometimes set up new structures alongside old ones that have become unreformable and unremovable. She takes the example of the German vocational training system. From time to time it has undergone crisis as economic and technological changes create an environment that no longer matches its assumptions. However, at each moment those responsible for implementing the system—a large number of agents in fact—have found ways of adapting it, always by returning to the generic point of the apprenticeship concept. Initially designed for the *Handwerk* sector, it was successfully adapted to large-scale industry (Streeck 1992); designed for manufacturing, it had to adapt to services sectors; designed for the lower levels of educational qualifications, it was adapted to the rise in educational achievements (Crouch, Finegold, and Sako 1999: ch. 5). Designed for specific skills, it adapted to polyvalency; most recently it has been adapting to the new highly flexible occupations in mass media industries (Baumann 2002). There was often a time lag while this adjustment was made, while those concerned either persisted with the old version or failed to find a means of adaptation. However, the fact that change was possible without either a total collapse of the model or exogenous borrowing means that the problem was solved by considering *hitherto unrealized potentialities of the system itself*.

This procedure is well captured by Levi's analogy (1996) of path dependence with an exfoliating tree. The trunk branches into large boughs, which then exfoliate into smaller branches, and then into twigs. One might assume a limited number of boughs (Q, R, S, T) representing different approaches to solving, say, collective action problems. Each is divided into branches 1 to n. A set of agents develop a path dependence along branch $q1$. When faced with a need to change paths, the agents will find it easier to try another branch within Q than to shift to an approach within R, S, or T, because a shorter distance is involved in retracing steps down to the generic origin in Q than in seeking out a new bough. Thus it was always easier for German vocational training reformers to go back down the familiar apprenticeship branch rather than cross over into a new, untried system.

Our approach is limited to dealing with endogenous change, as fundamental to it is the claim that agents can change to new ways of behaving if they have some endogenous access to appropriate new behaviour. It is not concerned with totally exogenous, bolt-on institutional borrowing. A practical example from a business context would be the efforts of car manufacturers in Britain, Germany, and elsewhere to introduce Japanese work practices in the 1980s. To the extent that efforts to adapt to these new challenges made use of older, pre-existing institutional repertoires that were rediscovered (Morris and Imrie 1992; Braczyk and Schienstock 1996), the model may contribute to the understanding of such change. (See also Herrigel (1993) on the conditions under which internationally oriented large firms have sought to make use of, or alternatively displace local paths of development, in their efforts to respond to a changed environment.)

As noted, these arguments highlight a relatively underappreciated implication of path dependence theory: that more than one path of institutional development is possible, even if only one becomes established. Alternatives exist somewhere within agents' repertoires, but have become forgotten or hidden through disuse or failure to appreciate their possible relevance. Something like this is embodied in Douglas's adaptation (1987: 66–7) of Lévi-Strauss's (1962) idea of *bricolage*, a rummaging around in disused but available practices for ways of solving new problems. For Lévi-Strauss this behaviour was specific to 'primitive' societies. Douglas sees that it might equally happen in 'advanced' ones. But her idea remains essentially conservative, rather than being a potential springboard for true innovation. But once we consider the transfer of practices from one field to another in which they have not previously been applied (as in the extensions), there is a possibility of true innovation. Campbell (2004), in a study of responses to the challenges posed to central and eastern Europeans during the 1990s, similarly treats *bricolage* as a creative process: access to new elements can increase the chances for revolutionary and not just evolutionary combinations. For Campbell it can be both substantive and symbolic. He brings an important twist to the argument, arguing that while the evolutionary economics school have been very good at identifying the selection process, they are not so good at the innovation process that precedes selection. This is where *bricolage* can help, but because it can be symbolic and follow a logic of appropriateness it does not necessarily lead to better outcomes.

A First Extension: Redundant Capacity as Subordinate Path Dependence

Path dependence theory necessarily deals only with situations in which actors can pursue one and only one path. This has been a useful base for most neo-institutionalist theory, which assumes, or asserts, that actors are confined to one typical course of action, usually dictated to them by their nation-state context. However, if we are to model the responses of entrepreneurial actors, it is essential that this assumption is relaxed, since entrepreneurial action consists in springing surprises, and clearly this is not possible if actors are constrained to one predictable repertoire. If the diversity available to them is very extensive, then path dependence does not apply; actors can more or less choose as they wish from an open menu of repertoires. Our concern here is with the scope for innovation available to actors subject to path dependence constraints. This scope can exist if such actors *are involved in a small number (greater than one) of constraining paths, movement between which is difficult but not impossible.*

To examine this in the terms of our model, we have to show A operating in two different contexts: that is, the environment now draws from two urns (E_1 and E_2). After every n rounds of the red-ball game already described (now called the dominant game, E_1) A plays one round of a subordinate game in a second environment, E_2, in which the path dependence is reversed, white balls being the subject of increasing returns. R is the same for both urns. The two environments are represented by two separate urns, which refill according to their opposite path dependences, but A has only one urn. If A has an understanding of the basic parameters of the game, she will have different Bayesian probability expectations for the two environments.

For most values of n, red will again establish a dominance in A's urn, as in the simple game. If white-ball dominant rounds are relatively infrequent, and/or searching for balls is relatively expensive, A may simply ignore the white rounds as a nuisance and take notice of red alone, behaving as in the original game, albeit with lower overall rewards. But if the white rounds come round relatively often, and search costs are low—the 'interesting' cases from our point of view—A may seek rewards from both paths, but again will have lower overall rewards than in the original game. She will not be able to take full advantage of the possibilities of creating path dependence on either colour in her own urn, and will have to incur higher search costs in matching both E_1's and E_2's draws. While A knows which game she is playing at any one time, the chances of finding a red ball at first attempt in the game with E_1 are less than in the original game, while the game with E_2 usually requires search costs to locate a white ball. There is a considerable amount of redundancy.

Let us now assume that at a certain point, as in the first game, E_1's urn changes to white dominance; there is no change in E_2's urn; white is dominant everywhere. If A has been following the two-colour strategy, she will now be able to adjust to the new path dependence more quickly than in the simple game, because she has a considerably higher proportion of white balls in her urn. A now finds that playing the two-environment game had greatly eased the transition. This version of the model represents the advantages of serendipitous redundancy, in which the need to switch between two different environments prepares actors better for completely unexpected changes in one of them.

An example of its practical application appears in Hollingsworth and Hollingsworth's study (2000) of the institutional contexts of major scientific discoveries. The Hollingsworths found that institutions with particularly large numbers of such discoveries to their credit typically encouraged, even possibly constrained, specialists in one area of science to sustain knowledge and interest in other areas:

[M]ajor discoveries occurred repeatedly because there was a high degree of interdisciplinary and integrated activity across diverse fields of science (thus, scientists with diverse perspectives interacted with intensity and frequency).... (ibid.: 222)

Sometimes these scientists might have found this redundancy irksome, as they could have made more progress with their 'own research' had they not had to sustain the subsidiary areas. They may even have fallen behind colleagues in more specialized institutes. However, at points of major new breakthrough, where new combinations of knowledge were needed and therefore where continuing an existing line would have been inadequate, they had major advantages over those who were more specialized. The two-environment game enables us to anticipate this outcome—but also to explain why the majority of academic institutions are structured in the opposite way and avoid redundancy by encouraging specialization. They do not take the risk of losing predictable routine returns by gambling on the chance of major discoveries.

Garud and Karnøe (2001*a*; 2001*b*) present several similar examples of such unplanned synergies in their accounts of technological innovations, and develop an argument concerning redundancy when they say of entrepreneurs that they:

[M]ay intentionally deviate from existing artefacts and relevance structures, fully aware that they may be creating inefficiencies for the present, but also aware that such steps are required to create new futures. (Garud and Karnøe 2001*b*: 6)

Campbell (2004) similarly sees entrepreneurs as located at interstices; and the broader their repertoire, the richer their *bricolage*. For Schumpeter (1936), the pioneer of entrepreneurial theory, entrepreneurs made 'new combinations'—implicitly of already existing components.

Neoclassical economists acknowledge that their models have extreme difficulty in dealing with how actors confront uncertainty, as opposed to risk. Insofar as actors are willing to incur costs in order to take advantage of future uncertainty, they are acting within a Schumpeterian rather than marginalist framework. Hollingsworth and Hollingsworth's research (2000) organizations were Schumpeterians, willing to take risks avoided by those engaged in marginal adjustments in order to reap large rewards when they suddenly arose. Within the economy as such, the chances for super-profits occur because the entrepreneurial agent is willing to take a risk which others refuse, making possible temporary rents. The super-profits of the Hollingsworths' scientists (2000) are rewards like Nobel Prizes, which can be seen as a kind of permanent rent.

Individual scientists within the institutes may occasionally have pre-ferred to be marginalists, but they were constrained by the rules of their game. In a Schumpeterian framework, entrepreneurs are agents who either sustain redundant capacities, or engage in temporarily less profit-able activities, so that at certain moments they may boldly grasp new opportunities. Schumpeter himself insisted on the importance of monopoly for entrepreneurs, arguing that continual strong competition under-mined the risk-taking that they required. This insight has been developed by evolutionary economists in their arguments about the need to protect research and development departments from erosion by competitive pressure (Nelson and Winter 1982), which is often more easily accomplished by monopolies (Lazonick 1991). North (1990a: 74–81) anticipates the problem of incentives to acquire pure knowledge—which has no immediate pay-off, but might have some in the future—and sees the particular structures chosen by firms as putting them into better or worse positions for dealing with it. Within the constraints of pure path dependence theory he has however no way of modelling different potential solutions.

We are here able to go beyond these accounts and identify as fundamental, not monopoly as such, but the capacity to retain redundant capacities in order to be able to cope with new or changing environments. Monopoly and limited competition are particular examples of how redundancy might be maintained. Other examples might be external constraint or simultaneous participation in different fields of activity, between which crossover is encouraged. For Hage and Hollingsworth (2000) the essential point is a number of separate specialized areas which are connected to each other through an innovation network.

Such arguments about redundancy in scientific and economic entrepreneurship have clear relevance to paths of institutional development too. In so far as agents or their institutions are regularly exposed to different sets of environmental pressures, they will be likely to develop substantial redundancies. These redundancies will often make it easier for agents to adapt these institutions to new and unexpected sets of environmental circumstances.

A Second Extension: Solutions Already Used in Adjacent Fields

In the first extension, I assumed that the agent has to take 'time out' from one game in order to play the other; there were opportunity costs, in particular in playing the subordinate game. However, in the case of a complex collective agent—such as a government with several ministries and agencies, working in diverse contexts—this will not necessarily be the case. Such an agent can simultaneously play different games in its different components. This increases the capacity of the entrepreneurial agent to spring path dependence traps. Our model must therefore be extended in order to deal with such a situation.

Components of the collective agent can learn from each other, even as each acts out her own path dependence. While the character of learning is one of the reasons why actors find themselves caught in path dependence traps, it can also be the means by which they might break dependence (see Pierson 2000*b*; Williamson and Masten 1995). One interesting historical example would be the way in which late nineteenth-century Dutch elites began to apply lessons they had learned about conflict management in the religious field (the *verzuiling* system) to conflicts emerging in industrial relations which could no longer be tackled in traditional ways (Hemerijck 1992). They could do this because of their acquired experience of using these mechanisms, understanding how they operated, and trusting them; *verzuiling* in the religious arena had become a self-reproducing path dependence, involving substantial increasing returns to learning. It would have been far more difficult, say, for French elites suddenly to imitate emerging Dutch industrial relations policy, because they did not have the prior learning experience from a proximate field. The neo-Darwinian synthesis of evolutionary biology is also relevant here; Gould (2002: 1234) talks at length about processes of 'exaptation;' 'the evolutionary result of functional co-optation from a different source of origin'.

Another example would be the case of Norway in Karl's comparative study (1997) of petroleum. She found path dependence theory of considerable value in explaining why states that had become dependent on petroleum revenues almost always failed to diversify their economic activity, even when it had become clear to them that oil dependence was harmful to their economies. At any one point in time it was always more profitable to continue with oil and not diversify. Almost alone among the oil-dependent states, Norway has long had a political system which makes changes through extensive and widely representative discursive processes; it alone succeeded in avoiding the trap. Path dependence theory has to recognize the Norwegian case as one that was able to escape its laws, but is unable to explain how or way. Our model enables us to see that, because Norwegian elites were subject to influence by and could access the perspectives of a diversity of organized interests, many of whom were not connected to petroleum, they were able to have access to alternative paths and to develop diversified strategies.

By making some further simple amendments to the situation presented in the first extension, we can model such possibilities. We now give A two urns, A_1 and A_2, provided that she pays each time she chooses to move between them. (It is a basic assumption of the whole model that all changes of action are costly in one way or another.) The original search cost C is now C_x; the urn swap cost becomes C_y. The relationship between C_x and C_y is not determined *ex ante*. As in the previous example, we assume that E_1 develops a red-ball dominance, and E_2 a white-ball dominance. In this extension A will swap her urns to match the different path dependences of E_1 and E_2, if C_y is not set at an unreasonably high level. We assume for simplicity that A will use urn A_1 to operate in environment E_1, and will switch to urn A_2 in E_2. A will seek to establish a red-ball dominance in A_1, and a white-ball dominance in A_2. It should be noted that we should still provide for search costs in this use of different urns: interdepartmental and interpersonal rivalries, desires to build little empires, personal jealousies all serve to make cooperation difficult in organizations formally considered to be subunits of a large structure.

While net profits are *ceteris paribus* lower than in the first, simplest version of the game, they will be the same as or higher than those in the first extension. When E_1's urn changes to white dominance, the relative values of C_x and C_y, as well as A's Bayesian beliefs will determine her response. If, as we already assume, C_y is low enough that A has been prepared to switch urns on turns when E played E_2, A will switch to urn A_2 in order to respond to E_1 as well as E_2, and will quickly start to draw white balls. This allows us to model a situation that is somewhat different from the redundancies modelled in the previous extension. Now, an agent who has followed two paths of institution building in two different environments or sets of circumstances may borrow from one in order to escape from an institutional path dependence in the other which is no longer appropriate. At its simplest level, this may involve lateral thinking, or, more broadly, as in the Dutch *verzuiling* case mentioned above, *Wahlverwandschaft* (Hemerijck 1992). This kind of innovation is more than mere *bricolage*, because taking responses originating in one action sphere and applying them in a new one can result in entirely new actions and institutions.

A Third Extension: Embeddedness in Networks of Policy Fields as a Resource

By incorporating innovation through learned behaviour from proximate fields, we have already gone some way towards bringing the insights of the sociology of 'embeddedness' (Granovetter 1985) within a framework of path dependence. Such learning allows agents to 'capture' external paths of institutional organization in a limited way; by recognizing this possibility, we open the way to dealing with more obviously exogenous phenomena, like imitations and impositions. In an open world it should not be assumed a priori that the walls around national or any other systems are impenetrable. Multinational firms, educational institutions, immigrants and consultants regularly penetrate them. As noted in Chapter 2, most neo-institutionalist literature is unable to deal with the implications of this, because it rests on assumptions that actors exist within bounded, coherent systems (usually nation-states). If neo-institutionalism is to deal with the more open reality of the contemporary world, it must develop path dependence theory in a way that *relativizes* pure endogeneity and pure exogeneity, making them end points of a continuum. This is, by the way, the best way to deal with the debate over nation states and globalization. For example, is the contribution of a staff member who has returned with new ideas and experiences from a secondment with an organization in a very different environment endogenous or exogenous? Or the headquarters staff of a multinational firm who bring new ideas to a remote branch? (It should be noted that we are here dealing with the endogenous or exogenous nature of the *response* made by actors, not of the *shock* which stimulates the need for change.) We can incorporate this new flexibility within the model while retaining the basic constraints of path dependence and avoiding creating situations in which anything is possible by developing two ideas already implicit within the second extension: that of different levels of 'proximity' of different urns in the game; and that of costs of switching from one urn to another.

Let us assume that there are N urns, which are used by N agents all playing the simple game in N different environments. Each player has an urn with two of B different coloured balls. These agents are not in competition with each other—indeed they do not interact directly, although they may copy each other's actions (i.e. draw from one another's urns)—and A is one among them. Further, they are situated on a plane in which some urns are more distant from A than others; closer urns are those that are less costly for A to emulate, and further urns are progressively more costly. Let us assume that A is playing the simple game in which both she and E have one urn. At some point E begins to draw a new colour, which may be any one of B. When this occurs, A may draw (blindly) from other urns in order to find the colour which will bring the reward. A has no prior knowledge of the colours of the balls in the different urns, but may have some knowledge of the underlying probability distribution, and may remember the colour of balls in urns that she has previously drawn from. To draw from another urn A must pay cost dC_y, where d is a positive function of the distance of the urn from A. This embodies the hypothesis that the difficulty of acquiring access to new practices increases with distance from the initial practice. 'Difficulty' may be constituted in various ways, such as a learning curve, or difficulty of communication with those in a remote location. 'Distance' may similarly have various meanings; it may be literal distance, or differences degrees of access determined by power relations, or just general institutional remoteness.

A's willingness to search out new balls as her environment changes will depend on: (i) as always, her Bayesian beliefs; (ii) her acquired stock of knowledge of urns $N-1$; and (iii) the relationship between t, d^*, C_y and A's expected future earnings from finding the proper ball, where t is the expected number of searches necessary to find the appropriate ball, and d^* the expected distance from the urn containing the right ball.

As in all other forms of the model, these parameters may have values that make anything other than continuing to pursue the original path dependence too costly or difficult. Here, condition (iii) in particular may be especially burdensome. A may be faced with a choice of: (a) trying to find a remote solution at possibly ruinous cost; (b) of searching intensively among more proximate urns, even in situations where she knows from the underlying probability distribution that the solution is unlikely to be found close by; or (c) continuing to follow the now failing path. This models a situation often faced by agents required to adopt exogenous solutions which do not fit with their past experience and institutional structures. Even if new ways can be learned given time, they may be so remote from the agent that success cannot be achieved before a total crisis arrives. There may be several examples of this in the history of central and eastern European countries during the 1990s. Firms and political elites were in a position where all available paths of development from the state socialist period seemed to have failed completely. International agencies and western governments advised these actors that they must imitate approaches that were extremely remote in terms of their previous experience. The responses adopted provide examples of all three above possibilities (a, b, and c).

This extended form of the model requires considerable operationalization before it can be used in research. The researcher must identify the relevant continuum of actors, the types of institutional practice in which they are engaged (i.e. the character of their urns), and the environments in which they operate. The idea of a full set of N possible solutions set at varying degrees of accessibility from A not only replaces the dichotomy between endogeneity and exogeneity of responses with a continuum, but enables us to consider constraints on and possibilities of action caused by relationships between A and a given social structure of opportunity. She is not endowed with perfect knowledge as in much neoclassical theory, but is dependent on her location within that structure for both knowledge of and capacity to use innovations.

The institutional lock-in that Grabher (1993b) found in the Ruhr during the crisis of the metals sector in the 1980s can be seen to be a case of this extension. All actors within the region were committed to metal manufacture, so that all attempts at solving the crisis involved attempts to reform that sector and no measures for developing new activities. In the terms of my model, all new possibilities were too remote from A to be practicable, while all other reasonably accessible players were committed to play the same colour as A herself. However, Glassmann (2004) has shown that some Ruhr cities at least have eventually been able to find new paths, largely through the actions of the Land government of Nord-Rhein Westfalen. This agent, which Grabher (1993*b*) argued was just as embedded as the Ruhr cities themselves in the metal-industry model, was nevertheless far from coextensive with that industry but also involved in many other policy areas and issues. The Land government provided an example of the argument demonstrated mathematically by Anderlini and Ianni (1993) in their locality model, where agents on the edge of a particular network of embedded relations have an access to other, adjacent networks not possessed by those in the middle of the net. The eventual success of these cities in changing their course of economic development is compatible with my theory, which expects lengthy periods of adjustment and failed attempts to sustain previous paths before actors accept the need for more radical change, but does not rule out eventual success as impossible.

In addition to the analogy of the net, we might also adapt that of molecules within a substance. The velocity of molecules at the edge is greater than that of those in the middle, enabling the former occasionally to travel to a considerable distance. We might apply this to Streeck and Thelen's observation (2005*a*) that change can take place *within the range* of a path-dependent practice. Where the actors engaging in such change are situated at the edge of the institution (i.e. they are in contact with others outside the institution), the range of path-dependent change on their part might extend considerably further than that of actors at the centre.

In practice it is often difficult to determine whether simple path dependence or a more complex sociological embeddedness is at work in a lock-in (Thelen 1999); and the two may reinforce each other. For example, consider the case of the so-called Bismarckian systems of social insurance established in Germany and a number of other countries, which have become deeply embedded, and which are frequently described in the literature as having produced path dependences. Did these systems originate as the result of the chance prior appearance of some instances of these particular schemes, which fact later led to their being adapted as a national standard? Or were they conceived because they corresponded to a particular balance of power and set of social relationships and compromises? If the former, we have a relatively pure case of path dependence, first-mover advantage and increasing returns as described in the probability theory literature. If the latter, we are instead dealing with something that needs explanation in terms of the balance of social relationships, for which path dependence theory is less suited, and perhaps even unnecessary. However, it may not be easy to disentangle these two phenomena in empirical situations; indeed, social structural reasons for the persistence of institutions may change over time, as for example new groups acquire vested interests in old institutions.

For our present purposes disentangling historical origins is not so important as the other end of the chain of events: understanding the character of practices which have become locked in, so that change and innovation are difficult. However an institution originated, some elements of learning curve and returns to scale may support its persistence against potential alternatives. This is a kind of quasi path dependence, with different origins from those discussed by Arthur (1994), but acquiring some characteristics of that model along the way. There is very likely to be a cluster of supporting and opposing interests, cross-institutional links, etc., creating a structure of embeddedness.

A Fourth Extension: Functional Equivalents and Renewed Path Dependence

Finally, let us consider how the model might be extended to deal with a frequently occurring, difficult question. Given the strong possibility that functionally equivalent alternative solutions exist for many problems, how can agents ensure that, in a situation of widespread availability of alternative institutional models, they have an opportunity to choose among various viable possibilities, hopefully finding one which most 'suits' them? This dilemma presents itself frequently to many groups in the post-communist societies of central and eastern Europe. How can they, acting under conditions of difficulty and a need to make rapid changes, ensure that they make those reforms which are best suited to their capacities and needs? We can adapt our model to demonstrate such a context of choice; it strongly suggests the conclusion that such actors may have very little chance of making such optimal choices. The powerful logic of the original path dependence concept is in fact likely to reappear.

To show this, I modify the third extension (in which A could search through the urns of her neighbours in order to find a new matching ball when E changes urns). Now, when E changes the ball colour which it rewards from the initial red, it is in principle willing to reward any one of a certain number of new colours. For the purposes of illustration, let us assume that it will reward white, blue, and magenta. A has decided to incur the search costs, searches for a ball until she finds one for which a reward is presented, and finally happens upon a magenta one. She learns that she will be rewarded if she presents further magenta balls; however, she has no knowledge that blue and white would also be rewarded, and if she finds any of these in the urns of her neighbours she will reject them and continue to look for magenta. While we do not specify any search function, it is reasonable to expect that under many circumstances, A will start to build up a path dependence in magenta balls. The possibility of offering blue or white balls will never be discovered, *even* if presenting either of these would be more lucrative, or less costly. Under these circumstances, Bayesian decision-makers can 'lock in' to inferior choices (Arthur 1994). The actual beliefs of agents themselves have many of the characteristics of path-dependent phenomena; they tend to lock into repeated patterns that are not necessarily optimal. One might go beyond these arguments, to suggest that in a context where agents observe each other, such effects may be contagious. Another actor, observing A's success, might conclude that A had indeed discovered an optimal response to a given set of environmental problems, and might copy her. This demonstrates how the idea of 'one best way' can become rapidly established even if in reality a 'world of possibilities' (Sabel and Zeitlin 1997) exists, discovery of some among which would better suit the interests of some agents than the proclaimed one best way. Cultural cognitive processes, important in seeking legitimacy, help explain why firms imitate each other as much as actual economic performance (Scott 2001); legitimacy can certainly be a source of path dependence. Schneiberg and Clemens (forthcoming) discuss how conformity to practices trickles down from international organizations, etc. giving a priority to imitative behaviour irrespective of its real value. As Scott (2001: 164) argues, in the early stages of institutionalization adoption of a practice is based on purposive rationality. But for latecomers the rationality is in doing that which is deemed appropriate. Nelson and Winter (1982) similarly argues that new technological advances create new frameworks, which then become the sources of new path dependences. This is the common fate of boundedly rational actors, the most common type of human actor. Nugent (2005) stresses the importance of the endemic nature of information deficiencies and asymmetries, which are central to this final problem. He then tries to push forward the new institutional economics approach so that it can account for change and development, but wonders whether this can be only carried out *ex post*.

Conclusions

We have now come full circle and shown how innovative actors, bent on breaking out from a suboptimal path dependence may well put themselves into a new path that repeats the same process. It is now time to show how the model of innovative actors presented here relates to the arguments of the previous chapters. Our agent, *A*, could find new paths only when there were some 'mongrel', even incongruent elements in her environment. *We can therefore observe innovations of this kind only if our models of real-world institutions have allowed us to find elements of complexity and incoherence. This will not happen if a false interpretation of the law of parsimony requires us to simplify the cases we study so that they seem to be the embodiments of ideal types.*

Although in the course of the discussion we have departed a long way from the probability theory base of pure path dependence theory, the essential logic of that base and of the constraints it imposes on social actors in many circumstances has remained important, making it necessary to explain why actors cannot simply change strategies as an act of volition when confronted with the failure of the habitual paths, but must follow a strictly limited number of possibilities, always with uncertain prospects of success. (I say 'possibilities' rather than 'strategies', because, even if agents behave rationally at each stage of the process, they do not choose a path with perfect knowledge of its consequences, so that accident, serendipity, and structured opportunity play an important role in the adoption of particular routes.)

In order to do this, we have extended and combined path dependence theories in the following ways, resulting in the identification of a number of path-changing possibilities:

- Through incorporating a Bayesian decision-maker with her 'own' urn, more accurately to model the relationship between actors and their environments;
- By introducing into the model the possibility of costed searches into other paths concealed within agents' own past experience, to enable them to stand a chance of pursuing possibility one: the use of hidden or dormant alternatives within their own repertoires;
- By introducing the possibility of agents playing simultaneous games, to enable them to pursue possibility two: transfer of experience from different action spaces;
- By introducing the possibility of agents having costed access to additional games, to enable them to pursue possibility three: transfer of

experience from other agents through networks of structured relationships—which in turn helps break down the rigid dichotomy between
endogeneity and exogeneity as sources of actors' responses;
• By introducing the possibility of several viable alternatives, only one of
which is likely to be discovered, to model how ideas of 'one best way'
solutions become established.

Our overall conclusions are similar to those already reached by Garud
and Karnøe (2001a: xiii) in their model of entrepreneurs as embedded
path creators, as 'neither insiders nor outsiders, but boundary spanners'.
They reject the conventional idea of entrepreneurs and innovators as
completely original, even exogenous, forces; entrepreneurs develop
along the paths provided by history, but attempt mindfully to depart
from it. By 'mindfulness' Garud and Karnøe (2001b: 23) mean conscious-
ness of embeddedness and knowledge of when to use it and when to
depart from it. They invoke Schumpeter's stress (1934) on the need for
entrepreneurs to escape from the strict dictates of rational action. Their
entrepreneurs therefore proceed through a path of 'chain-linked deviation' (Garud and Karnøe (2001b: 26). This differs from a random walk
in that at each step the agent places its next step purposively, though it is
acting with only imperfect knowledge.

Notes

1. The argument in this chapter is developed more fully and technically in Crouch
   and Farrell (2004). I am heavily indebted to Henry Farrell for very many of the
   insights into the argument.
2. In a simple random walk, each step starts from where the last one landed, but
   can go anywhere within a specified range from that point. If the walk is on a
   convex plane, it will be biased towards movements down the slope, the extent
   of bias expressing the shape of the curve.
3. For my purposes an agent can be an individual person, a firm, or another
   collective actor, provided that it is reasonable to assume that the agent makes
   decisions as a unit. By 'environment' I mean the context within which the agent
   acts and from which she derives rewards. In the case of a firm, the environment
   would be the markets within which it sells its products. For policy- and
   decision-makers it would be the action space within which they operate and
   learn whether or not their actions have led to desired results.

5

A Strategy for the Analysis of
Economic Governance

If neo-institutionalist analysis is to account for the actions of institutional entrepreneurs, it must be able to model fine detail and not just the broad characterization of institutional forms, because these actors depend on complexity in order to make their innovations. It is also necessary to be able to locate them historically and in context, and not leave them in an abstract space. Institutions therefore need to be specified in the research programme in such a way that we can identify the points at which the actors might try to gain a purchase on them, engage with them, and shape them. Lütz (2003), in her account of changes in European financial regimes, has provided an example of how this can be done. She shows, not just more than one governance mechanism, but also *parts or fragments* of some of them, being combined in new and different ways, with the result that the diversity of forms of political economy is itself increased. This is exactly the kind of approach that is needed. It must be remembered that for present purposes we are interested in *institutional* entrepreneurs: those who are concerned with changing the structure within which economic and other activities take place. We are not concerned with entrepreneurship within those activities themselves. Institutional entrepreneurs may be found in many places, including within public policy, consultancies, or representative associations.

Let us start by assuming a given field of action, F. This could be anything from the production of innovative biopharmaceutical products to organizing a religion. Within any such field there is a potential set of capacities, C, relevant to its performance, such that, if they possess them, actors will be able to accomplish certain tasks. The constituent items in the list will change over time. (For example, the list of capacities needed to produce books changed dramatically with the invention of the printing press, some old ones being lost and new ones added.) But let us assume that the list is stable at any one point in time. The fundamental hypothesis of neo-institutionalism is that different types of institutional context (I', I'', etc.) make available different subsets or patterns (C', C'', etc.) of these capacities. (For the present we set aside the question of what constitutes an institutional context, the usual assumption that it is always a nation-state being problematic.) Thus, once we know that a particular actor is located within a particular context I', we know that she has available C' capacities within F, where normally $C' < C$. The problem confronting a potential institutional entrepreneur is to change the institutional context, such that it delivers further elements of C not contained within C'.

For example, assume that C_{1-j} constitutes the full range of capacities that are needed to build and market successfully motor vehicles; and that I', I'', etc., are institutional contexts representing different national social systems of production (SSP) (Hollingsworth and Boyer 1997), which provide actors within them with parts of this range. Institutionalist theory tells us that if motor-industry firms are located within SSP I', providing capacities C', and if this pattern constitutes the capacities needed to produce high-performance cars alone, then firms within I' will be able to produce successfully only that kind of vehicle. If capacities C'' constitute those needed to produce basic mass-production cars alone, and if I'' provides only those capacities, then firms within I'' will be able to produce successfully only those, and so on. An institutional entrepreneur in I'', who wants car producers within his zone to be able to produce high-performance cars, needs to discover ways of changing institutions such that capacities C' become available to them.

These different repertoires of capacities possessed by actors within a given context may be envisaged as a series of combinations of presences and absences of individual capacities within each relevant field. Thus, if in field F_1 there are eight potential capacities, ($C_{1-h} = C_{1-8}$), institutional context I' might enable actors within it to possess pattern C', which provides five of these, distributed in the following way:

Context I'
Capacities 1 2 3 4 5 6 7 8

field F_1. 1 1 0 0 1 1 0 1

while context I'' might enable its actors to possess C'', which provides four, distributed differently, say:

Context I''
Capacities 1 2 3 4 5 6 7 8

field F_1. 0 0 1 1 0 0 1 1

This, expressed formally, is what neo-institutionalist analysis is telling us: Particular patterns of capacities are sustained by the institutions of a particular context, with the result that certain capacities are available to actors located within that space, while others are denied to them. (We temporarily assume no functional equivalents.) The observable pattern is a consequence of various conscious decisions, opportunity costs, and path dependences, such that it cannot easily be changed even if actors within the context perceive advantages in so doing. (If capacities can be changed at will, they are not of interest to the present task, which is concerned with innovation in the face of the constraints exercised by institutions.)

As we saw in Chapter 3, a second fundamental claim of much institutionalist theory is that governance modes, or certain combinations of compatibility and *Wahlverwandschaft*, ensure that similar, isomorphic patterns or combinations of capacities are found repeatedly across fields within a given individual context, such that these contexts become coherent, homogeneous wholes. Therefore, if C' is found in field F_1, it will also be found in fields F_{2-j}:

Context I'

Capacities   1 2 3 4 5 6 7 8

field F_1.	1 1 0 0 1 1 0 1
field F_2.	1 1 0 0 1 1 0 1
field F_3.	1 1 0 0 1 1 0 1
field F_4.	1 1 0 0 1 1 0 1
. . . .	
field F_j.	1 1 0 0 1 1 0 1

We can deepen the analysis if we consider different fields as comprising subfields, which can themselves then be analysed in the same way, treating the above framework as a kind of Russian doll, much in the manner of Parsonian social theory. Thus, for example, the economy comprises a financial system, a form of corporate governance, a labour market regime, a system of research and development, and so on. The main expectation of neo-institutionalist theory would be that the dominant pattern of capacities is reproduced in each of these, reinforcing strengths and magnifying weaknesses as in the reproduction of pedigree breeds of dog.

Complementarity

However, it is essential that analysis also be capable of dealing with fields that present different patterns. This is particularly important in the case of strictly complementary institutions, where theory claims that if actors have available patterns of capacities in some fields that compensate for gaps in others, they will sometimes possess strengths superior to those of a completely congruent system. For example,

Context I'

Capacities   1 2 3 4 5 6 7 8

field F_1.   1 1 0 0 1 1 0 1
field F_2.   1 1 0 0 1 1 0 1
field F_3.   1 1 0 0 1 1 0 1
field F_4.   1 1 0 0 1 1 0 1

. . . .

field F_j.   0 0 1 1 0 0 1 0
field F_k.   0 0 1 1 0 0 1 0

Here, fields F_j, F_k provide perfect complementarity in the sense of compensation for the others. An example of this would be the claims of some authors (e.g. Wood 2001), considered in Chapter 3, that the centralized and autonomous political system of the UK is a field F_j for the country's economy. Whereas the latter is rooted in markets and individualistic competition, the political system provides centralized order. Another example would be the role of venture capitalist 'angels' within Californian high-tech sectors. These contingently provide a form of patient, non-anonymous capital (and thus an 'F_j', contrasting with the stereotypical model of US finance capitalism) that *complementarily* provides long-term stability for firms which otherwise thrive on the high mobility of other factors of production (usually seen as the fields F_{1-4} of US economic institutions.

Perfectly complementary institutions of this type will be exceptions. In practice many institutions which differ from a dominant pattern are merely different, or even present negative capacities. As we have seen, such 'untidy' elements are highly important to the approach being proposed here, as they may constitute serendipitous redundancies, of potential use to endogenous institutional entrepreneurs trying to achieve change.

Links and Barriers

In the interests of parsimony we start by hypothesizing a strain towards similarity across fields and subfields within an identifiable context. Such an hypothesis is plausible if we can demonstrate the existence of unifying factors—probably forms of governance—working to achieve institutional homogeneity within a bordered framework. In the case of presumed 'national systems', the main examples of bordered frameworks used in the literature, state policy and national legal institutions provide such plausibility. These unifying factors produce strong links between institutional forms: for example, ensuring that a neoliberal corporate governance system is paralleled by a neoliberal labour market regime. It follows from this hypothesis that contrasting institutions, those following a different structural logic and providing different patterns of competences that might form complementarities, can exist only when there are identifiable barriers which protect them from the dominant linking, homogenizing forces. It is therefore an important research task to identify any such barriers. We should expect to find institutional entrepreneurs at work forging and breaking both links and boundaries.

We cannot predict a priori where links will be at their weakest, or where barriers will exist; they may be quite arbitrary, historical, accretions. But we can specify some likely sources, and identify both diffusion mechanisms and barriers. First, to the extent that, as proposed in Chapter 4, we can order fields of institutions as being at some kind of 'distance' from each other, we can hypothesize that diffusion is more likely between proximate complexes than remote ones. (For example, we should expect to find more strains towards similarity between the structure of the financial system and that of the labour market than between the former and the structure of religious life.) Second, if it can be established that the patterns found in some fields (or even subfields) are more 'powerful' than those in others—as in the dominant path dependences considered in Chapter 4—we should expect pressures for diffusion from the powerful to the powerless. 'Power' might here refer to the resources that can be wielded by the interests dominant in certain (sub)fields. For example, behaviour favoured by the authorities within stock markets is likely to be more influential than that favoured by sport authorities.

Where we find fields F_j, F_k as described above, we should expect to find an institutional barrier separating them from F_{1-4}. Without this it is unlikely that the former, as a minority system, could survive. Such barriers may take many empirical forms. An example would be the community mechanisms that sustain the religious norms of an ethnic minority; these then make it possible for that minority to sustain strong patriarchal family norms in defiance of majority practice, which in turn sustain forms of family business which are not possible for the majority community. (On the other hand, the lack of strong family norms in the majority may give it different kinds of advantage; for example, it may make possible high levels of geographical and social mobility.) If, over time, the institutions of the minority community weaken, it is likely that the practices of the majority will 'leak' into it, gradually eroding its contrasting practices. A very different example would be the formal provisions that prevent the manufacture and sale of nuclear weapons from being subject to the same rules as the rest of a market economy, and make their manufacture a monopoly of certain states. This enables a form of state involvement that assists large-scale investment in this sector, without spillover into parts of the economy that are governed by market criteria. When such diversity provides complementarities for an overall system, interests in the dominant fields will be quite happy to accept the diversity of norms. There is not necessarily any conflict around it.

The above discussion enables us to present the institutional map that confronts actors of the kind anticipated in Chapter 4: realizing that their path-dependent practices have reached as point of diminished utility, and preparing to seek costly but necessary new paths, using the limited number of possibilities we there made available. Patterns of capacities, running across fields and subfields, and possibly including elements of complementarity, constitute the paths that in Chapter 4 had been presented simply as balls of different colours. We can now see a number of possibilities of actions that these actors might take. They are seeking for sources of different combinations of 1, 0 than those which have emerged from their past practice. Where an existing institutional context included complementary and not just isomorphic components, the actors have a chance to work on these, trying to extend their operation, in a manner similar to that represented in the first extension of the game in Chapter 4. Or they might turn their attention to the links and barriers, and try to rearrange these, creating links to new combinations of complementarity by linking up with other fields and subfields, and possibly creating barriers where links had existed before.

An Actor-centred Model of Governance Mechanisms

We must now be more precise about what it is that institutional entrepreneurs need to change when they engage in these activities. In Chapter 1, we identified governance mechanisms as the means whereby the predictability and regularity fundamental to institutions are ensured. It is therefore these that must be changed. We therefore need a model of different modes of governance. The main scheme that will be used will be that derived from the work of Campbell, Hollingsworth, and Lindberg (1991), as further elaborated by Hollingsworth and Boyer (1997) and Hollingsworth (2002), with a particularly useful amendment from Van Waarden (2002).

In fact, the number and variety of mechanisms that perform governance functions ranges wider than the mechanisms usually considered in governance studies, even when these include the informal institutions of community governance. Regularities may be imparted by the presence of institutions that ostensibly have nothing at all to do with the field of action at stake. For example, a growing number of studies of contemporary developments in high-tech sectors demonstrate the role of universities in sustaining local and other clusters of commercial innovation and firms (Powell 1996; Kenney 2000a; Crouch et al. 2001, 2004; Jong Kon Chin forthcoming). The university as such stands outside the commercial activity concerned and has no formally acknowledged position within it, but it can play a strongly determining role within a high-tech sector. Through its own departmental structures it can, serendipitously and even unconsciously, make it more or less likely that certain scientists will remain within an area and work together in certain ways. Its rules about how its professors spend their time and exploit patents and the proceeds from commercial application of their research can affect the kind of access that firms have to the public research base (Jong Kon Chin forthcoming; Proudfoot 2004). This base itself, of course, exists by definition outside the market, which is firms' primary governance mode.

To take another example: Patterns of women's labour force participation and hours of employment will be affected by norms and rules prevailing in local family structures. Thus, the family is among the institutions which govern the labour market, though it is usually ignored in studies which would expect to concentrate on the state, the industrial relations system, employers, and the market (Crouch 1999: pt: I). Therefore, although we need analytical lists of typical governance mechanisms, we must also be ready to find unfamiliar, even coincidental and serendipitous institutions playing such a role and to add them to the list, at least for specified purposes.

These wider possibilities will not be considered in this initial presentation of a model, but they need to be borne in mind. The components of whatever scheme we eventually use can be usefully understood in relation to each other by defining them against a shared conceptual framework of abstract attributes, which will be developed first. For the sake of clarity, these will be presented as a series of binomial choices, the resulting pattern of choices defining governance modes in contrast with each other. In reality a more 'fuzzy logic' usually prevails rather than the clear distinction of an on/off switch. However, theory must always proceed by simple steps. If we first establish clear distinctions, we can proceed later to the greater realism of complexity. Therefore the set of capacities becomes a set of binomial possibilities, and if a pattern is valid for one field, it is assumed in this first cut to be valid for all, leading to:

Context I'   Characteristics of governance mode
              1 2 3 4 5 6 7 8 9

all fields   1 0 1 0 1 0 1 0 1 0 1 0 1 0 1 0 1 0

Production of a list of the elemental characteristics of governance is an inductive and nominalist task; and therefore no list can be considered final or beyond criticism. It is therefore also important to avoid the assumption that it must be possible to give an answer for every item in the list for every form of governance, as though these are functions that have to be performed. With that caveat, we can propose (no stronger verb can be used) the following approach to constructing a list. The model presented here differs from that of Hollingsworth and Boyer (1997:9) in that their 'general taxonomy of institutional arrangements' has only two criteria: horizontal versus vertical coordination; and self-interested or obligational action motives. The former is included in my list (point 5 below), but it is notable that in a further elaboration of their model to form 'models of coordination or governance' (ibid.: 12), they interpret horizontal versus vertical to mean 'no discrete organizational structure' versus 'bureaucratic administrative control structure'. This incorporates some ideas not found in the simple opposition of horizontal and vertical. Their contrast between self-interest and obligation is also problematic. For example, market contracts are usually enforced by law (obligation) as well as by self-interest. Further, whether a constraint operates through self-interest or obligation depends on ease of exit from the relationship. I have therefore tried to develop a more thorough list of relevant variables within which to contain the principal points of Hollingsworth and Boyer's scheme.

The Elemental Choices of Governance Modes

1. *Exogeneity versus endogeneity.* A governance mechanism may be either external to the institution being governed or internal to it. For example, the market is always exogenous to the firms that work in it. The hierarchy of managers that runs a firm itself, however, is endogenous to it.
2. *Formality versus informality.* The character of the rules through which governance is expressed can be either formal (that is explicit, in principle clearly specifiable) or informal (implicit, subject to nuance and

variable mutual understanding). For example, both market and law operate through formal rules; while regulation of behaviour through the understandings of a community is informal.

3. *Substance versus procedure.* In the former there is direct intervention by agents responsible for governance to give incentives to behaviour by allocating resources. In the latter a set of procedures affects the behaviour of ordinary actors within the institution. For example, an association provides substantive resources (usually, club goods) to its members; legal codes offer procedural sanctions for breaches of rules.

4. *Signalling versus dialogue.* This choice concerns the forms of communication that are used by the governance mechanism when relating to members of the institution. Signalling simply indicates what constitutes compliant behaviour (as in the pure market). Dialogue provides for complex exchanges of speech acts and negotiation of terms (as in most other governance forms, particularly at the local level).

5. *Verticality versus horizontality.* Communication also has a directional dimension. Vertical communication implies an authority centre (as in an association, or a corporate hierarchy). Horizontality presupposes a system of rules in place, enabling communication itself to be lateral and not itself embodying a command structure (as in the market).

6. *Strong versus weak enforcement.* Fundamental to governance is enforcement capacity: How effective is the governance mechanism in ensuring compliance? We can initially model this capacity simply as being either strong or weak.

7. *Extensive versus limited reach.* There is a second aspect of enforcement: its reach. Do the enforcement mechanisms in question extend generally across the society or indeed the world, or are they limited to those directly connected to the institution? We can again initially model reach dichotomously as being either extensive or limited.

8. *Difficult versus easy exit.* Related to the strength and reach of enforcement capacity is the possibility of exit from the institution. This can be difficult, leaving units and individuals trapped within the enforcement scope of the governance mechanism, or easy.

9. *Public versus private goods.* All governance provides goods for a collectivity of some kind, but the character of the collectivity so served can vary from a pure public one (in the economist's sense) to a private, defined group. For example, the actions of the state (particularly the procedural state) are in principle available to all, whereas an association normally provides benefits only for its members.

The resulting scheme is shown in Table 5.1.

TABLE 5.1 Attributes of governance

1. Relationship to institution/territory	Exogenous	1	0	Endogenous
2. Character of governance rules	Formal	1	0	Informal
3. Character of implementation of governance	Substantive	1	0	Procedural
4. Form of communication prescribed	Signalling	1	0	Dialogue
5. Structure of communication prescribed	Vertical	1	0	Horizontal
6. Strength of enforcement of rules	High	1	0	Low
7. Reach of enforcement	Extensive	1	0	Limited
8. Ease of exit from relationships	Difficult	1	0	Easy
9. Character of collectivity served	Public	1	0	Private

The Standard Forms of Governance

We can now attempt an allocation of the standard governance forms identified in the literature to this model, allocating them to the three frequently identified regulatory zones of polity, economy, and (residually) society. The polity and the economy can be distinguished from other social institutions by the clarity and abstract character of what actors within them are trying to maximize: in the former, power; in the latter, material wealth. It is this characteristic which early on enabled study of the state and the market to become distinct disciplines—political science and economics respectively—rather than remain part of a general science of society, or sociology, and to develop their bodies of theory more strongly than that discipline.

Central to the modern polity is the state. While those within the state, or struggling to have access to it, have a diversity of substantive goals, they can function effectively only if they can gain control over the capacity to give orders on the assumption that they will be obeyed. Following Weber's famous formulation (1922: pt. I, ch. 1, sec. 17), it is the distinctive feature of the state that in the last resort it commands a monopoly of the legitimate use of violence to support its authority. Politics, the name of the activity that focuses on access to the state, is therefore always action focused on the maximization of outcomes through command, through the attainment of power. Similarly, while actors within the economy seek a diversity of substantive goods and services, within a capitalist economy they can do this effectively only if they possess the means of exchange. Economic behaviour is therefore always focused on the maximization of the means of exchange, or wealth. It is difficult to find fundamental goals of similar abstract and type in other social institutions. The only exception is religion, where action is focused on the overwhelming general need to appease powerful figures in a world beyond this one—achieving a state of grace with God in Christian terms.

This pattern within the structure of the social sciences is also found in many actual social representations. In formally structured societies the *virtuosi* of state and market, and those of religion, are picked out as privileged social classes: in European history these were the orders of respectively aristocrats, bourgeoisie and priests; a similar pattern existed in the core caste order of Mogul India, though with the priestly caste accorded pride of place. Stratification in the rest of the population was far less systematic and clear; they were just a residuum, even though a vast majority. Similarly, the classic Greek and Roman city embodied a seat of government, a market and a temple as the most important buildings, normally located formally in relationship to each other in the most prominent part of the city. The medieval European city followed the same pattern, with town hall, marketplace and church similarly located. Other parts were less distinct and prominent; society in general was literally the poorly differentiated residuum that simply filled up the rest of available space. Bereft of religion as a clear source of governance, 'society' today remains a vast residual group of institutions. In practice, there are ways of defining it so that it becomes amenable to study, but never in the clear way that we can do with polity and economy.

In the following discussion, attention is limited to the governance of economic behaviour, though a similar scheme could be produced for other spheres of life.

The Polity

The most obvious form of governance is that provided by the state. The institutions around the state have the provision of governance as their principal *raison d'être*. Hollingsworth and Boyer (1997) include it as one of their principal forms of institutional arrangements, characterized by vertical coordination and obligational action motives. When modelling it as a form of governance, they also see it as embodying a bureaucratic administrative control structure. They therefore see the state solely in the form considered below as the 'substantive' state.

However, Van Waarden (2002) has demonstrated the importance of considering the state in two forms. The first is where the state intervenes as a direct actor; the second is where it exercises governance by making available to persons and groups within its jurisdiction a range of laws that they can use to regulate their affairs with each other. The state further provides and guarantees enforcement of the outcomes of this regulation. Here the state does not appear as a bureaucratic administrative control structure, but as legislator and as a system of courts and police forces. Individuals (or firms) make contracts with each other, these contracts taking a form prescribed (or permitted) by either statute or case law. In European systems this is the field of private law, but the law of contract of course also exists in Anglophone systems. Van Waarden points out how this role of the state is often not perceived as state action, because the initiatives are taken by citizens, and decisions are shaped by judges rather than by government officials. Also, Anglophone systems include the myth of Common Law, that law is something 'discovered' by judges working out the implications of rational and reasonable behaviour. But the modern law of contract, particularly where it relates to economic conduct, is heavily determined by statute and therefore by political and administrative activity, as discussed in Chapter 1 with respect to the law of intellectual property. I here therefore consider the polity in two aspects, the substantive and the procedural states.

The substantive state (S). In its simplest form, just specifying a state that operates a system of command and control by the manipulation of substantive incentives, the substantive state gives the following pattern according to the elements in Table 5.1:

1.	2.	3.	4.	5.	6.	7.	8.	9.
1	1	1	1	1	1	1	1	1

The ideal, in the sense of pure or extreme, concept of the substantive state is one in which its central command capacity shapes the entire environment of the territory. Governance is exogenous; collective competition goods (Crouch and Trigilia 2001) may be made available at a local level, but it is the central state that provides them or at least ensures their provision. Rules are formal and substantive. (This latter characteristic is *per definitionem*.) The state allocates competition goods through its administrative structure. Relations are vertical; the state assumes superiority over its society, and it has in principle a high capacity for enforcement. If a state fails to be able to enforce its rules, as in some third-world cases, a question mark is posed over its viability. The state is also characterized by the extensiveness of its general reach. It is not easy to leave the scope of a state, as it claims a general jurisdiction over units its national territory; a local territory that challenges this is engaged in secession, normally a highly dangerous activity. It is also usually not easy for individuals to gain membership of a new state, while being without a state creates difficulties. This condition is not so true for multinational companies; but the more important these become within the boundary of a particular state, the more this loses its state-like characteristics. In principle, the state is the core defender of the 'public' arena; therefore the goods it provides, including collective competition goods, are public ones. Indeed, 'public' and 'state' (as an adjective) are frequently used as synonyms.

When and if they ever operated according to their basic principles, the state socialist economies of the former Soviet bloc worked something like this. Firms were simply state units.

If we specify that the state is also a *Rechtstaat*, it must also itself respect private law relationships and hence procedural as well as substantive practices:

1.	2.	3.	4.	5.	6.	7.	8.	9.
1	1	1/0	1	1	1	1	1	1

If we specify a democratic substantive state, we have to amend this further to involve communication through dialogue as well as signalling. This form of state continues to operate simply as a state, through a centralized and potentially coercive structure, but it does not restrict its relations with its citizens to command and control, but consults them and lets them talk back to it:

1.	2.	3.	4.	5.	6.	7.	8.	9.
1	1	1/0	1/0	1	1	1	1	1

It is also necessary to model separately nation-states and territorially lower authorities. The relationship between these may be complex, depending on the extent to which key actors within both share perspectives and on the degree of autonomous power possessed by the local level(s). Principally, local government is likely to be endogenous to the territory concerned (unless that territory is a small part of the nearest local government unit). To the extent that local government is thus closer to actors within its territory than is a central state, there may be greater informality and something approaching horizontal communication. Strength of enforcement may be weaker, and both reach and control of exit are considerably weaker:

1.	2.	3.	4.	5.	6.	7.	8.	9.
0/1	1/0	1/0	1/0	1/0	1/0	0	0	1

The local state is therefore a far less heavily determined actor than a central, national one; the importance of this to institutional entrepreneurs (including those working within central and local government themselves) will depend on the relative autonomy of the local level. To the extent that it has autonomy, these entrepreneurs may find it particularly useful.

The procedural state (P). Following Van Waarden's insights noted above, we can model the governance of the procedural state as follows:

1.	2.	3.	4.	5.	6.	7.	8.	9.
1	1	0	1	0	1	1	1	1

This governance is exogenous and formal, law being formal. Regional and local government have some limited scope for establishing law, depending on the particular context concerned. However, at least within Europe, a capacity to make procedural law is primarily a characteristic of the national state. It is a procedural form of governance *per definitionem*, and, like the market, provides only rules as collective goods. Communication is solely through contract signals and judicial decision. Contract relations are horizontal. There is in principle a high capacity for enforcement through legal process, and this capacity has extensive reach throughout the society. Exit is difficult, as discussed in relation to the substantive state. Law in the modern *Rechtstaat* is in principle made available to citizens as a collective good, but there are no other collective goods in a pure procedural state model.

The Economy

Two separate forms of economic institutional arrangements appear in Hollingsworth and Boyer's scheme (1997): markets and hierarchies. Both are seen to be characterized by self-interest, but the latter, like the state, has a bureaucratic administrative control structure, while the former does not. The market is subdivided as a mode of governance into pure competitive spot markets and oligopolistic markets. The hierarchy is subdivided into vertically integrated firms and (with a higher level of obligation in the arrangements) holding companies or conglomerates.

This recognition of how the economy is endogenously regulated, not just by the market, but also by the internal authority structure of individual firms, is fundamental to an understanding of capitalism, but its implications for governance are frequently overlooked. Another good account of the issue has been set out by Windolf (2002: ch. 2). The argument derives from the elementary propositions of the Coasian theory of the firm (Coase 1937). While many economic contracts can be fully managed by a market deal codified and enforced by the procedural state, many contracts are what lawyers call 'incomplete'. Typically, an employee agrees, in exchange for a wage, to be generally at the disposal of his employer for a specified range of tasks. There is not a precise contract specifying the duties exactly. As a result, a firm does not comprise solely a web of contracts, but has a managerial authority structure. From this derives the concept of the firm as a corporate hierarchy, talking down to its employees, and not as just a mass of contractual relations among equal partners. This then becomes a form of governance in its own right.

The market (M). In the pure concept of a neoclassical market economy, firms are linked to each other and to resources and factors of production solely by relations of supply and demand as signalled by price under conditions of perfect competition among anonymous individuals.

1.	2.	3.	4.	5.	6.	7.	8.	9.
1	1	0	1	0	0	1	0	0

The market is exogenous to the individual firm; its rules are formal and purely procedural; the only collective goods that it produces are its own rules, all other goods being necessarily capable of being privately appropriated. Communication is solely through signals; participants in the market are anonymous and therefore cannot participate in dialogue. Relations are horizontal; and the market has a low capacity for autonomous enforcement because of the criterion of anonymity of its participants. Where autonomous enforcement takes place through the market's own processes, this is because it has become a hybrid with another form (like community, network, or association, where participants are identifiable). However, if its functioning can be guaranteed, its reach is extensive, all transactions being in principle commensurable. Exit from it is easy, *per definitionem*. Goods are allocated precisely to those purchasing them, and are therefore non-collective.

The market is in theory not place-sensitive. In reality one can distinguish local from national or even global markets, in the sense that in local markets actors can gain information other than that conveyed by market signals themselves. This is because other, more locally rooted forms of governance (mainly community and networks) are combining with the market. Territorially rooted markets are therefore examples of hybrids between the market and these other modes.

The corporate hierarchy (H). In the pure concept of a corporate hierarchy, all questions are handled through the managerial structure of firms themselves, including hierarchical relations between customer and supplier firms:

1.	2.	3.	4.	5.	6.	7.	8.	9.
0/1	1	1/0	1/0	1	1/0	0/1	1/0	0/1

All governance is endogenous to this hierarchy, though it is exogenous in relation to an individual territory. Rules are formal, though subject to the same qualification as in the case of the association. Incentives and sanctions can be substantive or procedural as the management chooses. Similarly, communication is through both signals and dialogue as management chooses. Relations are *per definitionem* vertical. There is a high capacity for enforcement within the hierarchy, because of the authority of management, but reach is limited to the hierarchy itself. Whether this reach extends more generally to a territory depends on the dominance of the firm or firms in question over that territory, in terms of both the proportion of persons in the territory employed in the firm(s) and the importance of locally based supplier chains. Exit may or may not be easy, depending on the availability of alternatives. No public goods are provided, but within the hierarchy goods may be made available which then benefit wider categories; there can therefore be collective competition goods for members of the hierarchy. For example, in some localities inward investing firms provide training for employees and suppliers that remains as an upgrading of the capacity of the area even if the firm subsequently departs. However, in many other instances this does not occur; it is a matter of empirical variation within the mode.

Society

For students of governance the residuum left over as 'society' after institutions have been assigned to polity and economy can initially be reduced to a few forms of identifiable collectivities. Hollingsworth and Boyer (1997) usefully identify communities, associations, and networks as institutional arrangements. The first of these is characterized as horizontally coordinated and obligational. Associations stand right in the centre of their matrix, with networks overlapping heavily but inclined towards the obligational. This scheme changes when they elaborate forms of governance from this base. Following Campbell, Hollingsworth, and Lindberg (1991), Hollingsworth and Boyer here separate community as the most obligational of a group of non-organized structures, with 'clans' and 'clubs' appearing as respectively less obligational but more structured. Corporatist business associations they separate completely from associations in general, and present them as even more obligational than the state. Networks are perceived as 'joint ventures, strategic alliances, and other forms of interfirm agreements', and are depicted as less structured organizationally than in the 1991 presentation.

The confusion here is not the fault of the authors, but of the protean nature of the social residuum in modern societies. Here I shall concentrate on the three forms: associations, communities and networks, but there is potentially more diversity. For example, in studying the so-called 'black economy' it is necessary to provide for a form of governance that has to be informally structured and unable to call on law as a support, and therefore capable of providing its own vertical enforcement methods. This is mafia rather than community (Crouch 2005).

The association (A). An association is a formal body bringing together as members persons and firms engaged in a particular economic activity. Membership provides access to collective competition goods useful or even necessary to the conduct of the activity. In exchange for acquiring this access members accept certain obligations on their behaviour, in relation to both other members and, often, the outside world. The association has its own rules for determining how these obligations should be determined and implemented. It is through this offer of access to collective competition goods in exchange for obligations that governance is exercised. It matches our model in the following way:

1.	2.	3.	4.	5.	6.	7.	8.	9.
1	1	1/0	0	1	1	0	1/0	0/1

This governance is exogenous to both firms and to territories. Regulation is formal *per definitionem*, as this is one of the means by which associations are distinguished from communities and networks. (In practice there is likely to be considerable informal governance within an association, but this is because networks and even communities develop within the framework of the association. These are strictly admixtures of other governance forms alongside the strict associational form.) Associations are likely to provide both procedural and substantive competition goods. Communication with members is through dialogue, because associations are defined as membership organizations; it is similarly dialogistic in relations with other actors in a territory, as associations possess no repertoire of signalling for such communication. Regulation is vertical, because it proceeds from a leadership to a membership. There is some diversity in relations between associational centres and local branches. The association has a high capacity for enforcement among its members (as it can exclude them if they are deviant), but its reach is not general. With the exception of single-industry areas, such as industrial districts, several different associations will be active within a given national or local territory, each representing only a proportion of its economic activity. Confederations of associations sometimes exist at national levels, exercising some autonomous govern-ance functions, particularly in smaller nation-states. There is wide diver-sity in the ease of exit from associations, ranging from those where it is impossible to practise the activity concerned without being members of them (as in the case of Austrian and German *Kammer*), to those where membership is voluntary. Associations normally produce competition goods for their members only, though these may be provided collectively within the association rather than solely privately. They therefore exist in a kind of halfway house on this dimension.

Associations may have local branches, which may be endogenous to the area and also differ in other ways from the sopra-local association as does the local from the central state, depending on the level of autonomy they achieve. This applies a fortiori to associations that are purely local.

1.	2.	3.	4.	5.	6.	7.	8.	9.
0/1	1/0	1/0	0	1/0	1/0	0	0	0/1

The guild economies of medieval Europe functioned partly according to this model.

The community (C). In the pure concept of community economy, individ-uals are strongly embedded in informal and usually local and enduring, multiply interlocking webs of relationships, which constitute all their links with the external environment. It is a form of governance that can exist only at a local level.

1.	2.	3.	4.	5.	6.	7.	8.	9.
0	0	1	0	0	1	0	1	1

This governance is endogenous to its territory. Regulation is informal *per definitionem*, as this is one of the means by which communities are distin-guished from associations. Community-provided collective competition goods are typically substantive, there being no explicitly defined rules. Communication is through dialogue. Regulation is horizontal. Through the interlocking nature of its relationships, the community has a high capacity for enforcement within its territory, but its reach beyond is almost non-existent. It is a definitional aspect of community in the strict sense that exit from it is difficult. It provides competition goods on a public basis to all within the community. Many subsistence peasant economies function(ed) partly according to this model.

The network (N). This concept has been formed more or less in contrast with that of community, to express the possibility of informal local groups that are lightly rather than heavily embedded. In a network economy, individuals and groups are linked loosely with others in limited understandings concerning reciprocity. But if a network is to function as a mode of governance, it cannot exist on a purely 'take it or leave it' basis, or it would have no capacity to constrain and encourage various forms of behaviour. Thus, the only firms accepted into networks of exchange are those known to be willing to collaborate (Windolf 2002: 127–8). Networks can also be exclusionary and monopolizing (ibid.: 9).

Networks are of two kinds: those, like communities, which have a local territorial character; and those that are not territorial; the examples of networks listed by Hollingsworth and Boyer were of this form. To deal first with the former:

1.	2.	3.	4.	5.	6.	7.	8.	9.
0	0	1	0	0	0	0	0	0/1

Local networks are *per definitionem* endogenous to their territories in the sense that the network is predominantly confined to actors working within a local area. Regulation is informal *per definitionem*, as in community, and is again typically substantive; communication is through dialogue, and regulation is horizontal. It contrasts with community in its looseness, implying a low (but greater than zero) capacity for enforcement among its members. Its reach beyond the network is weak, and it is an important definitional aspect of the network that exit from it is easy. Unlike the community, the local network provides local collective competition goods only for its members, though, as with associations, there will be collective components within the network. The links between scientists, entrepreneurs, venture capitalists, lawyers and others typical of high-tech districts are examples of territorially rooted networks. Territorial networks are often important among science-based firms, even though these are also nested in no-spatial ones of global extent, because technology-sharing within a common pool of tacit, frequently exchanged knowledge is necessary to make innovations (Trigilia 2004).

Other networks are not geographically confined, but link members through remote means of communication. They are therefore exogenous to a particular territory, but otherwise have the same attributes:

1.	2.	3.	4.	5.	6.	7.	8.	9.
0	0	1	0	0	0	0	0	0/1

Arrangements among small numbers of multinational firms to develop new products together, as described by Ohmae (1985) would be examples of non-territorial networks, as would those among scientists who communicate through telephone, email, letters, and participation in conferences. Already in the late 1950s Penrose (1959) had anticipated that rule-governed alliances of firms were possibly the only way in which very expensive developments in some high-science sectors could be executed. More recently, Quéré (2003) has pointed out how this kind of 'cooperation as coordination 'exists alongside the firm and the market.

The Normality of Hybrid Governance

A striking conclusion from an inspection of true ideal types of these forms of governance is that hardly any of them is likely to be fully autonomous, certainly not in dealing with economic relations of any complexity. Some display a rigidity of resource allocation that makes it difficult for them to respond to changing demand among consumers (the substantive state, association, community). In practice, these forms are likely to exist empirically only alongside elements of the market. This happens either openly and willingly, or (as in the former Soviet bloc economies) in the form of black markets. If we are considering capitalist economies alone, then the market is by definition always present to some degree, even if associations, communities and other governance modes are also active. The market is only absent from institutions within a capitalist society where those institutions are kept (through various institutional means) outside the realm of economic exchange (as in friendship and love relationships). Some forms of governance lack autonomous enforcement capacity (networks, markets), and are almost certain to co-opt external agencies, in particular the procedural state. In fact, in anything beyond a very primitive system, what is called the free market economy is always really a hybrid between the pure market and the procedural state (MP, using the notation adopted in the above list).

For example, when the German government wanted to move to a more 'US-type' stock-market system it had to replace voluntarist self-regulation for more centralized, statutory regulation *à l'américaine* (Deeg 2001a; Lütz 2000, 2003); more market implied more (procedural) state. Ironically, this system is said to operate only for a small number of firms who are the 'very largest and most influential in Germany' (Deeg 2001a: 35), that is, firms which do not really match the neoclassical model of the firm. This further draws our attention to the mix between market and corporate hierarchy in any functioning model. Krippner (2001) cites research by Baker (1984), showing the role of networks where one might have expected to find only pure markets—on stock-exchange trading floors. Contrary to the expectations of neoclassical theory (which expects markets to function more perfectly, the large the number of participants), there was more volatility in dealings among large groups. This was because there were major barriers to information flows among large groups, enabling dealers to find anonymity and deal simultaneously at various prices. Among smaller groups networks could ensure speedy transmission of information and inhibit such practices. In later research Baker (1990) showed how firms built long-term relational ties as well as short-term transactional ones in order to maximize control over banking partners, that is, using both market and network. Krippner also reports Uzzi's work (1997, 1999) on the US garment industry, showing a similar combination of different forms of relationships. Burt (1988) also studied the role of networks in stabilizing relations among US firms. Considine and Lewis (2003), in a study of new forms of provision of public services in Australia, found networks becoming increasingly important as simple distinctions between the public and market sectors no longer function, and had to be bound together in new ways. Contracts (central to procedural state governance), too, may be found in various combinations. Macneil (2001) identifies three types of contract: classical (spot) contracts, which would be the simplest compound of MP; neoclassical with third-party assistance (i.e. making use of corporate hierarchy too: MPH); and relational (making use of networks, MPN).

In fact, what passes in common (and unfortunately much academic and public policy) discussion for the 'market economy' is usually a compound of market, procedural state, and hierarchy: MPH. Virtually all large firms constitute hierarchies, and as has been seen above, hierarchy differs from market at some important points. The compound of these three forms therefore provides considerable complementarity and ranges of options to firms, who will rarely find in practice that the governance regime which predominantly surrounds them absolutely prevents them from doing something that they want, though they may experience difficulty and transient rigidities when the transaction costs of changing paths appear high while the need for change does not seem overwhelming.

Within this compound form of economic governance (which characterizes all advanced capitalist economies), the other governance modes operate by interposing themselves between firms and the MPH amalgam. For example, a firm embedded in community within a market economy is not engaged in a subsistence economy, but reaches out through its community to a market. A substantive state within a capitalist economy changes the way in which firms subject to its interventions encounter the market, but it does not suppress markets, and has to be careful of the impact of its actions on market forces.

It is possible to formulate other compound types, which would comprise those combinations of ideal types also likely to be encountered in empirical research. MPH will always predominate, but minority or even trace components of other governance forms can still be important, even decisive in making niche characteristics available to certain kinds of producer in specific national or regional economies. Similarly, while H_2O will always be by far the dominant constituent of water, it is different combinations of sodium, potassium, and other elements that impart distinctive flavour and other properties that determine the market niches of particular brands of bottled water—even when they appear only as trace elements. For example, one possible form is MPH with associations (MPHA)—economies in which associations play a particularly important role (one form of what is often seen as the *modèle rhénan*, or a coordinated market economy (Albert 1991; Hall and Soskice 2001*b*). Another form, MPH with substantive state (MPHS), would express the model of the post-war French economy (Hancké 2002; Schmidt 2002). For an example at a micro level, we can consider how the process of standard setting can be an activity in which solely public, or public mixed with semi-private (as in the International Standards Organization) or even solely fully private (as with ratings agencies) organizations are active (Sinclair 2001).

To shift the chemical analogy, another source of variation is the relative strength of the component elements within a compound. For example, while both the US and the Japanese economies are cases of MPH, the relative importance of H is considerably higher in the latter. (If the US economy might be stereotyped as M_2P_2H, the Japanese might be MPH_2.)

These empirically observable compounds must never be confused with ideal types, as they embody more than one logic of governance, and the exact form of the compromise, or structure of the complementarities, among them might vary considerably. In a full research programme on economic governance it would be finally possible to estimate the relative importance of all the different modes within an individual economy (temporarily accepting that national economies constitute whole economies). Therefore, in the US case, we would take account of the role of high-tech military expenditure as an important example of the substantive state, rather small roles for associations and community, but a larger one for networks in certain regions.

It should also be noted that there is often some indeterminacy in the pure forms themselves; they do not always have unambiguous approaches to the questions. Also, given that empirical forms often deviate from ideal types, and given that the types chosen are merely rationalized empirical generalizations rather than deductive categories, it is possible for 'deviant' elements to appear. Sometimes these may even become systematic. For example, very often actors in otherwise more or less pure market situations may move from signalling to dialogue: this happens, for example, when large, bespoke contracts are being negotiated. It is possible and necessary to recognize such variations, perhaps using adjectives to distinguish them if they appear sufficiently frequently to be treated as more than just a rare deviation. It is important to give these forms of variation an important role in analysis, in order to avoid a determinism that asserts that actors within particular forms of governance simply cannot engage in certain forms of behaviour. These forms, the results of 'kaleidoscopic governance', are those ruled out by the pure theory of the governance mode within which the theorist has deemed to classify them. Theory will from time to time be taken by surprise by innovation. Scientific knowledge progresses, not by allocating cases to a priori categories, but discovering the range of diversity around such categories that seems to be possible, including scope for innovation by actors pushing at what had hitherto been considered to be clearly established forms.

This does not mean that 'anything goes', and that modes of governance can change at any time into any of a thousand different forms. Governance implies regularity, predictability, and constraint. When practice is seen to deviate from a well-established pattern in a systematic way that cannot be written off as occasional exception, there must be an explanation. Possibly the theory was always wrong to have asserted the previous regularity, and possibly had ignored certain characteristics not given by the logic of the ideal type; these types are after all only constructed, they have no necessary place in reality. In such cases theorists need to look into their previous work and adjust it. Alternatively, it may be that a change has taken place, and that which was once regular has become transcended, or that a combination of elements previously found to be impossible has now been found able to coexist. In that case, theory has to be updated, not in terms of its own past errors, but to take account of the creativity of human actors.

It will be noted that in this account the market is one form of governance *inter pares*. It is neither privileged, nor seen as the Other against which institutionalist analysis sets itself. The market's own forms are ambiguous and problematic. I here follow Krippner (2001: 782–7), who builds on Polanyi's insight (1944) that the market is always inextricably a social object, and rarely autonomous. She contends that the neo-institutionalist writers do considerably better than most in sociologizing the market, but still go on to treat it as the 'other' against which their own theory works; they do not thoroughly internalize it. For example, she points out that Granovetter's use of embeddedness (discussed in Chapter 1) paradoxically leads him to take the market for granted, as he accepts that 'somewhere there is a hard core of market behaviour existing outside of social life (and hence that needed to be "embedded")' (1985: 778). She argues (ibid.: 797–8): 'It is both telling and deeply troubling that, given the way in which the paradigm of economic sociology has been formulated, sociologists have only been able to study markets by stripping them of the features that most make them social.' As she points out, Fligstein (2001) has a better grasp, seeing markets as always emergent, forged through political contestation over shifting cultural beliefs that provide a template for interaction in market settings.

Deconstructing the Principal Modes

We have clearly reached the point where we must attempt a deconstruction of the recognizable modes of governance: if these modes can be analysed in terms of the formal characteristics considered above, should not these constitute a more basic level of theory construction? Chemists are familiar with both 'water' and 'H_2O'. For much of the time they can use the common expression, which is a kind of shorthand for the correct term. But at times, particularly when breaking down water molecules into their component atoms, or recombining them with others, it is necessary that they are aware of H_2O. Very frequently, as chemists recombine known, frequently occurring chemicals with new ones, they have to invent new names.

For readers who prefer a different kind of analogy, we can look to music. In the western musical tradition there are twelve recognized notes in the scale that constitute the building blocks of all music. These can be combined, synchronically and diachronically, in many ways, but some combinations are recognized as constituting keys. Composers (at least between the sixteenth and late nineteenth centuries) would root any one of their works in a small number of these keys, but every so often would use notes foreign to those in which they were working. Sometimes this heralds a change to a new, also recognized key; sometimes they are just passing exceptions, discords adding interest to the sound; sometimes they constitute more systematic distortions of an existing key, designed to produce a special effect.

Similar processes are at work in governance. There are familiar, recognized shapes that represent particular combinations of basic elements, such that we can name them as market, state, community, etc. Occasionally, however, there are 'impure' patterns. These might be hybrids; they might constitute specific subforms (as with the democratic as opposed to simple substantive state); or they might be new forms in the making. We can take account of these possibilities only if we move to a level of analysis that does not take the dominant forms for granted. In theory there are forty-nine combinations of the different elements in the model. The seven recognized forms discussed above therefore constitute a small minority. Other combinations constitute hybrids, or slightly amended forms, or are perhaps not viable at all. For example, as already noted, although in theory the pure market implies an absence of dialogistic communication and communication only through price signals, in practice this condition is often changed. Where the number of participants in a market exchange is small, participants in the market will often discuss at length within social settings before reaching a deal. This is a variant of the pure market form, and from the point of view of the neoclassical paradigm it implies inefficiencies. If participants in the market start to limit their interactions to those whom they know in a social context, they will not carry out searches that will maximize their returns. In fact, from the neoclassical perspective what is happening is that the participants have decided that the gains that might come from searching widely for a better deal are outweighed by the costs of such a search. This form of market is sufficiently widespread to be accepted as a particular form rather than as an occasional aberration.

We should also note (following Immergut 2005) that institutions do not generally exert their effects in a continuous manner. Particular combinations come together and have particular outcomes, but they do not necessarily remain together. (To return to the chemical analogy, one might liken these to unstable compounds, the bonds of which never fix.) One can find spurious correlations by assuming that such elements are somehow associated, argues Immergut, but only by ignoring the importance of contingency. She therefore pleads for a restoration of a historical rather than a systematic methodology. One might take as an example the diversity of relations between managers and shareholders that have existed in the USA over the years. Today it is common to characterize this system as one of the maximization of shareholder value, placing emphasis on market governance. However, at many other times there has been a clearer dominance by single owners or managers—a purer hierarchy model (Lazonick and O'Sullivan 1996, 1997; Windolf 2002; Whitley 2005).

Modelling Recombination

A major conclusion from this account is that virtually all empirical cases are combinations of fragments of various modes. This brings us to the hypothesis already enunciated in Chapter 3: *that institutional heterogeneity will facilitate innovation, both by presenting actors with alternative strategies when existing paths seem blocked, and by making it possible for them to make new combinations among elements of various paths.*

Within fragmented governance, actors seek out those elements of one governance mode that seem to be associated with certain desired outcomes, and elements of others that give different ones, recombining them in order to maximize their performance. For Schumpeter too, entrepreneurialism consisted primarily in making new combinations of exiting components. Deeg (2005) sees scope for change within institutions in the following ways: loose integration, increasing differentiation (with successful buffering), variable complementarity, multiple, coexisting orders, tight integration, such that a change at one point will affect many others. He uses such a framework to show how, contrary to arguments about the tight coupling of production and financial spheres, German firms seem able to work with a diversity of financial regimes as these change over the years. Höpner (2003b; 2004) has similarly shown how co-determination in German industry can coexist with a variety of financial systems.

Let us assume that there are three governance modes, which seem to be associated with capacities as follows:

```
              1 2 3 4 5 6 7 8 9
Governance mode          G′
field F₁        1 1 1 0 0 0 0 0 0
Governance mode          G″
field F₁        0 0 0 1 1 1 0 0 0
Governance mode          G‴
field F₁        0 0 0 0 0 0 1 1 1
```

Actors in context I' therefore try ideally to achieve the following:

```
Context I′
              1 2 3 4 5 6 7 8 9
Governance   G′    G″    G‴
field F₁      1 1 1 1 1 1 1 1 1
```

The recombinant governance possibility redirects attention to the problem of how, if the actors in I' are trapped within their context and the practices made available by it (a starting assumption above), they can gain access to alternative modes in order to experiment with recombination. This returns us to some of the alternatives discussed in Chapter 4. First was the strategy of actors making costed searches back into their own past experience, trying to use hidden or dormant alternatives within their own repertoires. Here we can envisage dormant alternatives as a kind of palimpsest; modes G'' and G''' had been present in I' before, but had become obscured by G', perhaps by the latter's more frequent use or by its role in a dominant power coalition.

Second was the case of agents operating simultaneously in different arenas, enabling them to transfer experience from different action spaces, or secure cosseted access to the arenas of others, to enable them to transfer experience from other agents through networks of structured relationships. This is anticipated in the idea of segregated zones within an institutional context, within which other patterns of capacities, and hence other forms of governance, are found. An important aspect of the costs of transferring experience here comprises the barriers that exist to 'protect' the various governance modes and the ease of negotiating them.

The third possibility was that, of several viable alternatives, only one is discovered, leading to possibly false 'one best way' solutions. This can be easily accommodated to the search for recombinant elements of governance, but it also directs our attention to an issue that until now we have neglected: exogeneity and the strength of the boundary around an 'institutional context'. Just as, between fields within an institutional context, we have to account for both boundaries and their absence, we need to do the same to boundaries that define those contexts themselves. The contexts with which we usually work may well be set within wider ones: national systems may be set within world-regional or global ones. This is then a matter of a larger Russian doll, a wider system within which I', I'', etc., are located. It is possible that within such a wider system (W) particular governance modes are dominant which clash with those within I' or I''. As these latter are drawn within W (i.e. their external barriers melt), their locally dominant patterns might weaken; though they may remain concealed as redundant capacities, available for future use. This may well be happening, for example, as the German and Japanese corporate governance systems are forced to change in line with the requirements of the Anglo-American form which is globally dominant (Dore 2000).

Conclusion

In this chapter we have:

1. Established what can be understood by the establishment of a model of sets of institutions based on the principle of similarity; contrasted that with two forms of complementarity, and constructed abstract models that accommodate both.
2. Identified the role of governance within this model; elaborated a typology of governance modes, their varied relationships to the resources with which they must deal, and the different kinds of resource involved, all as seen from the perspective of the firm as a set of positive or negative capacities; and discovered the importance of compound forms of governance in empirical cases.
3. On the base of this last, established the possibility of recombining governance modes, and the hypothesis that institutional heterogeneity will facilitate innovation, both by presenting actors with alternative strategies when existing paths seem blocked, and by making it possible for them to make new combinations among elements of various paths.
4. Considered the importance of this for the work of institutional entrepreneurs, bearing in mind problems posed for the analyst by functional equivalence and power asymmetries.

It remains to demonstrate how this approach can be applied in practice.

6

Recombinant Governance Mechanisms

In the following pages I shall try to demonstrate some of the advantages of the method of institutional analysis that has been developed to this point by applying it briefly to two quite different cases. First, the greater explanatory power of detailed governance analysis over the typological 'national systems' approach will be displayed in a consideration of the governance structures of the biopharmaceutical and information technology sectors of the Californian (more specifically, the San Francisco Bay Area and 'Silicon Valley') economy. This is a relatively static analysis, largely concerned with showing the importance of existing diversity in governance modes. Second, the capacity of the approach to deal with conflict, change, and institutional entrepreneurs will be demonstrated by considering the shift from Keynesian to neoliberal economic policies in the UK during the 1980s.

Compound Governance in California

According to the logic of the Varieties of Capitalism approach, it should be reasoned that: the USA being an LME; and the pharmaceuticals and information technology sectors of California being located in the USA; these sectors should therefore have the characteristics of an LME. A simple set of syllogisms of this kind has been combined with a fourth in order to recommend to many countries throughout the world: Therefore, countries wishing to develop Californian economic dynamism need to deregulate their markets.

In practice, Hall and Soskice (2001a: 29) fully acknowledge departures from their LME model with respect to the US pharmaceuticals industry where financial institutions are concerned. However, these highly innovative sectors are precisely the elements of the US economy that their project regards as emblematic of the capacity for radical innovation of the LME form of capitalism. Emblematic cases should not present strong exceptions from the types of which they are considered to embody the consequences. This immediately alerts us to the fact that matters may be more complex and will require more than the allocation of cases to one of two types. According to the hypotheses of recombinant governance, in contrast, the high level of innovation in these sectors should be related to their having access to diverse modes of governance, enabling firms to choose from a range of possibilities those modes helpful to the logic of the science that they are exploiting. And recombinant governance theory can make a special model for California that is not necessarily just a local version of a wider US model.

We shall examine these issues in relation to the following resources: finance, labour, and knowledge.

Financial Resources

Casper (2002: 286), writing within the framework of the Varieties of Capitalism theory, states that Californian 'biotechnology start-ups need access to a continuous stream of high-risk finance'. This, he argues, is provided by the high mobility of the US financial market, which enables investors to exit easily from a venture which has become doubtful. This posits a pure market model of finance. Among the characteristics of pure markets considered in Chapter 5 were communication restricted to market signalling and ease of exit. The latter in particular corresponds to what Hall and Soskice contrast with the 'patient' capital of the coordinated market economy. In reality it is difficult to imagine a form of capital that has to be more patient than that invested in new biopharmaceutical discoveries. Research is extremely costly and has to begin a long way from the stage of finally developing a consumer product. Once a new medicine has been developed, it has to go through a very substantial testing process governed by both the substantive and procedural state. The former lays down absolute rules concerning health and safety; the latter establishes, particularly in the USA, a number of rights of consumers of a medicine to sue firms if they are damaged by their products. Capital in this industry has to be *both* high-risk *and* patient. It certainly will want to be able to exit from a development that seems to be failing, and that will be the price of initial willingness to offer support, as Casper argues. The German *Hausbank* model is clearly not suited to these needs. But investors also need to wait for results. Investors in really radical biotech also need to have knowledge of the product and its possibilities.

This sector therefore needs a hybrid: the mobility of the spot market combined with possibilities of dialogue and making long-term commitments not found there. This combination is in fact found in the networks that bind knowledgeable, embedded, sector-specific business 'angel' venture capitalists to the firms. This is a model that began first with the computing industry in Silicon Valley, where venture capitalists often take seats on the boards of companies in which they invest, assist in recruiting key personnel, provide introductions to potential suppliers, customers and partners (Kenney 2000*b*: 7). As Kenney (ibid.) comments: 'they have created a practice that is "hands-on" rather than "arm's-length"'. Indeed, they have some of the attributes of *Hausbanken*. These approaches then spread to the biotech sector through inter-sectoral local networks (Prevezer 1998: 160–1). The venture capitalists know the industry, share its tacit knowledge, and live close to it, becoming part of the social networks that link them with entrepreneurs, scientists, suppliers, sector-specific lawyers, and others. The geographical character of the cluster is fundamental to this, and explains why the industry is not spread out across the USA but concentrated in a small number of locations. This is one reason why we speak of a Californian biopharmaceuticals sector and not a US one. The investors certainly make deals that have time limits to them (unlike classic *Hausbanken*). And if necessary they can exit and switch their funds within the stock market. But the exit is a 'sticky' process; it does not resemble the rapid and impersonal movements of shares in spot markets. They have the sunk costs of their considerable knowledge investment in the sector, which in turn confer on them distinct advantages within that sector. In the terminology of this book, network governance combines in a complementary way with that of the market to link the firms to venture capitalists, overcoming at least some of the paradoxical demands for flexible but embedded capital needed for radical innovation over lengthy time periods.

The radical innovation in the information technology sector that peaked during the 1990s ('Silicon Valley') has had a financial structure conforming more closely to the LME model. Developments in software and Internet applications could be completed and launched quickly into a market that was largely unregulated. After the initial research had been carried out in the 1960s and 1970s, there was a large fund of exploitable knowledge. The long research lag times characteristic of biopharmaceuticals have been absent, and there are not the safety and regulatory hazards of the health sector. Evidence of the fact that relations between capital and the firms took a market form alone was provided when the collapse of the share market in the sector at the end of the 1990s demonstrated the lack of knowledge of many investors and the speculative nature of much of the investment. While biopharmaceuticals firms suffered from the general crisis of the US share market at the time, there was no equivalent crisis produced by investor ignorance of the products being developed.

However, in the longer term the ICT sector as a whole has not depended on spot markets alone, as the points cited above from Kenney (2000*b*: 7) concerning the hands-on character of its financial arrangements make clear. Indeed, Prevezer (1998: 128–9) has argued that stock exchanges (combined with venture capital) have been more important in biotech than in at least the computer part of the ICT industry. At certain stages of development embedded, knowledgeable capital has also played a role. The venture capitalists who initiated the truly innovative projects in no way resembled the largely poorly informed spot market investors who powered the extraordinary growth and sudden collapse of the sector in the 1990s. They were, like their opposite numbers in biotech, locally resident, networked actors. According to Gilson (2003), the venture capital market enables start-ups to solve the problem of extreme uncertainty and information asymmetry, the venture capitalists taking a close interest in the firms. He describes important complementarities: intensive monitoring (i.e. in terms of the model set up in Chapter 5, adding dialogue to the formal signals of the market, and an important role for repeat play and reputation mechanisms (ibid.: 1078)). The venture capital firm acquires 'disproportionate' representation among the firm's directors (ibid.: 1082) (in Chapter 5's terminology, using market to acquire hierarchy). Networks, even communities, link the investors to the firms (ibid.: 1087). Kenney and Florida (2000) similarly report venture capitalists taking more than a 50 per cent stake in a firm and having representation on its board, sometimes as chair. They also become involved in the firm, give it advice, and help find customers (ibid.: 100–1). They team up with clearly identifiable institutional partners: a university endowment, a pensions fund, a wealthy individual. Locally embedded venture capitalists and entrepreneurs themselves built the rules and the institutions of Silicon Valley together, with strong networks and other institutions which assist information sharing and trust-based deals (ibid.: 123) Their offices are all located in the same street (ibid.: 115). In this sector too, therefore, at least in the early stages of an investment, venture capitalists behave like a hybrid between a *Hausbank* and stock-market investors.

Similarly fundamental to the networks are the local law firms, who act as intermediaries in the development of the Silicon Valley system (Suchman 2000). They are deeply embedded in the area and become important repositories of knowledge about it, not only in its legal aspects. They transmit much of the tacit knowledge of the sector and maintain its normative properties (ibid.: 76). While today these lawyers are busy with the enormous and growing edifice of intellectual property law, when they and the sector began the regulatory environment was very sparse, and lawyers had to operate as general business advisers rather than just legal experts (ibid.: 78). They remain crucial in sustaining the networks of the sector, and in particular in linking firms to venture capitalists, suppliers and customers. They also assist new entrants surmount the social entry barriers that otherwise develop around insiders in such a networked sector (ibid.: 79–82). These are not the giant law firms typical of the US system, but essentially local, endogenous, dedicated enterprises (ibid.: 73–4). These relationships, being personal and based on acquaintanceship, are non-market relations. Much the same can be said to the relations that link firms and academic institutions (Coriat, Orsi, and Weinstein 2003).

It is also important to note that many firms in both biopharmaceutical and ICT sectors are also linked to corporate hierarchies. They are either large firms themselves, with large endogenously generated investment funds, or exist in client relations to such firms. This reduces their dependence on highly mobile, pure market funds.

One general conclusion that we can draw from this discussion concerns the extremely important role of network governance in any sector where access to rapidly and radically advancing substantive knowledge of the sector is necessary to rational investment behaviour (Saxenian 1994). Neoclassical economics has tried to avoid the need for recognizing this through the model of perfectly discounted future expectations. The argument works as follows. In a perfect stock market the participants do not need knowledge of the technology or product markets in which they invest. It is enough that they can calculate their capacity to sell stock on to third parties. The market's knowledge is autopoedetic; provided that participants in the stock market have confidence in the stock market itself, it does not matter whether these values correspond to what is going on in the product markets. And that condition is fulfilled if those participants have confidence that each other has confidence. Those who acquire complete knowledge of the market for stocks will succeed in that market, while those who participate without such knowledge will be driven out. Over time the market becomes one of perfectly rationally anticipating players; the acquisition of knowledge is not a problem. But knowledge of technology and products must enter this sealed model at certain points. In the information technology sector during the 1990s many Internet companies that had never even produced a product had extremely strong stock-market valuations because of the extraordinary internal confidence effect within the stock markets. At a certain point some participants began to lose confidence that the gap between the stock and product markets would be covered, and there was an abrupt collapse. Eventually, therefore, the rationality of the market reasserted itself; but there was a lengthy period of considerable distortion. The fundamental problem was that it is not possible for the stock market indefinitely to act as a proxy for product markets that do not yet exist. The long-term rational investors in these sectors are those who acquire substantive knowledge of the technology and the product possibilities. This will be particularly true of the venture capitalists who decide at a very early stage to commit themselves for some years, not the few minutes of the spot market. Since the knowledge bases of such sectors are developing rapidly and radically, this knowledge cannot be gained from textbooks or market reports. It is tacit knowledge, available only within the network. This fundamental role of network governance is produced by the need to link to tacit knowledge among the innovating scientists and entrepreneurs themselves (Swann and Prevezer 1998: 4–8; Trigilia 2004), but the key investors also have to be part of the network.

Hall and Soskice (2001a: 27–8) present the financial system of LMEs as one in which investors lack inside information about the progress of companies and are therefore heavily dependent on balance sheets and publicly available information. But many US and UK firms have demonstrated that in practice investors find ways of solving the information deficit that this implies, without moving towards some kind of overall coordinated economy. (The significance of differences in national financial systems for investment strategies has itself been greatly exaggerated in the literature. Firms in most economies depend overwhelmingly on internally generated funds for investment rather than on any distinctive external institutions (Corbett and Jenkinson 1996).) Large institutional investors—who make up a very large proportion of the investment community in these economies—are not small, anonymous actors of the kind necessary to neoclassical theory or assumed by the LME model. They are known and identifiable, perfectly able to speak directly to the management of firms. Similarly, Schmidt (2002: ch. 5) shows how a French analysis (Morin 2000) which claims to demonstrate the dominance of the financial markets over French firms in fact describes CEOs using this language largely to legitimate what they wanted to do anyway— and their relations with institutional investors were rooted in direct communication and did not conform to the model of arm's-length market links. (See also O'Sullivan 2001; Hancké 2001; and, making the same point with reference to Germany and Japan (Dore 2000).)

Temple (1998: 268) points out the completely fundamental role of military programmes in establishing and in coordinating through procurement policy and massive programmes in the Californian high-tech concentration. From the years after the First World War onwards naval and other military contracts had been important to the industrial development in the region. Reasons of military security were used to exclude foreign competition for contracts, creating a protected set of industries (Sturgeon 2000). Leslie (2000) calls the military 'the biggest angel of them all' in the history of Silicon Valley, with military contractor Lockheed Missiles and Space being the area's main employer for most of its history. The Cold War was fundamentally important in this process, with a further boost coming in the years of the Reagan presidency as the US government used high-tech military developments as its highly successful strategy to defeat the Soviet Union. The computing industry in particular was heavily dependent on government funds from this source (Swann 1998). As Kenney (2000b: 5) puts it, US defence policy created 'price-insensitive lead customers' for the new computing industry. Firms like Sun Microsystems, the major players in information technology industry, are significant defence contractors; and many semiconductor firms have the military as a major customer. In the early stages of Silicon Valley, military contracts provided, in addition to protection from foreign competition, huge volumes of guaranteed sales on a cost-plus basis, research and development alongside production. At the beginning there was no need for either venture capital or stock markets (Kenney 2000b: 50). Stanford University worked hard to achieve government research contracts in radar, electronics, and aerospace.

Most recently, the support of the Defense Department was essential to the establishment of the Internet in its early stages. This latest symbol of radical innovation was in fact the joint product of the Pentagon and certain university departments—neither market actors. Observers usually concede this, but then argue that, as the sector matured, it moved on to a more purely free-market model. The implication that as the 'real' fully mature form of the sector emerges, it is seen to be a pure market one, and that, therefore, the earlier stage can be disregarded—becomes in effect so much noise. But the fact that a particular form of an industry existed at an early point does not mean that, had actors thought about things more expertly, they would have seen that they did not need these early stages and could have gone straight to the pure market. Particularly important, it is precisely at the early points of radical innovation that market governance seems to need most support from other modes.

The industries that benefited most directly from military support were aerospace and various aspects of computing, but the natural sciences in general benefited from the rich infrastructure thereby produced in public

and private universities alike. Since biotechnology benefited only indir-
ectly from this strong action by the state governance mode, firms were not
placed under particular constraints, but could gain from the resources
produced. Universities have been even more important to the biopharmaceuticals sector than to ICT, playing a fundamental role within, and
sometimes being the hub of, the regional networks. Because universities
do not move geographically, firms have a strong incentive to remain
within the region. While the software industry also has important links
to universities, and benefited from the existing presence in the region of
the university-attached hardware firms, much of its own knowledge was
emerging *ab initio*, and its dependence on the codified knowledge base
represented by universities was less strong (Prevezer 1998: 128–30). The
networks were weaker, and the market played a stronger role in governance. It should also be mentioned that the leading district for this industry
is not in California but Seattle in Washington state, an area dominated by
the corporate hierarchy of Microsoft.

The Labour Market

The second characteristic identified by Casper (2002) is the very high
labour mobility produced by the pure labour market of the Californian
biotechnology industry, with firms easily able to poach staff from each
other, producing considerable cross-fertilization of ideas across companies. However, there is a contradiction here, just as there was between
the high mobility preference of investors and the long-term needs of firms
in the capital market. If poaching is so easy, there are severe, classic
agency problems. There would be considerable gains in the Californian
industry from firms that, without investing in the early stages of research,
just watched until key staff had the knowledge to take developments to
the next stage, and recruited them—offering higher salaries because of
low investment in the costly and risky stages of research.

   This is a clear and real contradiction, not a paradox: both employee
movement and employment stability are functional to a high rate of
innovation, but they are opposed to each other. It is remarkable how
many authors resolve this dilemma by stressing one side of the argument
only. For example, Gilson (1999) and Hyde (1998) both place exclusive
attention on the importance of a rapid circulation of staff and ignore
completely the damaging effects that this might have on a firm that
had made real breakthroughs as a result of team effort, but where individuals could leave abruptly with that knowledge. Similarly, Casper
and Kettler (2001: 9) celebrate the importance of 'competency destroying

environments' in producing radical innovation in biotechnology, forgetting that according to their own estimates there is a 7- to 10-year time horizon between discovery of a new product and final regulatory approval (ibid.: 8). Providing institutions that will operate according to such a time horizon requires something other than simple competency destruction. These sectors need a delicate balance: too much mobility and firms lose all capacity to protect their intellectual copyright; too little mobility and the gains from knowledge transfer are lost. This requires a certain level of sticky mobility, but such levels are difficult to plan for and to predict. If the balance is somehow 'right', this will be fortunate and serendipitous. It cannot be guaranteed. Shifts in the balance that produce negative effects can happen at any time.

Casper (2002) recognizes the dilemma, and shows how firms developed the use of share options and other ties to bind employees to the firm. If the employing firm is able to offer enough in stock options to offset the offer being made by the poaching firm and therefore retain the employee, then the market favours its continuing retention of an advantage in the research programme concerned. The disadvantages of extreme high mobility are resolved. If the poaching firm is able to offer more, then it takes over the programme. However, if the poaching firm is able to outbid the first firm because it has saved resources by not itself investing in the research programme, the net outcome is still likely to be a decline in the position of firms investing in research and a rise in those poaching staff and not investing, to the overall detriment of the sector.

The share option is in fact a good example of how the logic of corporate hierarchy operates complementarily to the market. True, it was presented initially as one of the means by which senior management accepted the dominance of the shareholder value model of the firm over the managerial one, because it led senior staff to share shareholders' aspirations for a high share price in the stock market rather than an internally well-funded organization—a major step on the perceived shift to purer markets of the 1990s. But share options involve increasing the number of claims on a firm's capital without increasing the size of that capital; and the decision to do this is taken by management, not by the markets, according to the perceived needs of the organization. In other words, it was a perfect example of corporate hierarchy changing the terms of the market. During the 1990s, when share markets were rising almost continuously, share market investors did not object. However, following the collapse of those markets in the early 2000s, the market challenged corporate hierarchy, as one of the first reactions of many dominant institutional shareholders was to demand the limitation and even scrapping of stock option schemes (though it should be remembered that dominant institutional share-holders are themselves an example of corporate hierarchy rather than the pure market). Firms are today seeking ways round this, with far more limited schemes, but many of them feel that levels of circulation of staff are running at levels too high for maximal development of long-term programmes. The virtual disappearance of the stock option solution has left firms with a problem of staff retention, which has certainly made the market a purer, high-mobility one again, but possibly at the expense of radical innovation.

A second mechanism used by firms to prevent staff taking important knowledge to a rival is the use of contract clauses that prevent an employee leaving a firm to go to another working on the same programme within a certain period of time. But, interpreted strictly, this contradicts the need of a highly innovative system to have rapid mobility among scientific personnel. Here most observers point to paragraph 16600 of the California Business and Professions Code, which prevents firms from imposing covenants not to compete on employees who subsequently leave their service. Casper and Kettler (2001: 9) compare this with the situation in Massachusetts, where no such clause exists, and where the information technology sector has declined in relation to that in California. However, Jong Kon Chin (2002) has challenged this, pointing out that firms in Massachusetts have continued to perform well in the biotechnology sector despite the existence of such covenants, implying that different explanations should be sought for that state's decline in information technology. He further points to evidence that firms have other, non-legal ways of limiting the mobility of key employees. It is also the case that these authors ignore the role of intellectual property law, even in California, in enabling firms to prevent former employees from working on specified, patented research programmes, even if they cannot impose a more general covenant not to compete. (It must be acknowledged here that Casper and Kettler (2001) do see potential in hybrid cases.)

This combination of paragraph 16600 with intellectual property protection may result in exactly the right mix of employee movement and employee stability, but this cannot be ensured. In any case, it is likely that no one really knows what the ideal mix is. Meanwhile, these legal complexities provide a good example of how the procedural state is used to both support and modify the market. It is impossible to say a priori exactly what constitutes the purer market: permitting poaching to maximize freedom of movement, or protecting intellectual property rights. These two fundamental characteristics of the market are in contention, and the issue becomes increasingly important as 'knowledge sectors' constitute a major part of economies. The exact state of the law at any one time depends on complex political processes as well as the differential abilities of different lawyers (Van Waarden 2002).

Finally, there is again the role of network governance. Firms understand their dependence on the links and tacit knowledge of the network, and know that were they to break its tacit norms by extensive poaching, they would risk exclusion. (See Helper, MacDuffie, and Sabel 2000 on the role of collaboration in both advancing knowledge and controlling opportunism.)

The network nature of this economy also reconciles another paradox of a pure labour market: the insecurity it brings to employees who never know for how long their job will last. Because the concentration of firms in both biotechnology and ICT sectors is so intense, and because the network includes venture capitalists as well as research and production firms, there are usually many opportunities within a fairly limited geographical area. Some authors (Kenney 2000*a*) have depicted Silicon Valley as a kind of organism, and a similar observation could be made about the biotechnology sector. Firms are formed, flourish, decline and disappear, but the clustered, networked nature of the region limits the waste, whether of labour, finance or knowledge, involved. As these resources are let go by a declining or dying firm, they remain within the network, and are quickly snapped up by new ventures. Again, the network provides creative complementarities for the market's destruction.

The role of immigrants in these industries in California is also interesting (Kenney 2000*b*; Saxenian 1994). The reasons why communities of immigrants are often repositories of entrepreneurial skills have been well demonstrated by Granovetter (1985). In brief, the strength of their community links embeds them in support structures that enable them to bear entrepreneurial risk. On the other hand, since these communities are minority ones, they do not dominate their members' lives as thoroughly as strong majority communities may do, leaving them the space in which to become entrepreneurial. For our present purposes a different aspect is important. Immigrants, whose socialization and education had been largely completed outside their country of arrival, seriously challenge the Varieties of Capitalism assumption of a strong relationship between the general (as opposed to specialized) education model of US schooling and radical innovation. The specific characteristics of the US national education system may be less relevant in these sectors than the coming together of US, German, Indian, Chinese and many other backgrounds. Dynamism and innovative capacity often result from the conjunction and mutual accessibility of different kinds of and approaches to knowledge. The general education model may have some relevance to the early days of the ICT industry. Then, as a new set of activities, there were no tailored courses for the industry, and there was scope for the high-school dropouts working in their fathers' garages who form the legends of ICT in the same way that heroes with log-cabin origins provided an earlier generation of American myths. But the secrets of the genome were not laid bare in this way, but by highly trained, specialized scientists with Ph.D.s from US universities, recruited from earlier education in many national systems, by no means all resembling US institutions.

The Knowledge Base

As this last discussion has shown, firms in the high-tech sectors need access to new scientific knowledge, so that they can exploit its implications for making new products, which they can develop commercially. Here the market-driven hypothesis for explaining the Californian cases can point to a major phenomenon: the close links between scientists in the universities of the region and the firms. In fact, it is the scientists themselves who found and then manage the firms. In doing this, they take advantage of US law, which apportions shares in rights to patents that exploit scientific advances to the universities in which the original research was conducted. This leads the universities themselves to be market-oriented, encouraging and assisting their scientists to become entrepreneurs. The great Californian (and many other US) universities are market-driven institutions.

However, if we step back and examine the institutional environment more closely, we observe certain things that challenge the simple hypothesis. First, the public knowledge resource base, primarily expressed through universities, remains fundamental to the system, particularly in biotechnology (Prevezer 1998: 124–93; Coriat, Orsi, and Weinstein 2003). Firms in the biopharmaceuticals sector have not internalized the entire research process. Universities are important for the production and dissemination of the public research base. In a pure market society there would be no public research base, as all knowledge resources would take the form of private property which could be acquired in the market. Individual firms would then have to bear the full costs of all their research, duplicating each other's efforts. They might buy and sell specified pieces of knowledge, but there can only be an efficient market in knowledge when its value is known. The point about radical innovation is that it requires ventures into the unknown, and these involve the highly costly acquisition of redundant capacities. (There are important cases in other industries where major innovative projects are taken on by individual firms. However, given the very high costs that these have to incur before they produce anything that can be marketed, they can be undertaken only by large corporations using the resources of corporate hierarchy. They are therefore not examples of pure market governance. Some particularly interesting cases involve partnerships among groups of multinationals, who make contracts together to pool resources at a shared, R&D phase, moving to competitive mode once they are in a position to produce and market their final products. This is an interesting example of the frontier between market and hierarchy modes.)

The public research base is a non-market resource that supports the market, and to survive it has to have a system of governance that protects it from the market. The academic community is a particularly specialized compound form of governance. It includes an important element of the procedural state, universities taking a particular legal form. Sometimes, including some of the Californian examples, they are entities created by the state itself; in other instances they are private legal foundations of a particular kind. The scientists within them manage their work through formal associations, communities and informal but highly important networks. They engage in many market activities, and their internal management structure often resembles that of the corporate hierarchy. They are therefore complete hybrids, capable of considerable diversity in their modes of operation, provided they are not captured by particular path dependences.

The Californian environment is institutionally diverse in other ways. The substantive state is further present. Prevezer (1998: 188) asserts:

It would be wrong, therefore, to think of the initial clusters in California and Massachusetts as having grown up in the absence of policy initiatives and inducements and being entirely 'market-driven'. Both states have cultivated a range of policies, and several of the biotechnology centres were located in those states and helped to create the type of infrastructure that has encouraged start-up companies, especially in high-technology areas.

Central to this state role are of course the military research activities discussed above.

Summary: The Californian High-tech Economy

The most striking characteristic of both these sectors in the southern Californian institutional environment is that this paradigmatic region of radical innovation exhibits a complex hybrid of governance forms. It is an environment that maximizes institutional choice. Markets are clearly central, but in both sectors these are unusual markets where

financial arrangements are concerned, as dialogue replaces market signalling in the role of venture capitalists. Particularly in biopharmaceuticals, venture capitalists lack the extreme ease of exit characteristic of pure
markets, as they have important sunk costs in the knowledge bases of the
firms. Not only are markets themselves unusual, but in a very important
way they share governance with networks in financial arrangements,
labour markets and the use of knowledge alike, and across both sectors.
Further, these are networks that deliver public as well as private goods.
They retain all three kinds of resource within a kind of local organism
whether or not individual firms come and go. And the university-rooted
public knowledge base is brought into the network, available to newcomers as well as to existing firms. The procedural state plays more than
its usual role, as intellectual property law is so important to exploitation
of research in these fields. The substantive state is particularly important
in the ICT sector, in providing both finance and the knowledge base. And
in both sectors corporate hierarchies are significant, for example, in providing investment funds and managing the stock option problem. Only
community and associational governance seem to be lacking.

From the perspective of the individual firm, this kind of mixed and
flexible governance is highly useful. For example, the firm may want to
have secure financial resources of the kind made possible by associations
or hierarchy, but to deal with its labour through pure market relations.
We cannot tell a priori how these combinations will operate. They will be
determined by path dependences, other forms of strong ties, and by
different political power relations.

Neo-institutionalist approaches which were defined in Chapter 3 as
labelling theories rule out examination of these possibilities by assuming
that the knowledge which is most accessible to actors always comes from
a logically coherent source; that is, if the primary context can be identified
as neoliberal, then actors will have access only to neoliberal possibilities.
If actors are presented solely with functionally integrated institutions of a
pure model, they can innovate only within its predictable functionalist
terms, at best achieving very limited *bricolage*. The disastrous effect of
learning from the USA the lesson that all that institutional entrepreneurs
need to do is to purify and open their markets, reduce the role of the state
and restrain associations could be seen throughout central and eastern
Europe in the years after the collapse of communism. The initially extremely naive beliefs that, once all barriers were cleared away, free markets would appear and flourish, were vulnerable to rapid disillusion as
criminality spread. This was quickly remedied by appreciation of the fact
that a market system needed to be protected by a strong and sophisticated

legal framework (the procedural state). But it has been a much harder lesson to learn that considerable institutional complexity lies behind successful innovating economies. Institutional entrepreneurs need a pluralist environment, just as do economic and also scientific entrepreneurs. As Kenney and Van Burg (2000) argue, in the course of its successful rise, Silicon Valley moved from being a set of isolated individuals (on the neoclassical model) to a complicated interactive community. It is for that reason that it is difficult to replicate elsewhere, as several localities have found who had been told that, provided they created deregulated, pure market environments, little Californias would emerge, and phenomena like high-tech industries would grow.

Much in this account bears out the argument that radical innovation seems to be favoured by hybrid characteristics. Neither strong ties nor no ties seem to provide the appropriate environment, but weak ties. Discoveries seem to be facilitated by moderately high scientific diversity (see also Hollingsworth 2004): too much, and knowledge is inadequate and also difficult to exchange; too little, and there is inadequate creativity.

The British Neoliberal Turn[1]

During the late 1970s it was common for observers of British political institutions to see the country as fixed in a highly unsuccessful set of macroeconomic institutions. A legacy of post-war corporatism had survived in a set of institutions which gave a considerable role to trade unions and employers' associations, but neither these nor governments had had either the will or the structures to make these institutions function in a way that produced sustained positive outcomes (Crouch 1977). Most attempts at reform concentrated on trying to make British institutions more closely pursue neocorporatist stability. There was a long record of this, starting with attempts at incomes policy in the early 1960s, and culminating in the attempted social contract of 1974–9 (Crouch 1977; Middlemas 1979, 1986–91). However, none of these attempts had more than a temporary success. Meanwhile, macroeconomic policy continued, with rather greater achievements to its name, along a Keynesian path (Shonfield 1964; Middlemas 1986–91; Stewart 1972, 1977). Governments used fiscal policy to keep levels of unemployment and inflation at low levels. However, whenever these objectives came into serious opposition, there was recourse to incomes policy and similar forms of restraint to try to ensure that increased demand produced by action to reduce unemployment did not lead to a general rise in prices; but these attempts ran into the problem that British interest organizations did not easily behave in a neocorporatist way. British Keynesianism, unlike the Scandinavian variety, was not intrinsically linked to neocorporatist industrial relations, though it came to depend on them. Policymakers were therefore left pursuing an impossible policy mix.

Although the theory of path dependence had not been applied to political theory at that time, academic observers in effect diagnosed such a condition as explaining why nothing seemed able to shift the UK from an apparently doomed course. (Major examples of such arguments were Beer 1982; Middlemas 1979.) But by the 1980s there had been a dramatic change in policy of a kind that very few 1970s observers had predicted: Industrial relations institutions of employers and employees alike had lost their public-policy role; Keynesian policy had been abandoned; there was no longer a commitment to maintain low unemployment through direct government action. Control of the supply of money had replaced unemployment reduction as the main concern of macroeconomic policy. By the 1990s several other European countries had begun to adopt elements of this new policy, but the UK has been the case where the changes started first, moved fastest and proceeded furthest.

This is a good example of major policy change in a context of path dependence. It is clear that Keynesianism had initially delivered returns. British wartime and post-war decision-makers learned how to practise these policies, which in turn reinforced the position of a certain set of interests. When, by the end of the 1960s, decision-makers realized that the policy mix was no longer delivering success, they nevertheless continued to try to use it. However, by 1976 the Labour government had made some initial steps towards monetarist policies. When that government fell in 1979 its Conservative successor embarked on an initially still gradual but thoroughgoing reversal of the entire trajectory of neocorporatism and Keynesianism. By the mid-1980s the UK had completely changed path. A system of governance that had featured associations alongside its other components (MPSHA, in terms of Chapter 5), now dropped this mode completely. In industrial relations in particular, the roles of markets, law, and managerial hierarchies were particularly strengthened. How was such a change possible?

Power Dynamics

Any account of changes in the British power structure during this period must take account of certain major factors. By 1976 the government was in considerable debt to the International Monetary Fund and had to accept certain exogenous policy terms imposed on it. In the 1980s the Labour Party, which by the mid-1970s had become the partisan guardian of what earlier had been a Keynesian consensus, formally split for the first time since 1931. And in 1984–5 the trade-union movement also suffered bitter divisions and a major political defeat in a coal-mining strike. Peter Hall has also pointed to certain initially unintended long-term institutional changes caused by a series of reforms in competition and credit control in the early 1970s (Hall 1992: 99–106; 1993). These made British policy exceptionally vulnerable to short-term evaluation by the financial markets, giving the interests associated with them a power to break the Keynesian paradigm (Hall 1992: 108–9).

Hall (1992: 106–8) sees the case as showing how institutions, as well as hindering change, can assist it, provided they take a certain form. Here the relevant form was the centralization of power in the British political and mass media systems. He also points out how the initial social learning which fostered the introduction of monetarism took place in powerful structures outside the state but able to influence it. He argues that this demonstrates the weakness of state-centric theories that look at the logics of action embedded in political institutions alone to find explanations of government policy change (Hall 1993: 288). The impetus came from the party-political (as opposed to government) system, from within the Conservative Party, and these groups engaged in a successful power struggle to oppose the paths familiar to both the public administration and the rest of the political system, including other parts of the Conservative Party. What was happening was an initial shift in the balance among subgroups of actors, such that those securing some increasing returns from the continuity of the neocorporatist Keynesian system were displaced by those representing the monetarist alternative.

The Weak Foundations of British Neocorporatism

As mentioned above, neocorporatist Keynesianism was never strongly implanted in the UK in any case. The Keynesian component of policy was, and very powerfully so, but its necessary neocorporatist accompaniment was weak. Apart from the war years and immediate aftermath, when emergency structures were in place, trade unions and employers' associations were not structured in ways that enabled them to play a neocorporatist role; and government was ambiguous about whether it wanted them to do so. Certainly, the system did not produce successful outcomes of the kind generated by the Scandinavian cases at that time, or the differently structured, non-Keynesian corporatism of Germany, the

Netherlands, Austria and Switzerland (Crouch 1993: ch 7). The early stages of an incomes policy might bring an initial gain, both in a temporarily better balance between inflation and unemployment, and in organisational prestige for the participant associations. However, as the strains of participation in restraining their constituents became a burden, these associations experienced diminishing returns.

Neocorporatism was embedded in the UK between 1940 and 1979 in the limited sense that, certain initial, in fact wartime, conditions having established the strength of such a path, it was reinforced by continuing recourse to it, developing a learning curve that crowded out other possibilities. But at each iteration the approach would suffer reverses. A path dependence was present, and increasing returns were present in terms of the operation of the system itself, but there were diminishing substantive returns. Even insiders did not derive unambiguous rewards. Employer associations and unions, not being structured to operate in a neocorporatist way, were often wracked by conflict whenever they began to do so. Many parts of government were not organized in a way that enabled them easily to share public authority with interest representatives.

Availability of Other Paths

Finally and perhaps most importantly, one needs to take full account of the fact that the UK system had been, even during the post-war period, a complex hybrid between Keynesianism and a laissez-faire approach inherited from earlier periods. Neocorporatist Keynesianism never dominated the whole British political economy. An important part of the British mid-century compromise was a strong division of labour between sectors of political economy covered by the compromise and those excluded or exempted from it. Among the latter was the financial sector. This did in fact take a corporatist form; the City of London was not just corporatist in the analogous sense in which that term is used in contemporary analysis; it *was* (and is) a medieval corporation, and possessed everything that implied in terms of highly articulated collective organization and political access. It is in fact a perfect hybrid, with a set of some of the purest markets bounded by an instance of the purest corporatism. Nevertheless, it stood outside the terms of the Keynesian compromise. This latter was concerned mainly with two sectors of the economy: the production of goods (and services concerned with their distribution) and public services. The first was at the heart of the Keynesian cycle linking employment and consumption; the second provided the channels through which the public spending that powered the system was spent, and provided further employment. Employer and employee interests within production, distribution and public services enjoyed positive-sum interests within this framework. And the productive industries and public services were the main sectors represented by trade unions.

The investment and securities sector was an outsider to all this. Historically the UK financial sector had played only a small part in the financing of manufacturing. Its activities were mainly located offshore and it had little connection to the economic life of the geographical and political territory of the UK. With the exception of front-line banking and insurance, the sector was also weakly unionized. Its main interest in the British economy was in ensuring that the pound sterling, in which it conducted much of its business, was a stable currency, and that UK economic and financial policy would provide a stable basis for the operations of a global financial sector. City interests were therefore particularly averse to inflation and would always favour monetary stability over full employment. And, unlike industrial capitalism and some other sectors, British finance capitalism never became embedded in the rest of British society.

Despite this, the sector was usually extremely powerful within that society; it was in a way its absentee landlord. Even in the period of foreign exchange controls and regulated capital movements, finance had mobility, and would move out of a country that did not provide a favourable environment, while the City's earnings made a positive contribution to the country's balance of payments. Although firms in manufacturing and other non-financial sectors might occasionally criticize the low profile of the City in providing them with their own investment finances, they also welcomed the opportunity to make offshore investments and to liquidize their assets through City institutions. Also, within its highly organized, corporatist network, the City incorporated the UK central bank, the Bank of England, itself. This in turn enjoyed a special relationship with the Treasury, the most powerful ministry in the government. The sector therefore had a 'sponsoring ministry' considerably more significantly than, say, the agricultural sector. British financial interests therefore enjoyed a combination of autonomy from the UK economy and polity and a highly influential role within both.

There was therefore a very strong division of labour and of perspectives within the British post-war compromise; it was a compromise that allocated different interests a role in different sectors; it made fewer demands on them to come to terms with each other within a sector. The Keynesian part of British political economy did not make claims on the scope of the

City, and the latter largely tolerated the Keynesian policy framework. They certainly clashed from time to time over the relative importance of currency stability and full employment, but the modus operandi of the two remained distinct. By the 1970s, when the parameters of the Keynesian system were proving increasingly difficult to sustain, the City was also at one of its weakest moments. It had become highly marginal to the British economy; new share issues contributed a very small proportion of investment finance. Just as had happened during the recession of the 1930s, there was political debate over whether the City was serving the interests of the national economy. The sector was also in a period of internal uncertainty. The web of informal understandings, personal friendships, and family links that had sustained it for centuries as a kind of industrial district were being strained by the early stages of internationalization.

However, during the early 1980s a series of major institutional innovations was to propel the City to a new global importance. The so-called 'big bang' of reform brought together a liberalization of capital movements, a shift from an informal, private corporatist regime to a state-directed one, and the possibilities of new technology. Further, the processes described by Hall (1992, 1993), whereby government became increasingly dependent on the willingness of financial institutions to accept its policies, further strengthened the City's role. All this prepared it to play a major role in the new ascendancy of share markets that characterized the global economy of the 1990s. The monetarist, non- (pre-, anti-, post-) Keynesian practices that came to dominate during this period had always been the policy preferences of the financial sector; the secondary neoliberal path had run alongside the dominant Keynesian one throughout the post-war period. Abandonment of the Keynesian model did not therefore present any profound problems of policy preference or priorities to significant parts of the British political and economic elite.

The major components of Keynesian neocorporatism were rapidly demolished and replaced with neoliberal structures. Apart from the shift to monetarism, there were major changes to the industrial relations system. These partly took the form of legal reductions of trade union rights, but perhaps more important was an almost complete end to the tripartite consultation that had been taken for granted in previous decades. Spending on social services declined alongside Keynesian management, and gradually large parts of the public sector were privatized. Internal markets and commercialization were encouraged in activities remaining public. By the 1990s the process was so thoroughgoing that it had become a new path dependence.

Conclusions: The UK Case

That the UK was the first and remains the most thoroughgoing example of a turn from neocorporatism and Keynesianism towards monetarism and neoliberalism in Western Europe seems amply explained. The neocorporatist component of the former model had not in practice been successfully pursued; and the power balance that sustained it and the Keynesian model had collapsed and had been replaced by a very different configuration. In terms of two principal drivers of path dependence—power relations and the learning curve—the former requirement for change was clearly satisfied. Increasing returns now flowed to a UK policy system that pursued a neoliberal path, whereas the former model had been delivering decreasing returns for some time.

As Hall shows, there had also been considerable effort at the level of policy learning. Neoliberal academic economists and 'think tanks' supported by the power interests who would gain from the change had articulated the monetarist policy models that replaced Keynesian mechanisms. Measures of increase in the money supply were developed to replace the indicators used by the Keynesian approach. These provided technical solutions to the problem of how to govern the economy with different targets from those relating to the relationship between employment, inflation, growth, and currency stability. In practice they played a mainly talismanic role in policy steering. Governments adopted whatever definition of monetary targets their policies seemed able to achieve. The debate over what rate of monetary expansion would produce what level of inflation was never resolved. All that was necessary was that political and economic elites had a frame of reference that suited their preferences, could be presented publicly, and gave them some strategic orientation.

Hall points out the importance of not concentrating solely on structural institutional processes in our accounts of action; initiatives from outside that structure may be able to effect change. But, to return to the initial argument with which we are concerned, if our account of a society stresses the congruity and coherence of all its institutional parts this advice can only be used if the disruption comes from forces previously so weak within that society that they had no impact on its institutional formation and policy practices. Alternatively the new actors must be seen as entirely exogenous; such actors need to 'conquer' the system, so that they either take control of its institutions or acquire a position where they can give instructions to the endogenous agents who execute the tasks; or they need to have close allies within the field who had not possessed enough power before to shift the path.

But neither of these was the case with the British neoliberal turn. The interests that became favoured were deeply endogenous: those of the wealthier sections of society, business interests, and the financial sector of the economy in particular. These had always been powerfully present in the more general context of British political economy, even if they had been forced to compromise with other interests during the period of Keynesian consensus and post-war democratic pressure. We can take full account of this possibility if we have a model of institutions that allows for internal diversity and even incoherence, provided of course that we can identify the institutional barriers that protect the heterogeneity. In this case this is provided by the exemption of the offshore-oriented City from the institutions of the Keynesian consensus.

The sequences of actions and motivations described above fit what was set out theoretically in Chapter 4 as the second extension of the principal argument. An actor becomes dissatisfied with the substantive returns being received from an existing path. The actor has access to an alternative set of practices being used in an adjacent field. Once the price is paid for transferring those practices into the first field, the actor can change the path. This actor can certainly make this kind of change more rapidly than one who has no access to such alternatives. To carry out this kind of analysis we must have an approach that can perceive two or more, or fragments of several, not necessarily harmoniously related, institutional forms coexisting within one political economy. Whether the Keynesian system and the neoliberal financial sector existed in a complementary relationship, or were simply in contradiction with each other, is a separate question, well worth exploring, but not here. In either event, they were certainly not cases of isomorphism or elective affinity. What took place in the UK was a shift from one to another of two available, very different paths in a context of perceived 'failure' of one and a shift in the power relations between those committed to it and those associated with its rival.

Note

1. Another version of this discussion appears in Crouch and Keune (2005), which I wrote jointly with Maarten Keune.

7

Conclusions: A Reformed Neo-institutionalist Research Programme

When can we say that changes within a system have accumulated to such an extent that the system is a new one? When does a form of capitalism 'change' its nature? Yamamura and Streeck (2003) raise this question sharply when they show both remarkable continuities and extraordinary changes in their historical analyses of German and Japanese capitalism. Similar questions arise with studies covering far shorter periods. For example, Deeg (2005) has shown how, contrary to arguments about the tight coupling of production and financial spheres, German firms seem able to work with a diversity of financial regimes as these change over the years. And Höpner (2003*b*) has similarly shown how co-determination in German industry can coexist with a variety of financial systems. As Höpner himself asks: When has a national system changed, and when is it operating within the scope of its existing diversity?

We begin to answer these questions when we realize that systems are primarily constructions of theorists, not of society itself. As has been stressed many times in the above pages, elements of various systems are found within these cases; empirical cases are rarely simple examples of systems. When we note that actors in a particular context have started to behave in a different way, it may simply mean that they have slipped between one or more of our constructed frames; not necessarily that they have themselves crossed some paradigmatic Rubicon. Even if they do themselves conceive what they are doing as a major change, it may be because they are unduly influenced by some theorists who have presented to them the concepts of what they are doing.

This does, however, bring us to an important point: such presentations of what they are doing are inevitable and necessary if human actors are to develop proficiency. It is difficult to maximize our performance unless we have a clear sense of the paradigm within which we are working. We can only maximize fully when we know what we are trying to maximize, and this is given to us by the paradigm. For example, the artists of the Florentine Renaissance did (after a certain point) believe that they were involved in a major change of cultural paradigm away from what they pejoratively described as 'Gothic' aesthetic values towards humanistic, realistic, rediscovered Græco-Roman ones. They were not wrong; we can certainly see that something extraordinary happened at that time and place that influenced the visual arts until at least the end of the nineteenth century. However, when today we look at some of the work said by Renaissance scholars to represent the Gothic Other, we cannot avoid seeing incipient characteristics that the Renaissance came to believe were its own inventions. We see attempts at perspective, increased realism in the representation of the human figure, conscious imitation of classical models. Change in practice pre-dated change in perception of the practice; but the latter certainly accelerated the former.

Similar arguments apply to a different point with which we have also been preoccupied in this book. The hypothesis that institutional heterogeneity will facilitate innovation can be set against those that point to the advantages of institutional similarity, but neither can dispose of the logic of the rival arguments. There will be examples of both confusing and creative incoherence. Can we say anything about the kinds of conditions likely to be associated with each? There is in fact a meta-complementarity between complementarity and similarity. Although they are opposed principles, and tend to be advocated by rival theorists, they are likely in fact both to be present, and produce results together—like Nils Bohr's theory of light. This is particularly likely to be the case if we take an evolutionary approach to institutions: as they change they gradually reveal a particular shape that was not clear before, though elements of it were present, and will not be clear again in future after some further changes have taken place.

We need to be able to identify actors pursuing rules that actually contradict those they were using before. This is not just a question of breaking the first set of rules, but of erecting new ones that at certain points prescribe something very different from those followed before. Then a new paradigm has come into existence. However, we must still expect that the context in which the actors are operating will comprise a multiplicity of paradigms, which do not necessarily all change together or in the same direction. We can, to return to the earlier example, see how Renaissance ideals projected a relatively more realistic depiction of the human form than the far more formal and even abstract shapes of Byzantine art. But both shared a paradigm that required demonstrating considerable respect in depicting holy figures.

To return to more familiar territory for neo-institutionalists: we observe paradigm change when we can see actors using unprecedented means successfully to carry out tasks that we know had been difficult for them within the terms of their previous mode. If the second mode is simply different from the first, but not necessarily in ways likely to assist the firm in solving its problem, it might be more likely to create confusion and therefore inefficiency.

Let us assume that we are seeking to answer the question why Italy has not provided a successful environment for the producers of computer software. Using the method outlined above, the study would begin by enumerating the capacities that are needed for success in this industry, in terms of financial structure, human and other resources, markets, management structures, etc. The next step would be to show what pattern of capacities and (presumably predominantly) lack of capacities Italy possesses on this scale. Explanations can then be given by economists and other social scientists as to why Italy has predominately minus scores on this account. However, institutional analysis can simplify its task by being concerned with only one aspect of this question: What is the putative role of mechanisms of *governance* in providing the presumably appropriate set of capacities for computer software manufacture? And how does the pattern of governance found in Italy measure up this task?

But how good is our knowledge of the capacity of different governance forms? Some authors make strong claims. For example, several claim that the pure market is superior to most other forms of governance in stimulating radical innovation. Our analytical, not to mention prescriptive, capacity would increase considerably if we could confidently make statements of this kind. But, as Regini (1996) has shown, the existence of functional equivalents raises considerable difficulties for such simple means–ends associations: actors are able to bend governance mechanisms to carry out surprising tasks. In Regini's own main example, Italian machine-tool firms have demonstrated a capacity to provide training for a skilled workforce, even though the existing literature had argued that provision of such skills required forms of associational governance which Italy lacked. Functional equivalence, if it is strategically achieved by institutional entrepreneurs, can be described in terms of the model presented in Chapter 5 as a situation where actors within I'' refashion G'' so that, while retaining its own characteristics, it gives the same substantive outcome as G'.

This does not mean that anything is possible, and that we should therefore abandon all attempts at institutional analysis. The Italian machine-tool industry found a solution to its governance problem in the provision of machine-tool skills; but their British equivalents did not do so (Crouch and O'Mahoney 2004). On the other hand, the British did solve the governance problem of providing training for new film and television skills (Baumann 2002), while the Italians have not solved the computer software problem, except in some isolated (and therefore interesting) cases (mainly around Pisa (Biagiotti and Burroni 2004)). Different forms of governance are associated with different capacities, but knowledge of this cannot be derived in a mechanistic, a priori way. We are dealing with creative human actors who, faced with an institution that does not 'work' in a certain way, will sometimes fashion it until it does. We really need some synthetic works that pull together the results of the many individual case studies that are lying around in Ph.D. theses and journal articles, never incorporated into an emerging corpus. Unlike natural scientists, social scientists too often derive their reputations from showing how different they are from each other, how each one is making a new departure, and not contributing to a collective edifice of shared knowledge.

Functional equivalence and the process of recombining elements of governance forms together help us model the behaviour of institutional entrepreneurs. As we have noted, entrepreneurial actors will not be content with the overall structure of governance institutions they find around them, but will try to borrow and adapt components from a variety of them in a kind of institutional *bricolage* to produce new combinations that bring together the apparently incompatible functions of those which went before. Scott (2001: 188), who similarly insists that most structures contain multiple institutional systems, incorporating heterodox elements, uses a fine analogy when he points out that waters where fresh and salt water meet are particularly rich in marine diversity.

Combining the apparently irreconcilable is a major form of innovation. We can take the analogy of experimental fruit growers. If there seems to be a clear biological choice between a tomato that is sweet to taste and one that has a robust skin for transport, it can be guaranteed that in some tomato grower's laboratory there is a project for producing a sweet but robust tomato. Of course, the search is not guaranteed success. (In practice success is being achieved using the new botanical paradigm of genetic modification, which is in itself controversial.) And when the sweet, robust, genetically modified tomato finally appears, its invention does not suddenly render retrospectively false the knowledge that had shown these two characteristics to have been incompatible in the past. That knowledge had indeed served as a spur to the research that found a way, creating new knowledge. Research on governance and institutions operates in the same way. The capacity of humans to learn means that, where there is knowledge of the past (even inaccurate knowledge), there is no pure repetition of an action.

The repeatability of an experiment, said to be fundamental to the scientific character of knowledge, is not possible when creative human actors are involved.

This is not much comfort for social scientists who want to advise public policymakers on what they should do to achieve success in some specified aim; nor indeed is it any comfort for the policymakers themselves who want clear answers. The advice that follows from a book like this, suggesting a large diversity of as yet unknown possibilities, will always be unwelcome in these quarters, because it proposes acceptance of redundant capacity, which is costly. In Chapter 3, I recounted the example of railway operators who reduced costs by axing redundant capacity and retaining too few engine drivers to deal with absences. This is what took place in the UK in the mid-1990s. The staff members who devised the plan for the initial job reductions were probably rewarded handsomely for the savings they achieved; far more so than those who had the unglamorous task of trying to put it all back together again a few years later, incurring new costs. Matters will always be so; there is little learning curve here, as new cohorts are faced with similar incentives to propose cost reductions, the negative consequences of which will not be experienced for a period of time. After I had completed the final draft of Chapter 3 in summer 2004, the story broke in the UK that British Airways was in a staff shortage crisis, unable to man its check-in desks, because they had just completed a staff reduction plan, cutting out redundant capacity as had the railways less than ten years previously. In this field as in public policy, there are fashions. As several authors have noted, and as I have demonstrated in Chapter 4, fashionable policies will be followed even if they are suboptimal. At present, delayering and reducing staff levels are fashionable; therefore they will take place; and this will continue until the fashion changes.

The Role of Power Imbalances

Path dependence theory assumes initially randomly chosen paths. There remains a large class of non-randomly chosen ones that require consideration. In particular, why might leading actors within a particular governance mode deliberately favour one path rather than another, when in principle both are available and both are, in the simple case, likely to be equally effective? To answer these questions we must return to the question of the relationship between governance and power mentioned in previous chapters. Power is fundamental to governance, because if governance mechanisms sustain regularities of behaviour, they must have the capacity to lead actors to behave in ways other than maximizing their own conception of their interests. In Chapter 3, I outlined the example of a group that starts with perfect equality of influence, but where association with even randomly selected outcomes in early stages could confer considerable path dependences of unequal power and influence. In situations of this kind, which are found very frequently in real life, the path dependence differentially benefits the power-holding or insider interests, but all members of the group also benefit from the fact that a solution to the collective problem has been found.

These considerations are more important than any formal properties that render a particular type of governance mode more or less likely to encourage innovation. To illustrate: In principle the market form of governance encourages innovation—because to resist competitive challenge, a firm must keep introducing new products. On the other hand, the market also encourages short-term perspectives, because profits have to be realized. This may inhibit radical innovation that needs long lead times for research and considerable uncertainty as to outcome. In contrast, governance by formal business associations may be considered likely to inhibit radical innovation, because associations are defined by the sector in which they find themselves and therefore have little interest in encouraging activities which might challenge those boundaries. On the other hand, they are capable of restraining short-term incentives that might inhibit long-term decisions. The overall outcome whether the market or an associational regime is more likely to favour radical innovation is undetermined. In such a situation much will depend on the identity of the particular interests associated with the dominant governance form, *and* on how they, as Bayesian actors, perceive those interests.

Assume that delivery of health service resources in a particular society is governed by markets. Health providers, insurers and clients all realize their health needs through this mechanism, and therefore feel threatened by any attempt to shift to a different system of delivery. Meanwhile, those too poor to achieve much health care at all have hardly any voice within the market and will be ignored, even by highly innovative action within it. In this context, an attempt by interest associations in an exogenous area, but which can develop ways of influencing debate and conflict about health—for example a set of trade unions—could press for innovation in a way not likely to emerge from the market itself. On the other hand, in a health insurance system governed solely by associations, innovation in the interests of excluded actors might come through the market.

To illustrate the point further, we can turn to the example of the university as a form of governance of scientific communities. When the University of Oxford and its colleges were secure in their store of endowed resources and government grants, they took little interest in what relationship they might have with science-related business in the region around them (Proudfoot forthcoming). In fact, the predominant view in the university had been that engagement with anything local to the relatively low-population region around Oxford could even diminish the university's international status. It was far from being a regionally embedded institution. This view changed rapidly during the 1990s, as existing sources of resources seemed far less secure, and as university scientists and authorities perceived the advantages that its rival Cambridge was drawing from its associated high-technology local production system. The University of Oxford began to act less like a secure insider, and sought out means of innovation, including those which connected it to its surrounding local economy and society. As a consequence, university authorities and leading scientists took a number of measures which have brought the university to the centre of a flourishing biopharmaceuticals sector (Proudfoot 2004; Jong Kin Chin forthcoming).

We can therefore attribute safely to governance mechanisms only formal qualities; substantive ways in which they are used will depend heavily on power and varied patterns of insider and outsider relations.

Implications for the Neo-institutionalist Research Programme

It is now possible to specify how a research programme on institutional change should be pursued. By this I do not mean that every individual *project* should try to cover the whole specified field, but an overall programme of different projects related to a shared paradigm. It is thus necessary that individual projects see themselves as both drawing from and contributing to a developing edifice of knowledge which will gradually cover the field and be able to be drawn on by further researchers. This is especially important for those giving an account of how institutional entrepreneurs have been exploring the transferable, concealed and dormant institutional resources of their societies. At the same time, we have to remember that in all such work we are ourselves engaging in the construction of paradigms that might (if we are very fortunate) start to influence some actors in the real world. But, as researchers set off on the path dependence of their paradigm, they will gradually become blind to certain possibilities that are excluded from its framework. If the research programme is to be fully scientific, it should make recognition of this explicit and contain within itself alternative and even rival paradigms.

1. Defining the context. First, the relevant institutional context needs to be identified, and its points of openness and closure to external influence specified. The former is usually done in relation to nation-states, but this is not the only possibility: regions, economic sectors, cross-national entities like the European Union can also be studied in this way. Researchers are free to specify any level they wish, but the viability of such a level as an object of study, and in particular any assertion that a particular level constitutes *the* object of study must be presented as hypotheses and not as starting assumptions.

2. Specifying capacities. Evidence must then be gathered on what appear to be the available capacities (and absence thereof) in the various fields. Existing neo-institutionalist research programmes have made considerable progress in doing this, in so far as the capacities identified form part of a coherent whole. As already argued above, it is also necessary to search out subordinate systems that embody patterns different from any dominant one. Such an account then has to be nuanced in terms of both relative importance of the mechanisms within the ongoing situation, and whether they are currently in use or only potentially available, with different degrees of difficulty.

3. Specifying the available governance range. Second, the range of governance mechanisms available to actors within a context needs to be identified, related to capacities in their current mode of operation, and specified in terms of a theoretical model. To some extent this is a straightforward task. Working from the established list of governance mechanisms, the researcher looks for evidence of the presence of these in the day-to-day conduct of affairs. For example, let us assume a study of pension institutions within a particular nation-state. Is there a state role? If so, what is it? Is there a market role? If so, what is it? Is there a role for formal associations? If so, what is it? And so forth. There are then three less obvious parts of the analysis, which require more than behaviourist observation.

(*a*) Are some institutions present which, while not being within the a priori set of specified mechanisms, might in fact play a part in the activity concerned? The role of universities in the governance of high-tech clusters is an example, now well known but not originally considered part of governance theory. There is no clear research method that can be recommended to identify such mechanisms beyond the curiosity and detective skills of the researcher—essential tools in all scientists' equipment. It might be possible to use a more rigorous method of unexplained variance: if, after having examined all obvious candidates for examination, we find that there is still something unexplained in the situation, we are encouraged to search around for what it might be.

(b) More difficult to find are *potential* governance mechanisms: institutions which are not currently playing an observable role, but which, in a condition of crisis or necessary change, might do so. It is difficult to subject this part of the research to scientific rules, precisely because innovation cannot be fully predicted.

(c) Also important is the search for unusual, or non-typical, elements within the modes, leading occasionally to the need to deconstruct these.

4. *Ranking the modes*. Next, an attempt should be made to rank the modes found in terms of their relative dominance. Relationships between mechanisms also need to be specified. In particular, when we encounter mechanisms which may conflict with each other, can we anticipate:

(a) a clash between them, likely to end in confusion or the destruction of one by another;

(b) an unimportant relationship, for example in the case of a division of labour between the mechanisms, such that a potential clash never arises; or

(c) potential creative joint operation of the mechanisms, perhaps in changing relationships to each other?

At the end of these first four stages of the analysis is an account of governance, identifying, not 'an example of which form of governance is this empirical case?', but 'traces of what forms of governance can be found within this case?'

5. *Mapping the fields*. A conceptual map must then be developed of other fields within the society, described according to their proximity to the institutions at the centre of the research and their accessibility to agents within those institutions. The various modes of governance or institutional approaches at work within these other institutions must be specified, again in terms of theoretical models. An attempt must also be made to rank these in terms of their relative dominance.

The range of institutions covered in this way has to be limited to the scope of available knowledge. Thus, if there is well-established evidence that particularly forms of parliamentary government are associated with certain kinds of production, it is legitimate to cite such evidence in support of a hypothesized *Wahlverwandschaft*. But if thorough evidence of this kind is lacking, it is not legitimate merely to assume the link because of its theoretical appropriateness; instead it is appropriate to remain silent about it. This is particularly relevant to the problem of 'complementarities'—which also applies to what one might call sub-institutions within the initial institution of reference of the study.

There is an empirical difficulty in identifying which institutions should be considered as external to the field of prime interest and which should be seen as within it. Although for convenience and in building models from simple origins it is useful and necessary to distinguish between internal and external, endogenous and exogenous, in practice there are always continua. The analogy we use of the relationship of an institution to its environment should not be that of a closed but permeable bounded space in a wider field, but that of a net of a certain topography, like a spider's web. The strands in the centre of the net are thick and clear; as the net extends outwards they become faint, until at a more or less definable point they cease altogether. The model is then made more complex by envisaging a series of such nets within a wider overall net shape. Where thick strands cluster before a distinct thinning can be perceived, we can talk of a more or less bounded institution. Other institutions will exist at other thick clusters, located at various distances from our original focus; some will be so close that they overlap (as with political government and the economy); others will seem extremely remote (as with religious institutions and economy in contemporary industrialized societies). But changes of various kinds can suddenly make previously faint links in the net stronger, and strong ones fainter. This can happen through interventions, as powerful actors call on the aid of other but accessible institutions; or through borrowings and learning through contact with elements of such institutions. It is through interchange at weak points and adjustments that change is most likely across boundaries.

6. *Watching the actors.* The moves of, and conflicts among, actors observed in the research should be interpreted in terms of their attempts to sustain or to change the prevailing governance pattern; in the latter event, the new combination being sought, or inadvertently produced, by the moves and conflicts should be specified. Are particular class or other interests associated with a particular governance mechanism? And how does their relationship to that mechanism relate to their position in other fields of the society? Human actors will be among the forces that are particularly capable of recombining governance elements. They live their lives across a range of institutions, not necessarily following any

predictable pattern. (For example, marriage alliances can introduce actors to new and sometimes surprising patterns of shared interest—a fact well understood by monarchical and aristocratic families.) It is at this point of an analysis that it is particularly important to model the power positions of particular groups of entrepreneurial actors. A group which is generally powerful may be able to marshal resources and bring them unexpectedly across from some sectors of society to others, challenging an established governance mode or institutional or policy pattern.

Patterns of relations among actors will also be important in enabling us to describe embeddedness. Actors might find themselves in embedded relations for reasons exogenous to their particular action field. These relations may, and particularly if they are the products of path dependence, reinforce existing institutions, governance and ways of acting, inhibiting change. On the other hand, they might be the source of change, by giving access to alternatives to the actors.

A research programme based on these principles provides a richer description of an institutional configuration than do standard accounts, and makes it possible to study action and structure interactively as commended by Sewell (1992). It provides a full analysis of the state of governance in a particular context, and of the scopes for change and blockages of change to be found within it. It will lack the neatness and capacity for easy classification of national cases afforded by allocative approaches. However, it is not a lapse into description, as it has used generalizable, theoretically derived categories and theories of relations among categories in producing its accounts. The resulting accounts can therefore be used in comparative studies without difficulty, as different cases will be analysed in the same terms.

When we study complex macro-social phenomena like the wider institutional structure of an economy we often have to accept that, despite their theoretical identity, explanation and prediction are very different activities, and we may often have to limit ourselves to the former. When an event has already taken place it is possible with various methodologies to reconstruct how and why it occurred, and to delve back into the ensemble of wider institutional processes involved. It is not possible to do this for future events, because researchers cannot tell which surprising combinations of institutional resources will in practice be used by creative, entrepreneurial actors; if they can, the changes are not surprising.

We shall therefore continue to be taken by surprise by acts of true Schumpeterian entrepreneurialism. We can however at least conceptualize the likelihood of these occurring in terms of risk-taking. Schumpeterian actors can be conceived as those who make unexpected and daring leaps in innovation. As we considered in Chapter 4, if we retain the basic assumption of the theory, that even such leaps as these have to draw on knowledge which is somehow already available, an innovative leap can be theorized in terms of extended path dependence theory as a decision to start drawing balls from a very remotely located and unlikely urn. The idea of the 'leap' is very apt. In terms of the model, this is always possible; but it is costly. An important cost will be lack of knowledge whether the innovation will work, because the idea for it has been pulled from such a remote and unfamiliar institutional location. It is therefore reasonable to predict that most such attempts will fail, but a small but finite number will succeed. Further, we can specify the kind of conditions (e.g. redundancy) which will put agents in a position to carry out such innovations. And, while we shall always be surprised, we can at least be ready for surprise: We must always present the diversity of the governance we analyse as the dynamic and processual result of constant attempts to solve problems, rather than as static ensembles in place. As Weber so memorably argued, the rules required by bureaucratic and similar systematic arrangements can never fit all cases; they must therefore constantly respond and adapt as they are implemented. The same applies to both institutions and those who observe them.

REFERENCES

Albert, M. (1991). *Capitalisme contre capitalisme*. Paris: Seuil.

Amable, B. (2000). 'Institutional complementarity and diversity of social systems of innovation and production', *Review of International Political Economy*, 7/4: 645–87.

—— (2003). *The Diversity of Modern Capitalism*. Oxford: Oxford University Press.

Anderlini, L. and Ianni, A. (1993). *Path Dependence and Learning from Neighbours*, Economic Theory Discussion Paper 186: 1993, Cambridge, University of Cambridge Department of Applied Economics.

Aoki, M. (1994). 'The Contingent Governance of Teams: Analysis of Institutional Complementarity', *International Economic Review*, 35/3: 657–76.

—— (2001). *Toward a Comparative Institutional Analysis*. Cambridge, MA: MIT Press.

Arrow, K. (2000). 'Increasing Returns: Historiographical Issues and Path Dependence', *European Journal of the History of Economic Thought*, 7, 2: 171–80.

Arthur, B. (1990). 'Positive Feedbacks in the Economy', *Scientific American*, February: 92–9.

—— (1994). *Increasing Returns and Path Dependence in the Economy*. Ann Arbor, MI: University of Michigan Press.

——, Ermoliev, Y. M., and Kaniovski, Y. M. (1987). 'Path–Dependent Processes and the Emergence of Macrostructure', *European Journal of Operational Research*, 30: 294–303.

Bagnasco, A. (1977). *Tre Italie: la problematica territoriale dello sviluppo Italiano*. Bologna: Il Mulino.

Baker, W. (1984). 'The Social Structure of a National Securities Market', *American Journal of Sociology*, 89: 775–811.

—— (1990). 'Market Networks and Corporate Behaviour', *American Journal of Sociology*, 96: 589–625.

Barreto, H. (1989). *The Entrepreneur in Micro–Economic Theory: Disappearance and Explanation*. London: Routledge.

Baumann, A. (2002). 'Convergence Versus Path-Dependency: Vocational Training in the Media Production Industries in Germany and the UK'. Ph.D. thesis, Florence, European University Institute.

Becattini, G. and Burroni, L. (2004). 'Il Distretto Industriale come Strumento di Ricomposizione del Sapere Sociale', *Sociologia del Lavoro*.

Beer, S. H. (1982). *Britain against Itself*. London: Faber and Faber.

Berggren, C. and Laestadius, S. (2000). *The Embeddedness of Industrial Clusters: The Strength of the Path in the Nordic Telecom System*. Stockholm: Kungl. Tekniska Högskolan.

Bertoldi, M. (2003). 'Varietà e dinamiche del capitalismo', *Stato e Mercato*, 69: 365–83.

Beyer, J. (2001). 'One best way' oder Varietät? Strategischer und organisatorischer Wandel von Groaunternehmen im Prozess der Internationalisierung'. MPIfG Discussion Paper 01/2. Cologne: Max-Planck Institut für Gesellschaftsforschung.

Biagiotti, A. and Burroni, L. (2004). 'Between Cities and Districts: Local Software Systems in Italy', in C. Crouch et al. (eds.), Changing Governance of Local Economies: Response of European Local Production Systems. Oxford: Oxford University Press, 283–305.

Blanchard, O. J. (2004). The Economic Future of Europe. MIT Economics Working Paper No. 04–04. Cambridge, MA: Massachusetts Institute of Technology.

Bourdieu, P., Chamboredon, J.-C., and Passeron J.-C. (1973). Le métier de sociologue: préalables epistémologiques. Paris: Mouton.

Blyth, M. (2003). 'Same as it never was: Temporality and typology in the varieties of Capitalism', Comparative European Politics, 1, 2: 215–26.

Boyer, R. (1996). 'The Convergence Hypothesis Revisited: Globalization but still the Century of Nations?', in S. Berger and R. Dore (eds.), National Diversity and Global Capitalism. Ithaca, NY: Cornell University Press.

—— (1997). 'The Variety and Unequal Performances of Really Existing Markets: Farewell to Doctor Pangloss?', in R. Hollingsworth and R. Boyer (eds.), (1997a), q.v., 55–93.

—— (2004a). 'New Growth Regimes, But still Institutional Diversity', Socio-Economic Review, 2/1: 1–32.

—— (2004b). The Future of Economic Growth: As New becomes Old. Cheltenham: Edward Elgar.

—— and Didier, M. (1998). Innovation et Croissance. Paris: La Documentation Française.

—— and Saillard, Y. (eds.) (1995). Théorie de la régulation: L'état des savoirs. Paris: La Découverte.

Braczyk, H.-J. and Schienstock, G. (eds.) (1996). Kurswechsel in der Industrie. Lean Production in Baden-Württemberg. Berlin/Cologne: Kohlhammer.

Breen, R. (2000). 'Beliefs, Rational Choice and Bayesian Learning', Rationality and Society, 11/4, 463–79.

Burroni, L. and Trigilia, C. (2001). 'Italy: Economic Development through Local Economies', in C. Crouch et al., (2001), q.v., 46–78.

Burt, R. (1988). 'The Stability of American Markets', American Journal of Sociology, 94: 356–95.

Butzbach, O. (2005). 'Varieties within Capitalism? A Comparative Study of French and Italian Savings Banks'. Ph.D. thesis, Florence, European University Institute.

Calmfors, L. and Driffill, J. (1988). 'Bargaining Structure, Corporatism and Macroeconomic Performance', Economic Policy, 6.

Calvert, R. L. (1995). 'Rational Actors, Equilibrium, and Social Institutions', in J. Knight and I. Sened (eds.), Explaining Social Institutions. Ann Arbor, MI: University of Michigan Press.

Campbell, J. L. (2004). Institutional Change and Globalization. Princeton, NJ: Princeton University Press.

—— (2001). 'Institutional Analysis and the Role of Ideas in Political Economy', in J. L. Campbell and O. K. Pedersen (eds.), (2001l), q.v., 159–89.

—— and Pedersen, (2001a). 'The Rise of Neoliberalism and Institutional Analysis', in J. L. Campbell and O. K. Pedersen (eds.), (2001l), q.v., 1–23.

——— (eds.) (2001b). *The Rise of Neoliberalism and Institutional Analysis*. Princeton, NJ: Princeton University Press.

———, (2001c). 'The Second Movement in Institutional Analysis', in J. L. Campbell and O. K. Pedersen (eds.), (2001l), q.v., 249–82.

——, Hollingsworth, J. R., and Lindberg, L. N. (eds.) (1991). *Governance of the American Economy*. New York: Cambridge University Press.

Carlsson, B. and Eliasson, G. (2003). 'Industrial Dynamics and Endogenous Growth', *Industry and Innovation*, 10/4: 435–56.

Carruthers, B. G., Babb, S. L. and Halliday, T. C. (2001). 'Institutionalizing Markets, or the Market for Institutions? Central Banks, Bankruptcy Law, and the Globalization of Financial Markets', in J. L. Campbell and O. K. Pedersen (eds.), (2001l), q.v., 94–126.

Casper, S. (2001), 'The Legal Framework for Corporate Governance: The Influence of Contract Law on Company Strategies in Germany and the United States', in P. A. Hall and D. Soskice (eds.), *Varieties of Capitalism: The Institutional Foundations of Comparative Advantage*. Oxford: Oxford University Press, 387–416.

—— (2002). 'National Institutional Frameworks and High-Technology Innovation in Germany: The Case of Biotechnology', in Hollingsworth et al (eds.), q.v., 277–306.

—— and Kettler, H. (2001). 'National Institutional Frameworks and the Hybridization of Entrepreneurial Business Models: The German and UK Biotechnology Sectors', *Industry and Innovation*, 8/1: 5–30.

Castles, F. G. and Mitchell, D. (1991). *Three Worlds of Welfare Capitalism or Four?* Working Paper 63. Luxembourg: Luxembourg Income Study.

Coase, R. (1937). 'The Nature of the Firm', *Economica*, 4: 386–405.

Coleman, W. (1997). 'Associational Governance in a Globalizing era: Weathering the Storm', in R. Hollingsworth and R. Boyer (eds.), (1997a), q.v., 127–53.

Considine, M. and Lewis, J. (2003). 'Working with Networks: Exploring Service Delivery Strategies in Public and Private Organizations as Networking Effects', *Journal of European Public Policy*, 10, 1: 46–58.

Corbett, J. and Jenkinson, T. (1996). The Financing of Industry, 1970–1989: An International Comparison'. *Journal of the Japanese and International Economies* 10: 71.

Coriat, B., Orsi, F., and Weinstein, O. (2003), 'Does Biotech Reflect a New Science–Based Innovation Regime?', *Industry and Innovation*, 10/3: 231–54.

Cotts Watkins, S. (1991). *From Provinces into Nations: Demographic Integration in Western Europe 1870–1960*. Princeton, NJ: Princeton University Press.

Crouch, C. (1977). *Class Conflict and the Industrial Relations Crisis*. London: Heinemann.

—— (1993). *Industrial Relations and European State Traditions*, Oxford: Clarendon Press.

Crouch, C. (1999). *Social Change in Western Europe*. Oxford: Oxford University Press.

—— (2001). 'Breaking Open Black Boxes: The Implications for Sociological Theory of European Integration', in A. Menon and V. Wright (eds.), *From the Nation State to Europe? Essays in Honour of Jack Hayward*. Oxford: Oxford University Press.

—— (2005). 'The governance of emersione: Preparing the approach'. Working document for project 23, NewGov research programme, European Union Framework Programme. Florence: European University Institute.

—— and Farrell, H. (2004). 'Breaking the path of institutional development? Alternatives to the new determinism', *Rationality and Society*, 16/1: 5–43.

—— and Keune, M. (2005). 'Rapid Change by Endogenous Actors: the Utility of Institutional Incongruence', in W. Streeck and K. Thelen (eds.), (2005a), q.v., 83–102.

—— and O'Mahoney, J. (2004). 'Machine Tooling in the United Kingdom', in C. Crouch et al., (2004), q.v., 74–98.

—— and Streeck, W. (eds.) (1997). *Political Economy of Modern Capitalism: Mapping Convergence and Diversity*. London: Sage.

—— —— Boyer, R., Amable, B., Hall, P. A., and Jackson, G. (2005). 'Dialogue on "Institutional Complementarities and Political Economy" ', Socio-Economic Review, 3: 359–82.

—— and Trigilia, C. (2001). 'Conclusions: Still Local Economies in Global Capitalism?', in C. Crouch et al., (2001), q.v., 212–37.

—— Finegold, D., and Sako, M. (1999). *Do Skills Matter? A Political Economy of Skill Formation in Advanced Societies*. Oxford: Clarendon Press.

—— Le Galès, P., Trigilia, C., and Voelzkow, H. (eds.) (2001). *Local Production Systems in Europe: Rise or Demise?* Oxford: Oxford University Press.

—— —— —— —— (eds.) (2004). *Changing Governance of Local Economies: Response of European Local Production Systems*. Oxford: Oxford University Press.

Culpepper, P. D. (2001). 'Employers, Public Policy, and the Politics of Decentralized Cooperation in Germany and France', in P. A. Hall and D. Soskice (eds.), (2001l), q.v., 275–306.

Daly, M. (2000). 'A Fine Balance: Women's Labour Market Participation in International Comparison', in F. Scharpf and V. Schmidt (eds.), (2001l), q.v., 467–510.

David, P. A. (1992a). 'Path Dependence and Economics'. Center for Economics Research Working Paper. Stanford: Stanford University.

—— (1992b). 'Path Dependence in Economic Processes: Implications for Policy Analysis in Dynamic System Contexts'. Center for Economics Research Working Paper. Stanford: Stanford University.

—— (2000). 'Path Dependence, its Critics and the Quest for "Historical Economics" ', in P. Garrouste and S. Ioannides (eds.), *Evolution and Path Dependence in Economic Ideas: Past and Present*. Cheltenham: Elgar.

Deeg, R. (2001a). *Institutional Change and the Uses and Limits of Path Dependency: The Case of German Finance*, MPIfG Discussion Paper 01/6. Cologne: Max-Planck Institut für Gesellschaftsforschung.

—— (2001*b*). 'Path Dependence and National Models of Capitalism: Are Germany and Italy on New Paths?' Paper presented at annual meeting of American Political Science Association, San Francisco Aug. 30–Sep. 2.

—— (2005). 'Path Dependency, Institutional Complementarity, and Change in National Business Systems', in G. Morgan, R. Whitley, and E. Moen (eds.), (2005), q.v., 21–52.

DiMaggio, P. (1998). 'The New Institutionalisms: Avenues of Collaboration', *Journal of Institutional and Theoretical Economics*, 154/4: 697–705.

Djelic, M.-L. (1999). 'From a Typology of Neo–Institutional Arguments to Their Cross–Fertilization'. Unpublished paper, ICC Workshop. Evanston: Kellogg Institute.

Dore, R. (2000). *Stock Market Capitalism: Welfare Capitalism*. Oxford: Oxford University Press.

Douglas, M. (1987). *How Institutions Think*. London: RKP.

Drago, M. E. (1998). 'The Institutional Bases of Chile's Economic "Miracle": Institutions, Government *Discretionary Authority* (DA). Economic Performance under Two Policy Regimes'. Ph.D. thesis, Florence, European University Institute.

Ebbinghaus, B. (2001). 'When Labour and Capital Collude: The Political Economy of Early Retirement in Europe, Japan and the USA', in B. Ebbinghaus and P. Manow (eds.), (2001l), q.v., 76–101.

—— and Manow, P. (2001*a*). 'Introduction: Studying Varieties of Welfare Capitalism', in B. Ebbinghaus and P. Manow (eds.), (2001l), q.v., 1–24.

—— —— (eds.) (2001*b*). *Comparing Welfare Capitalism. Social Policy and Political Economy in Europe, Japan and the USA*. London: Routledge.

—— (2003). Global Economic Integration and Regional Attractors of Competence', *Industry and Innovation*, 10/1: 75–102.

Elster, J. (1989). *The Cement of Society: A Study of Social Order*. Cambridge: Cambridge University Press.

Esping-Andersen, G. (1990). *The Three Worlds of Welfare Capitalism*. Cambridge: Polity Press.

Estevez-Abe, M., Iversen, T., and Soskice, D. (2001). 'Social Protection and the Formation of Skills: A Reinterpretation of the Welfare State', in P. A. Hall and D. Soskice (eds.), (2001l), q.v., 145–83.

Ferrera, M. (1997). *Le trappole del welfare*. Bologna: Il Mulino.

—— and Hemerijck, A. (2003). 'Recalibrating Europe's Welfare Regimes', in Zeitlin and Trubeck (eds.), (2003), q.v.

—— —— and Rhodes, M. (2000). *The Future of Social Europe: Recasting Work and Welfare in the New Economy*. Lisbon: Report for the Portuguese Presidency of the European Union.

Fioretos, O. (2001). 'The Domestic Sources of Multilateral Preferences: Varieties of Capitalism in the European Community', in P. A. Hall and D. Soskice (eds.), (2001l), q.v., 213–44.

Fligstein, N. (2001). *The Architecture of Markets: An Economic Sociology of Twenty-First-Century Capitalist Societies*. Princeton, NJ: Princeton University Press.

Freeman, C. (1995). 'The National System of Innovation in Historical Perspective', *Cambridge Journal of Economics*, 19/1: 5–24.

Gamble, A. (1988). *The Free Economy and the Strong State: The Politics of Thatcherism*. Basingstoke: Macmillan.

Garrett, G. (1998). *Partisan Politics in the Global Economy*. Cambridge: Cambridge University Press.

—— (2000). 'Shrinking States? Globalization and National Autonomy', in N. Woods (ed.), *The Political Economy of Globalization*. Basingstoke: Palgrave.

Garud, R. and Karnøe, P. (2001a). 'Preface', in R. Garud and P. Karnøe (eds.), (2001c), q.v.

—— —— (2001b). 'Path Creation as a Process of Mindful Deviation', in R. Garud and P. Karnøe (eds.), (2001c), q.v.

—— —— (eds.) (2001c). *Path Dependence and Creation*. Mahwah, NJ: Lawrence Elbaum Associates.

Giddens, A. (1976). *New Rules of Sociological Method: A Positive Critique of Interpretative Sociologies*. London: Heinemann.

Gilson, R. (1999). 'The Legal Infrastructure of High Technology Industrial Districts: Silicon Valley, Route 128, and Covenants not to Compete', *New York University Law Review*, 74: 3.

—— (2003). 'Engineering a Venture Capital Market: Lessons from the American Experience', *Stanford Law Review*, 1067–1103.

Glassmann, U. (2004). 'Refining National Policy: The Machine-Tool Industry in the Local Economy of Stuttgart', in C. Crouch et al., (2004), q.v., 46–73.

—— and Voelzkow, H. (2001). 'The Governance of Local Economies in Germany', in C. Crouch et al., (2001), q.v., 79–116.

Goodin, R. (2003). 'Choose Your Capitalism?'. *Comparative European Politics*, 1/2: 203–14.

—— Headey, B., Muffels, R., and Dirven, H.-J. (1999). *The Real Worlds of Welfare Capitalism*. Cambridge: Cambridge University Press.

Gould, S. J. (2002). *The Structure of Evolutionary Theory*. Cambridge, MA: Harvard University Press.

Grabher, G. (1993a). 'Rediscovering the Social in the Economics of Interfirm Relations', in G. Grabher (ed.), (1993c), q.v., 1–32.

—— (1993b). 'The Weakness of Strong Ties: The Lock-in of Regional Development in the Ruhr Area', in G. Grabher (ed.), (1993c), q.v., 255–77.

—— (ed.) (1993c). *The Embedded Firm: On the Socioeconomics of Industrial Networks*. London: Routledge.

—— (2002). 'Cool Projects, Boring Institutions', *Regional Studies*, 36.

Granovetter, M. (1973). 'The Strength of Weak Ties', *American Journal of Sociology*, 78/6: 1360–80.

—— (1985). 'Economic Action and Social Structure: The Problem of Embeddedness', *American Journal of Sociology*, 91/3, 481–510.

—— (1990). 'The Old and the New Economic Sociology', in R. Freedland and A. F. Robertson (eds.), *Beyond the Marketplace: Rethinking Economy and Society*. New York: De Gruyter.

Grant, W. (1997). 'Perspectives on Globalization and Economic Coordination', in R. Hollingsworth and R. Boyer (eds.), (1997a), q.v., 319–36.

Grebel, T., Pyka, A., and Hanusch, H. (2003). 'An Evolutionary Approach to the Theory of Entrepreneurship', *Industry and Innovation*, 10/4: 493–514.

Greenwood, J., Pyper, R., and Wilson, D. (2002). *New Public Administration in Britain*. London: Routledge.

Hage, J. and Alter, C. (1997). 'A Typology of Interorganizational Relationships and Networks', in R. Hollingsworth and R. Boyer (eds.), (1997a), q.v., 94–126.

—— and Hollingsworth, J. R. (2000). 'A Strategy for the Analysis of Idea Innovation Networks and Institutions', *Organization Studies*, 21/5: 971–1004.

Hall, P. A. (1986). *Governing the Economy: The Politics of State Intervention in Britain and France*. New York: Oxford University Press.

—— (1992). 'The Movement from Keynesianism to Monetarism: Institutional Analysis and British Economic Policy in the 1970s'. In Steinmo, P. Thelen, K. and Longstreth, F. (eds.), *Structuring Politics: Historical Institutionalism in Comparative Analysis*. Cambridge: Cambridge University Press.

—— (1993). 'Policy Paradigms, Social Learning and the State: The Case of Economic Policy Making in Britain', *Comparative Politics*, 25, 3: 275–96.

—— (1999). 'The Political Economy of Europe in an Era of Interdependence', in H. Kitschelt et al. (eds.), (1999a), q.v.

—— and Gingerich, D. W. (2004). 'Varieties of Capitalism and Institutional Complementarities in the Political Economy: An Empirical Analysis'. MPIfG Discussion Paper 04/5, Cologne: Max–Planck Institut für Gesellschaftsforschung.

—— and Soskice, D. (2001a). 'Introduction', in P. A. Hall and D. Soskice (eds.), (2001l), q.v., 1–68.

—— —— (eds.) (2001b). *Varieties of Capitalism: The Institutional Foundations of Comparative Advantage*. Oxford: Oxford University Press.

Hancké, B. (2001). 'Revisiting the French Model: Coordination and Restructuring in French Industry', in P. A. Hall and D. Soskice (eds.), (2001l), q.v., 307–34.

—— (2002). *Large Firms and Institutional Change: Industrial Renewal and Economic Restructuring in France*. Oxford: Oxford University Press.

Hay, C. (2002). 'Common Trajectories, Variable Paces, Divergent Outcomes? Models of European Capitalism under Conditions of Complex Economic Interdependence'. Conference of Europeanists, Chicago, March 2002.

Hayek, F. A. (1973). *Rules and Order*. London: Routledge and Kegan Paul.

Hechter, M. (1990). 'The Emergence of Cooperative Social Institutions', in M. Hechter, K.-D. Opp, and R. Wippler (eds.), *Social Institutions: Their Emergence, Maintenance and Effects*. Berlin: Walter de Gruyter.

Helleiner, E. (1994). *States and the Reemergence of Global Finance*. Ithaca, NY: Cornell University Press.

170   *References*

Helper, S., MacDuffie, J. P., and Sabel, C. (2000). 'Pragmatic Collaborations: Advancing Knowledge while Controlling Opportunism', *Industrial and Corporate Change*, 9/3: 443–88.

Hemerijck, A. (1992). 'The Historical Contingencies of Dutch Corporatism'. D.Phil. thesis, University of Oxford.

—— and Schludi, M. (2000). 'Sequences of Policy Failures and Effective Policy Responses', in F. Scharpf and V. Schmidt (eds.), (2000a), q.v., 125–228.

—— Unger, B., and Visser, J. (2000). 'How Small Countries Negotiate Change: Twenty-Five Years of Policy Adjustment in Austria, the Netherlands, and Belgium', in F. Scharpf and V. Schmidt (eds.), (2000l), q.v., 175–263.

Herrigel, G. (1993). 'Power and the Redefinition of Industrial Districts: The Case of Baden-Württemberg', in G. Grabher (ed.), (1993c), q.v.

Hirst, P. and Thompson, G. (1997). 'Globalization in Question: International Economic Relations and Forms of Public Governance', in R. Hollingsworth and R.Boyer (eds.), (1997a), q.v., 337–61.

Hobbes, T. (1651). *Leviathan: or, the Matter, Forme and Power of a Commonwealth, Ecclesiasticall and Civil*. London.

Hodgson, G. (2002). 'Institutional Blindness in Modern Economics', in Hollingsworth et al. (eds.) (2002), q.v., 147–70.

Hollingsworth, R. (1997). 'Continuities and Changes in Social Systems of Production: The Cases of Japan, Germany, and the United States', in R. Hollingsworth and R. Boyer (eds.), (1997a), q.v., 265–310.

—— (2000). 'Doing Institutional Analysis: Implications for the Study of Innovations', *Review of International Political Economy*, 7/4: 595–644.

—— (2002). 'On Institutional Embeddedness', in Hollingsworth et al. (eds.) (2002), q.v., 87–146.

—— (2004). Oral Presentation at Conference on Health Care Industries, European University Institute, Florence, 2004.

—— and Boyer, R. (eds.) (1997). *Contemporary Capitalism: The Embeddedness of Institutions*. Cambridge: Cambridge University Press.

—— and Hollingsworth, E. J. (2000). 'Major Discoveries and Biomedical Research Organizations: Perspectives on Interdisciplinarity, Nurturing Leadership, and Integrated Structure and Cultures', in P. Weingart and N. Stehr (eds.), *Practising Interdisciplinarity*. Toronto: Toronto University Press, 215–44.

—— Müller, K. H., and Hollingsworth, E. J. (eds.) (2002). *Advancing Socio—Economics: An Institutionalist Perspective*. Lanham: Rowman and Littlefield.

—— Schmitter, P. C., and Streeck, W. (eds.) (1994). *Governing Capitalist Economies: Performance and Control of Economic Sectors*. New York: Oxford University Press.

Hopkins, T. K. and Wallerstein, I. (1982). *World-systems Analysis: Theory and Methodology*. Beverly Hills, CA: Sage.

Höpner, M. (2003a). *European Corporate Governance Reform and the German Party Paradox*. MPIfG Discussion Paper 03/4, Cologne: Max–Planck Institut für Gesellschaftsforschung.

—— (2003*b*). 'What Connects Industrial Relations with Corporate Governance? A Review on Complementarity'. Complementarity group unpublished paper. Cologne: Max–Planck Institut für Gesellschaftsforschung

—— (2004). *Unternehmensmitbestimmung unter Beschuss*. MPIfG Discussion Paper 04/8, Cologne: Max-Planck Institut für Gesellschaftsforschung.

Hyde, A. (1998). 'The Wealth of Shared Information: Silicon Valley's High-Velocity Labor Market, Endogenous Economic Growth, and the Law of Trade Secrets', http://newark.rutgers.edu/~hyde/.

Immergut, E. (2005). 'Historical-Institutionalism and the problem of Change', in A. Wimmer and A. Köessler (eds.), (2005), q.v.

Jaccoby (1990). 'The New Institutionalism: What Can It Learn from the Old?' *Industrial Relations*, 29: 316–59.

Jackson, G. (2001). 'The Origins of Nonliberal Corporate Governance in Germany and Japan', in W. Streeck and K. Yamamura (eds.), (2001), q.v.

—— (forthcoming). 'Varieties of Capitalism: A Review'. Unpublished manuscript.

Jong Kon Chin, S. (2002). 'Covenants not to Compete, Trade Secrets and the Emergence of High Tech Clusters'. M.Phil. thesis, Management Studies, University of Cambridge.

—— (forthcoming) 'The Birth, Dispersion and Adaptation of New Institutions Across Institutional Systems: A Study of the Emergence and Performance of Biotech Firms and Technology Transfer Officers in and Around Publicly Funded Research Centres in Three Regions'. Ph.D. thesis, Florence, European University Institute.

Karl, T. (1997). *The Paradox of Plenty: Oil Booms and Petro-states*. Berkeley, CA: University of California Press.

Kenney, M. (ed.) (2000*a*). *Understanding Silicon Valley: The Anatomy of an Entrepreneurial Region*. Stanford: Stanford University Press.

—— (2000*b*). 'Introduction', in M. Kenney (ed.), (2000*a*), q.v., 1–12.

—— and Florida, R. (2000). 'Venture Capital in Silicon Valley: Fuelling New Firm Foundation', in M. Kenney (ed.), (2000*a*), q.v., 98–123.

—— and Van Burg, V. (2000). 'Institutions and Economics: Creating Silicon Valley', in M. Kenney (ed.), (2000*a*), q.v., 218–40.

Keune, M., with Kiss, J. P. and Tóth, A. (forthcoming). 'Innovation, Actors and Institutions: Change and Continuity in Local Development Policy in Two Hungarian Regions', *International Journal of Urban and Regional Research*.

King, D. and Wood, S. (1999). 'The Political Economy of Neoliberalism: Britain and the United States in the 1980s', in H. Kitschelt et al. (eds.), (1999l), q.v.

Kitschelt, H., Lange, P., Marks, G., and Stephens, J. (1999*a*). 'Convergence and Divergence in Advanced Capitalist Democracies', in H. Kitschelt et al. (eds.), (1999l), q.v.

—— —— —— —— (eds.) (1999*b*). *Continuity and Change in Contemporary Capitalism*, Cambridge: Cambridge University Press.

Kjær, P. and Pedersen, O. K. (2001). 'Translating Liberalization: Neoliberalism in the Danish Negotiated Economy', in J. L. Campbell and O. K. Pedersen (eds.), (2001l), q.v., 219–48.

Knight, J. (1992). *Institutions and Social Conflict*. Cambridge: Cambridge University Press.

—— (1995). 'Models, Interpretations and Theories: Constructing Explanations of Institutional Emergence and Change', in Knight, J. and Sened, I (eds.), *Explaining Social Institutions*. Ann Arbor, MI: University of Michigan Press.

—— (2001). 'Explaining the Rise of Neoliberalism: The Mechanisms of Institutional Change' in J. L. Campbell and O. K. Pedersen (eds.), (2001l), q.v., 27–50.

Kooiman, T. (1993). *Modern Governance*. London: Sage.

Korpi, W. (1983). *The Democratic Class Struggle*. London: RKP.

Krippner, G. (2001). 'The Elusive Market: Embeddedness and the Paradigm of Economic Sociology', *Theory and Society*, 30: 775–810.

Kristensen, P. H. (1997). 'National Systems of Governance and Managerial Prerogatives in the Evolution of Work Systems: England, Germany, and Denmark Compared', in R. Whitley and P. H. Kristensen (eds.), (1997), q.v.

Lazonick, W. (1991). *Business Organization and the Myth of the Market Economy*. Cambridge: Cambridge University Press.

—— and O'Sullivan, M. (1996). 'Organization, Finance and International Competition', *Industrial Corporate Change*, 5: 1–49.

—— —— (1997). 'Big Business and Skill Formation in the Wealthiest Nations: The Organizational Revolution in the Twentieth Century', in A. D. Chandler, F. Amatori, and T. Hikino (eds.), *Big Business and the Wealth of Nations*. Cambridge: Cambridge University Press.

Leach, R. and Percy-Smith, J. (2001). *Local Governance in Britain*. London, Palgrave.

Le Grand, J. (2003). *Motivation, Agency and Public Policy*. Oxford: Oxford University Press.

Lepsius, M. R. (1990). *Interessen, Ideen und Institutionen*. Opladen: Westdeutscher Verlag.

Leslie, S. W. (2000). 'The Biggest "Angel" of Them All: The Military and the Making of Silicon Valley', in M. Kenney (ed.), (2000a), q.v., 48–67.

Levi, M. (1996). 'Social and Unsocial Capital: A Review Essay of Robert Putnam's *Making Democracy Work*', *Politics and Society*, 24/1: 45–55.

Lévi-Strauss, C. (1962). *La Pensée Sauvage*. Paris: Agora.

Luhmann, N. (1980). *Gesellschaftsstruktur und Semantik*. Frankfurt am Main: Suhrkamp.

Lundvall, B.-A. (ed.) (1992). *National Systems of Innovation: Towards a Theory of Innovation and Interactive Learning*. London: Pinter.

Lütz, S. (2000). 'From Managed to Market Capitalism? German Finance in Transition', *German Politics*, 9: 149–70.

—— (2003). *Governance in der politischen Ökonomie*, MPIfG Discussion Paper 03/5. Cologne: Max–Planck Institut für Gesellschaftsforschung.

Macneil, I. (2001). *The Relational Theory of Contract: Selected Works of Ian Macneil* (ed. David Campbell). London: Sweet and Maxwell.

Magnusson, L. (2001). 'The Role of Path Dependence in the History of Regulation', in L. Magnusson and J. Ottoson (eds.), *The State, Regulation and the Economy*. Cheltenham: Edward Elgar, 107–19.

Mahoney, J. (2000). 'Path Dependence in Historical Sociology', *Theory and Society*, 29: 507–48.

March, J. G. and Simon, H. A. (1958). *Organizations*. New York: Wiley.

Mayntz, R. (2004). *Organizational Forms of Terrorism: Hierarchy, Network, or a Type sui generis?* MPIfG Discussion Paper 04/4. Cologne: Max–Planck Institut für Gesellschaftsforschung.

—— and Scharpf, F. (1995). 'Der Ansatz der akteurzentrierten Institutionalismus', in R. Mayntz and F. Scharpf (eds.), *Steuerung und Selbstorganisation in staatsnahen Sektoren*. Frankfurt am Main: Campus, 39–72.

Middlemas, K. (1979). *Politics in Industrial Society. The Experience of the British System since 1911*. London: A. Deutsch.

—— (1986–91). *Power, Competition and the State*, 3 vols. Basingstoke: Macmillan.

Morgan, G. (2005). 'Introduction', in G. Morgan, R. Whitley, and E. Moen (eds.), (2005), q.v., 1–20.

Morgan, G., Whitley, R. and Moen, E. (eds.) (2005). *Changing Capitalisms? Complementarities, Contradictions and Capability Development in an International Context*. Oxford: Oxford University Press.

Morin, F. (2000). 'A Transformation in the French Model of Shareholding and Management', *Economy and Society*, 29/1: 36–53.

Morris, J. and Imrie, R. (1992). *Transforming Buyer–Supplier Relations*. London: Macmillan.

Naldini, M. (1999). 'Evolution of Social Policy and the Institutional Definition of Family Models: The Italian and Spanish Cases in Historical and Comparative Perspective'. Ph.D. thesis, Florence, European University Institute.

Nelson, R. R. (1993). *National Innovation Systems: A Comparative Analysis*. Oxford: Oxford University Press.

—— (2000). *Knowledge Management in the Learning Society*. Paris: OECD.

—— and Winter, S. G. (1982). *An Evolutionary Theory of Economic Change*. Cambridge, MA: Harvard University Press.

North, D. C. (1990a). *Institutions, Institutional Change, and Economic Performance*. Cambridge: Cambridge University Press.

—— (1990b). 'A Transaction Cost Theory of Politics', *Journal of Theoretical Politics*, 2/4, 355–68.

—— and R. P. Thomas, R. P. (1973). *The Rise of the Western World: A New Economic History*. Cambridge: Cambridge University Press.

Nugent, J. B. (2005). 'The New Institutional Economics: Can It deliver for Change and Development?', in Wimmer and Köossler (eds.) (2005), q.v.

OECD (1994). *The Jobs Study*. Paris: OECD.

Ohmae, K. (1985). *Triad Power: The Coming Shape of Global Competition*. New York: Free Press.

O'Sullivan, M. (2001). Equity Markets and the Corporate Economy in France'. Unpublished manuscript.

Parsons, T. and Bales, R. F. (1955). *Family, Socialization and Interaction Process*. New York: Free Press.

Pempel, T. J. (1998). *Regime Shift: Comparative Dynamics of the Japanese Political Economy*. Ithaca, NY: Cornell University Press.

Penrose, E. (1959). *The Theory of the Growth of the Firm*. Oxford: Blackwell.

Pierson, P. (2000*a*). 'The Limits of Design: Explaining Institutional Origins and Change', *Governance*, 13/4: 475–99.

—— (2000*b*). 'Increasing Returns, Path Dependence, and the Study of Politics', *American Political Science Review*, 94/2, 251–67.

Pizzorno, A. (1983). 'Sulla razionalità della scelta democratica', *Stato e Mercato*, 7, 83.

Polanyi, K. (1944). *The Great Transformation*. New York: Rinehart.

—— and DiMaggio, P. (eds.) (1991). *The New Institutuoinalism in Organizational Analysis*. Chicago: Chicago University Press, see their own chapter.

Powell, W. (1996) 'Inter-organisational Collaboration in the Biotechnology Industry', *Journal of Institutional and Theoretical Economics*, 152, 197–225.

—— and DiMaggio, P. (1991). *The New Institutionalism in Organizational Analysis*. Chicago: University of Chicago Press.

Prevezer, M. (1998). 'Clustering in Biotechnology in the USA', in G. M. P. Swann, M. Prevezer, and D. Stout (eds.), (1998), q.v.

Proudfoot, N. (forthcoming). 'The Governance of Innovation: Comparisons from the European Biopharmaceuticals Industry'. Ph.D. thesis, Florence, European University Institute.

Przeworski, A. (1985). *Capitalism and Social Democracy*. Cambridge: Cambridge University Press.

Putnam, R. D. (1993). *Making Democracy Work: Civic Traditions in Modern Italy*. Princeton, NJ: Princeton University Press.

Quack, S. and Djelic, M.-L. (2005). 'Adaptation and Recombination: The Story of Antitrust and Competition Law in Germany and Europe', in Streeck and Thelen (eds.) (2005), q.v., 255–81.

—— and Morgan, G. (2000). 'National Capitalisms, Global Competition and Economic Performance: An Introduction', in S. Quack, G. Morgan, and R. Whitley (eds.), *National Capitalisms, Global Competition and Economic Performance*. Amsterdam: Benjamins, 2–26.

Quéré, M. (2003). 'Knowledge Dynamics: Biotechnology's Incursion into the Pharmaceutical Industry', *Industry and Innovation*, 10/3: 255–74.

Radice, H. (1998). ' "Globalization" and National Differences', *Competition and Change*, 3: 263–91.

—— (2000). 'Globalization and National Capitalisms: Theorizing Convergence and Differentiation', *Review of International Political Economy*, 7/4: 719–42.

Ragin, C. (2000). *Fuzzy-set Social Science*. Chicago: University of Chicago Press.

Regini, M. (1996). 'Le imprese e le istituzioni: domanda e produzione sociale di risorse umane nelle regioni europee'; and 'Conclusioni', in M. Regini (ed.), *La produzione sociale delle risorse humane*. Bologna: Il Mulino.

—— (2003). 'Dal neo-corporativismo alle varietà del capitalismo', *Stato e Mercato*, 69: 388–93.

Rhodes, R. (1997). *Understanding Governance*. Buckingham: Open University Press.

Rodríguez-Pose, A. (1998). *Dynamics of Regional Growth in Europe: Social and Political Factors*. Oxford: Oxford University Press.

—— (1999). 'Convergence or Divergence? Types of Regional Responses to Socio-Economic Change in Western Europe', *Tijdschrift voor Economische en Sociale Geografie*, 90/4: 363–78.

Rosenau, J. N. (1992). 'Governance, Order and Change in World Politics', in N. D. Rosenau and E. O. Czempiel (eds.), *Governance without Government*. Cambridge: Cambridge University Press.

Sabel, C. and Zeitlin, J. (eds.) (1997). *World of Possibilities: Flexibility and Mass Production in Western Industrialization*. Cambridge: Cambridge University Press.

Saxenian, A.-L. (1994). *Regional Advantage. Culture and Competition in Silicon Valley and Route 128*. Cambridge, MA: Harvard University Press.

Scharpf, F. (1997). *Games Real Actors Play: Actor-Centered Institutionalism in Policy Research*. Boulder, CO: Westview.

—— and Schmidt, V. (eds.) (2000a). *Welfare and Work in the Open Economy*, Volume I: *From Vulnerability to Competitiveness*. Oxford: Oxford University Press.

—— —— (eds.) (2000b). *Welfare and Work in the Open Economy*, Volume II: *Diverse Responses to Common Challenges*. Oxford: Oxford University Press.

Schmidt, V. (2002). *The Futures of European Capitalism*. Oxford: Oxford University Press.

Schneiberg, M. and Clemens, E. S. (forthcoming). 'The Typical Tools for the Job: Research Strategies in Institutional Analysis', in W. W. Powell and D. L. Jones (eds.), *Bending the Bars of the Iron Cage*. Chicago: University of Chicago Press.

Schumpeter, J. A. (1934). *The Theory of Economic Development: an Inquiry into Profits, Capital, Credit, Interest, and the Business Cycle*. Cambridge, MA: Harvard University Press.

Scott, W. R. (2001). *Institutions and Organizations*, 2nd edn. Thousand Oaks, CA: Sage.

Selznick, P. (1957). *Leadership in Administration*. New York: Harper & Row.

Sewell, W. H. (1992). 'A Theory of Structure: Duality, Agency, and Transformation', *American Journal of Sociology*, 98/1: 1–29.

Shonfield, A. (1964). *Modern Capitalism*. Oxford: Oxford University Press.

Sinclair, T. J. (2001). 'The Infrastructure of Global Governance: Quasi-Regulatory Mechanisms and the New Global Finance', *Global Governance*, 7: 441–51.

Solokoff, K. L. and Engerman, S. (2000). 'Institutions, Factor Endowments, and Paths of Development in the New World', *Journal of Economic Perspectives*, 14/3: 217–32.

Soskice, D. (1990). 'Wage Determination: The Changing Role of Institutions in Advanced Industrialized Countries', *Oxford Review of Economic Policy*, 6/4: 36–61.

—— (1995). 'A Comparative Review of National Training Models: Germany, the UK, the USA, Japan', in R. Koch and J. Reuling (eds.), *The European Dimension in Vocational Training*. Bielefeld: Bertelsmann.

—— (1999). 'Divergent Production Regimes: Coordinated and Uncoordinated Market Economies in the 1980s and 1990s', in H. Kitschelt et al. (eds.), (1999l), q.v.

Stark, D. (2001). 'Ambiguous Assets for Uncertain Environments: Heterarchy in Postsocialist Firms', in P. DiMaggio (ed.), *The Twenty-First Century Firm: Changing Economic Organization in Comparative Perspective*. Princeton, NJ: Princeton University Press.

Steinmo, S., Thelen, K., and Longstreth, F. (eds.) (1992). *Structuring Politics: Historical Institutionalism in Comparative Analysis*. Cambridge: Cambridge University Press.

Stewart, M. (1972). *Keynes and after*. Harmondsworth: Penguin.

—— (1977). *The Jekyll and Hyde Years: Politics and Economic Policy since 1964*. London: J. M. Dent.

Stinchcombe, A. L. (1968). *Constructing Social Theories*. New York: Harcourt, Brace.

Streeck, W. (1992). *Social Institutions and Economic Performance*. London: Sage.

—— (1997). 'Beneficial Constraints: On the Economic Limits of Rational Voluntarism', in R. Hollingsworth and R. Boyer (eds.), (1997), q.v., 197–219.

—— (2001). 'Introduction: Explorations into the Origins of Nonliberal Capitalism in Germany and Japan', in W. Streeck and K. Yamamura (eds.), (2001), q.v.

—— and Yamamura, K. (eds.) (2001). *The Origins of Nonliberal Capitalism: Germany and Japan in Comparison*. Ithaca, NY: Cornell University Press.

—— and Thelen, K. (eds.) (2005a). *Beyond Continuity: Institutional Change in Advanced Political Economies*. Oxford: Oxford University Press.

—— —— (2005b). 'Institutional Change in Advanced Political Economies', in W. Streeck and K. Thelen (eds.), (2005a), q.v., 1–39.

Sturgeon, T. J. (2000). 'How Silicon Valley Came to Be', in M. Kenney (ed.), (2000a), q.v., 15–47.

Suchman, M. C. (2000). 'Dealmakers and Counselors: Law Firms as Intermediaries in the Development of Silicon Valley', in M. Kenney (ed.), (2000a), q.v., 71–97.

Swann, G. M. P. (1998). 'Clusters in the US Computing Industry', in G. M. P. Swann, M. Prevezer, and D. Stout (eds.), (1998), q.v.

—— and Prevezer, M. (1998). 'Introduction', in G. M. P. Swann, M. Prevezer, and D. Stout (eds.), (1998), q.v.

—— —— and Stout, D. (eds.) (1998). *The Dynamics of Industrial Clustering: International Comparisons in Computing and Biotechnology*. Oxford: Oxford University Press.

Swedberg, R. (1987). 'Economic Sociology: Past and Present', *Current Sociology*, 35/1.

Tate, J. (2001). 'National Varieties of Standardization', in P. A. Hall and D. Soskice (eds.), (2001l), q.v., 442–73.

Temple, P. (1998). 'Clusters and Competitiveness: A Policy Response', in G. M. P. Swann, M. Prevezer, and D. Stout (eds.), (1998), q.v.

Thelen, K. (1999). 'Historical Institutionalism in Comparative Politics', *Annual Review of Political Science*, 2: 369–404.

—— (2001). 'Varieties of Labor Politics in the Developed Democracies', in P. A. Hall and D. Soskice (eds.), (2001l), q.v., 71–103.

—— (2003). 'How Institutions Evolve: Insights from Comparative Historical Analysis', in J. Mahoney and D. Rueschemeyer (eds.), *Comparative-Historical Analysis in the Social Sciences*. New York: Cambridge University Press.

—— (2004). *How Institutions Evolve: The Political Economy of Skills in Germany, Britain, the United States, and Japan*. Cambridge: Cambridge University Press.

Teubner, G. (2001). 'Legal Irritants: How Unifying Law Ends up in New Divergences', in P. A. Hall and D. Soskice (eds.), (2001l), q.v., 417–41.

Trigilia, C. (1998). *Sociologia Economica*. Bologna: Il Mulino.

—— (2004). 'The Governance of High-Tech Districts', in C. Crouch et al., (2004), q.v., 321–30.

Uzzi, B. (1997). 'Social Structure and Competition in Inter-Firm Networks: The Paradox of Embeddedness', *Administrative Science Quarterly*, 42: 35–67.

—— (1999). 'Embeddedness in the Making of Financial Capital: How Social Relations and Networks Benefit from Firms Seeking Financing', *American Sociological Review*, 64: 481–505.

Van Waarden, F. (2002). 'Market Institutions as Communicating Vessels: Changes between Economic Coordination Principles as a Consequence of Deregulation Policies', in Hollingsworth, Müller, and Hollingsworth (eds.), q.v., 171–212.

Viebrock, E. (2004). 'The Role of Trade Unions as Intermediary Institutions in Unemployment Insurance: A European Comparison'. Ph.D. thesis, Florence, European University Institute.

Visser, J. and Hemerijck, A. (1997). *A Dutch 'Miracle'*. Amsterdam: Amsterdam University Press.

Watson, M. (2003). 'Ricardian Political Economy and the "Varieties of Capitalism" Approach', *Comparative European Politics*, 1, 2: 215–26.

Weber, M. (1922). *Wirtschaft und Gesellschaft*. Tübingen: Mohr.

Western, B. (2000). *Bayesian Thinking about Macrosociology*. Working Paper 2000/152. Madrid: Instituto Juan, March.

Whitley, R. (1997). 'The Social Regulation of Work Systems: Institutions, Interest Groups, and Varieties of Work Organization in Capitalist Societies', in R. Whitley and P. H. Kristensen (eds.), (1997), q.v.

—— (1999). *Divergent Capitalisms*. Oxford: Oxford University Press.

—— (2005). 'How National Are National Business Systems? The Role of States and Complementary Institutions in Standardising Systems of Economic Coordination and Control at the National Level', in G. Morgan, R. Whitley, and E. Moen (eds.), (2005), q.v., 190–231.

—— and Kristensen, P. H. (eds.) (1997). *Governance at Work: The Social Regulation of Economic Relations*. Oxford: Oxford University Press.

Williamson, O. E. (1985). *The Economic Institutions of Capitalism*. New York: Free Press.

—— and Masten, S. E. (1995). *Transaction Cost Economics*. Aldershot: Edward Elgar.

Wimmer, A. and Kössler, A. (eds.) (2005). *Understanding Change: Models, Methodologies and Metaphors*. London: Palgrave.

Windolf, P. (2002). *Corporate Networks in Europe and the United States*. Oxford: Oxford University Press.

Wood, S. (2001). 'Business, Government and Patterns of Labor Market Policy in Britain and the Federal Republic of Germany', in P. A. Hall and D. Soskice (eds.), (2001l), q.v., 247–74.

Yamamura , K. and Streeck, W. (eds.) (2003). *The End of Diversity? Prospects for German and Japanese Capitalism*. Ithaca, NY: Cornell University Press.

Zeitlin, J. (2003). 'Introduction: Governing Work and Welfare in a New Economy: European and American Experiments', in J. Zeitlin and D. Trubek, D. (eds.), (2003), q.v.

—— and Trubek, D. (eds.) (2003). *Governing Work and Welfare in a New Economy: European and American Experiments*. Oxford: Oxford University Press.

Zukin, S. and DiMaggio, P. (1990). *Structures of Capital: The Social Organization of the Economy*. Cambridge: Cambridge University Press.

Zysman, J. (1983). *Governments, Markets, and Growth: Financial Systems and the Politics of Industrial Change*. Ithaca, NY: Cornell University Press.

INDEX